THE POOR MAN'S REVOLUTIONARY

Thomas Spence
The Poor Man's Revolutionary

Edited by
Alastair Bonnett and Keith Armstrong

BREVIARY STUFF PUBLICATIONS
2014

First published 2014 by Breviary Stuff Publications,
BCM Breviary Stuff, London WC1N 3XX
www.breviarystuff.org.uk

A CIP record for this book is available from
The British Library

ISBN: 978-0-9570005-9-9

Contents

Gathering Nuts (1801) *Thomas Spence* ix

Acknowledgements xi

Contributors xiii

Introduction 1
Alastair Bonnett

1 Property in Land Every One's Right (1775) 7
Thomas Spence

2 Paine, Spence, Chartism and 'The Real Rights of Man' 13
Malcolm Chase

3 Four Roads from 'Genesis': Spence, Paine and Rights to Property 27
Gregory Claeys

4 Spence's *Property in Land Every One's Right*: Problems and Solutions 35
Rachel Hammersley

5 Thomas Spence and the London Corresponding Society, 1792-1795 53
Jon Mee

6 The Economic Ideas of Thomas Spence: The Right to Subsistence 65
John Marangos

7 Spence and the Politics of Nostalgia 75
Alastair Bonnett

8 Thomas Spence's Spelling Reform 89
Robert W. Rix

9 A Radical Plan for the English Language 103
Joan C. Beal

10 'Meet and Sing, and Your Chains Will Drop Off Like Burnt Thread': The Political Songs of Thomas Spence 109
Michael T. Davis

11 The End of Oppression (1795) 127
Thomas Spence

12 A Supplement to the History of Robinson Crusoe, Being the History of Crusonia, or Robinson Crusoe's Island (1782) 133
Thomas Spence

13 The Constitution of Spensonia (1803) 145
Thomas Spence

14 Poems and Songs 163
Thomas Spence

15 Poems and Song 171
Keith Armstrong

Appendices

A Contrast Between Paine's *Agrarian Justice*, and Spence's *End Of Oppression* 177

Spence's Tokens 182

The Thomas Spence Trust 190

Index 191

Portrait of Thomas Spence (dated April 2nd, 1810)

Gathering Nuts
(1801)

•

Thomas Spence

In order to show how far we are cut off from the rights of nature, and reduced to a more contemptible state than the brutes, I will relate an affair I had with a forester in a wood near Hexham alone by myself a gathering of nuts, the forester popped through the bushes upon me, and asking what I did there, I answered gathering nuts: gathering nuts! said he, and dare you say so? Yes, said I, why not? would you question a monkey, or a squirrel, about such a business? And am I to be treated as inferior to one of those creatures? Or have I a less right? But who are you, continued I, that thus take upon you to interrupt me? I'II let you know that, said he, when I lay you fast for trespassing here. Indeed! answered I. But how can I trespass here where no man ever planted or cultivated, for these nuts are the spontaneous gifts of nature ordained alike for the sustenance of man and beast that choose to gather them, and therefore they are common. I tell you, said he, this wood is no common. It belongs to the Duke of Portland. Oh: My service to the Duke of Portland, said I, nature knows no more of him than of me. Therefore, as in nature's storehouse the rule is, "First come, first served," so the Duke of Portland must look sharp if he wants any nuts. But in the name of seriousness, continued I, must not one's privileges be very great in a country where we dare not pluck a hazel nut? Is this an Englishman's birthright? Is it for this we are called upon to serve in the militia, to defend this wood, and this country against the enemy?

What must I say to the French, if they come? If they jeeringly ask me what I am fighting for? Must I tell them for my country? For my dear country in which I dare not pluck a nut? Would not they laugh at me? Yes. And you do think I would bear it? No: certainly I would not. I would throw down my musket saying let such as the Duke of Portland, who claim the country, fight for it, for I am but a stranger and sojourner, and have neither part nor lot amongst them.

This reasoning had such an effect on the forester that he told me to gather as many nuts as I pleased.

Source: *The Restorer of Society to its Natural State* (London, 1801)

Acknowledgements

Introduction by Alastair Bonnett. An earlier version appeared as 'The Other Rights of Man' *History Today* 2007, 57, 9, 42-48.

Paine, Spence, Chartism and 'The Real Rights of Man' by Malcolm Chase is an expanded and fully referenced version of the 2008 Paine Memorial Lecture, given at the invitation of the Thomas Paine Society. The latter subsequently published the lecture in pamphlet form and Malcolm Chase is grateful to the Society for its permission to draw on that text here.

The Economic Ideas of Thomas Spence: The Right to Subsistence by John Marangos. The chapter is a revised version of material included in J. Marangos, "Thomas Paine (1737-1809) and Thomas Spence (1750-1814) on Land Ownership, Land Taxes and the Provision of Citizens Dividend", *International Journal of Social Economics*, Vol. 34, No. 5 (2008): 313-325; J. King and J. Marangos, "Two Arguments for Basic Income: Thomas Paine and Thomas Spence", *History of Economic Ideas*, Vol. XIV, No. 1 (2006): 55-71; and J. Marangos, "Contrasting Primitive Conceptions of Basic Income Guarantee", *International Journal of Environment, Workplace and Employment*, Vol. 2, No. 1 (2006): 6-20.

Spence and the Politics of Nostalgia by Alastair Bonnett. This chapter draws on material previously published in *Left in the Past: Radicalism and the Politics of Nostalgia*, New York: Continuum, 2010.

Thomas Spence's Spelling Reform by Robert W. Rix. An earlier version of this article appeared as 'The Crusonian Alphabet: Thomas Spence's *Grand Repository of the English Language*' in *English Language Notes* 43.2 (2005): 69-92.

Contributors

Keith Armstrong
Poet, Author and Founder of the Thomas Spence Trust

Joan C. Beal
Emeritus Professor of English Language, University of Sheffield

Alastair Bonnett
Professor of Social Geography, Newcastle University

Malcolm Chase
Professor of Social History, University of Leeds

Michael T. Davis
Lecturer in History, School of Humanities, Griffith University

Gregory Claeys
Professor of the History of Political Thought, Royal Holloway, University of London

Rachel Hammersley
Senior Lecturer in Intellectual History, Newcastle University

John Marangos
Professor in the Department of Balkan, Slavic and Oriental Studies, University of Macedonia

Jon Mee
Professor of Eighteenth-Century Studies, University of York

Robert W. Rix
Associate Professor in the Department of English, Germanic, and Romance Studies, University of Copenhagen

Introduction

Alastair Bonnett

2014 saw the 200th anniversary of the death of an original voice in the history of radicalism, Thomas Spence. Spence described himself as 'the poor man's advocate'[1] but he may equally be described as 'the poor man's revolutionary', for what he advocated was a dramatic overturning of the existing social order.

Perhaps Spence can be best summed up by one of the inscriptions he placed on one of his self-minted coins, the coin his friends chose to place in his coffin. It depicts a cat. It stares straight out at us, around it the words, 'IN SOCIETY LIVE FREE LIKE ME'.[2] Spence wasn't interested in compromise, with reforms and half-freedoms. He was stubborn. Contemporaries described him as 'querulous' and 'single-minded'. One obituary observed he was 'poor and despised', yet 'not despicable'.[3]

But who was Thomas Spence? And why did he excite such passions? This collection of essays seeks to go some way to find answers to these questions. It offers a series of insights from contemporary experts on different aspects of Spence's life and times. We are also delighted to be publishing some pamphlets by Spence himself, including a long-lost treasure.

Leafing through a battered compilation of eighteenth century documents held by Newcastle's Literary and Philosophical Society, in June 2005 Dr David Gardner-Medwin chanced upon an intriguing one penny pamphlet. No author is indicated but the title is striking, *Property in land Every One's Right, proved in a lecture read at the Philosophical Society in Newcastle, on the 8th of Nov. 1775.*

Dr Gardner-Medwin immediately recognised it as the founding statement of Spence's thought and, hence, one of the founding texts of the English radical tradition. It is a work republished many times in later, altered, editions as 'The Rights of Man'. But for many years the original had been thought to have been

1 For example, the title of his journal ran as follows, *Pigs' Meat; or, Lessons for the Swinish Multitude: Published in Weekly Penny Numbers, Collected by the Poor Man's Advocate (an Old Veteran in the Cause of Freedom) in the Course of his Reading for more than Twenty Years.*

2 In *Trial of Thomas Spence in 1801* by Arthur W. Waters (Leamington Spa: Courier Press, 1917), p. 8 the following portrait of his funeral is given:

Thomas Spence was buried on 8th September in St. James' Burial Ground, Hampstead Road, with his favourite tokens, the Cat & The Meridian Sun, placed in the coffin. The funeral procession made its way up Tottenham Court Road, from his address in Castle Street, Oxford Street. About forty friends attended his funeral. They carried the scales after his body as an emblem of justice, the balance of which was decorated with white ribbon to denote the innocence of his life and example. As the mourners passed by the still open grave, many of his tokens were thrown upon the coffin. An oration was delivered by an advocate of his principles, William Snow, in which he showed what benefits would accrue to the working classes by the adoption of Spence's system of Land Reform.

3 *Newcastle Weekly Chronicle*, 4 November, 1888.

lost. We are proud to reproduce it here, for this first edition has not been in print since it first appeared, over 230 years ago.

Spence had been thrown out of the Philosophical Society for hawking this outrageous pamphlet on the streets of Newcastle. It was the start of a long and impoverished life on the furthest margins of British politics. Spence's story is a rags to rags tale of defiance and ingenuity. Today Spence's name is little known but this ignorance in no way reflects his significance. In the first two decades of the nineteenth century his name was synonymous with ultra-radical opinion. Thomas Spence was the subject of four contemporary biographical memoirs. Moreover, three years after his death an Act of Parliament was passed prohibiting 'All societies or clubs calling themselves Spencean or Spencean Philanthropists'.[4] Spenceanism appears to be unique: it has a good claim to be the only political ideology to have ever been outlawed by the British Parliament.[5]

One of his biographers, Francis Place, observed that Spence was 'as poor as any man could well be. And with some trifling fluctuation in his affairs he continued in this state to the day of his death'.[6] Yet his ideas had influence. Spence's scheme for local and democratic ownership of the land was eventually to find a receptive audience within sections of the labouring poor. In 1817 Thomas Malthus wrote that, 'an idea has lately prevailed among the lower classes of society that the land is the people's farm, the rent of which ought to be divided equally among them'.[7] This, in a nutshell, is 'Spence's Plan'. It sounds simple but, as John Marangos demonstrates in his chapter, it carried profound economic claims. In his contribution to this book, Mike Davis also explains that it was a message spread more by way of tavern meetings and ballads than by published treatise. Another form of dissemination was chalked graffiti. And amongst coin collectors Spence's name has always been revered. Both the currency Spence countermarked with radical phrases (such as 'War is starvation' and 'Full bellies, fat bairns'), or the thousands of new tokens he threw into the street (all with striking political images, such as a pig trampling on the symbols of monarchy, or the Prime Minister, William Pitt, hanging on a gibbet), continue to be prized as some of the boldest coinage ever cast. Today they are one of the few tangible relics of the phenomenon that was Thomas Spence.

Spence was born in 1750 on the Quayside in Newcastle. He was one of 19 children. His mother sold stockings; his father made fishing nets. Thomas received no formal education and at the age of ten he joined his father's trade. However, Newcastle was no back-water. As we shall see in Rachel Hammersley's chapter, this most northerly of English cities provided a fertile context for Spence's evolving ideas.

Spence was not a theoretician and always emphasised that his ideas were plain, that they were common sense; and that what radicals needed to produce was not merely criticism of the existing order but a concrete plan for a different

4 *A Bill For the More Effectually Preventing Seditious Meetings and Assemblies*, The House of Commons, 4th March, 1817.

5 Political parties have been banned, like the British Union of Fascists, but not other political ideologies.

6 Cited by P. M. Ashraf's *The Life and Times of Thomas Spence*, (Newcastle: Frank Graham, 1983), p. 287.

7 T. Malthus, *Additions To The Fourth And Former Editions Of An Essay On The Principle Of Population*, (London: John Murray, 1817), p. 40.

kind of society. What interested him was not theory but offering a model of how a new, democratic society, based on the common ownership of the land, would work.

Spence moved to London, setting up a bookshop on Chancery Lane. But one last incident from his Tyneside years demands our attention. In 1780 Spence went to visit 'Jack the Blaster', an ex-miner who 'had been ill-used by his landlords' and 'dug a cave for himself by the seaside, at Marsden Rocks, between Shields and Sunderland'. By the time of Spence's visit the cave had become something of a local tourist trap. Jack the Blaster must have been use to callers, but few are likely to have matched Spence's enthusiasm. He was jubilant to find a working man who had escaped the grasp of the land owning classes. Years later, whilst in prison in London on a charge of High Treason, Spence recalled that he 'wrote extempore with chaulk above the fire place of this free man, the following lines':

> Ye landlords vile, whose man's peace mar,
> Come levy rents here if you can;
> Your stewards and lawyers I defy,
> And live with all the RIGHTS OF MAN

Spence says this was 'as far as he knows' the first use of the phrase 'the rights of man'.[8] It is a significant assertion. For Spence was by then engaged in a doomed attempt to wrestle the phrase away from its association with Thomas Paine (whose *Rights of Man* was published in 1791). The relationship between the 'two Thomases', which is addressed in different ways by Malcolm Chase and Gregory Claeys in their chapters in this volume, is a fascinating and revealing window into late eighteenth century radicalism.

Spence sold Paine's book at his stall and went to prison for doing so. But he disagreed with Paine on a number of fundamental issues. Paine had no qualms about private property in land. Moreover, Spence thought that his proposed reforms were mere tinkering; they would not do away with poverty and tyranny. As Jon Mee shows us, having arrived in London, Spence plunged into the capital's turbulent radical sub-culture. Biographical portraits begin to appear at this time, written either by government informants or activists within the radical movement. One such sympathiser was William Hone, who tells us that,

> Spence was a native of Newcastle, small in stature, of grave countenance and deportment, serious in speech and with a broad burr in his accent. He would sometimes relax at little evening parties where his plan was discussed. On these occasions he sang a song highly characteristic of himself and his plan, in which is a sentiment denoting the pleasing state of being 'free as a cat'.[9]

In London Spence began issuing a penny weekly, *Pigs' Meat or, Lessons for the*

---

8 'The Rights of Man For Me' and note are reproduced in Kemp-Ashraf, M. and Mitchell, J. (eds) *Essays in Honour of William Gallacher: Supplement: Thomas Spence: The History of Crusonia and Other Writings* (Humboldt-Universitat zu Berlin, Berlin, 1966), p. 340.

9 Cited by Ashraf, p. 92.

Swinish Multitude. The odd title is a reference to Edmund Burke's characterisation of the revolutionary masses as a 'swinish multitude'. *Pigs' Meat* offered 'the Honey or Essence of politics'. Alongside new utopian visions of 'Crusonia' and 'Spensonia' (which we reprint in this book),[10] it provided short extracts from such writers as Volney, Harrington and Voltaire and serialised the revolutionary French Constitution.

Pigs' Meat could hardly have been more inflammatory. Spence was taking considerable risks in a dangerous city: spies, threats and conspiracy swirled around him. Within this murky world, Spence's naïve faith in his 'Plan' has a touching quality. Indeed, another sympathetic reformer, Francis Place, observed that he was,

> unpractised in the ways of the world to an extent few could imagine in a man who had been pushed about in it as he had been. Yet what is still more remarkable, his character never changed, and he died as much of a child in some respects as he probably was when he arrived at the usual age of mankind.[11]

Spence believed that if enough people came across democratic ideas there would be relatively peaceful revolution. Nevertheless, the would-be insurgents of the mockingly named 'Lambeth Loyal Association' drilled twice weekly above his shop. It seems these were rather ramshackle gatherings. Making use of a mixture of broomsticks and muskets were twelve or so labouring men, including two tailors, a miller, a hatter and a gun engraver (and Mr Frederick Polydore Nodder, a Government spy).

Spence's wish for 'perfect freedom' often took him one step further than his peers. He accorded women equal democratic rights. For the time it was a daring idea but Spence went even further. For what about the rights of children? Spence's *The Rights of Infants* no doubt provoked more than a few incredulous smiles when it was published in 1796. Yet cruelty towards children was a topic Spence returned to time and again and it is fitting that today he is cited as one of the world's first champions of children's rights.[12] In *The Rights of Infants* he argues that children have a right to be free from poverty, dirt and abuse. It is Spence at his angriest: a bitter dialogue between the contemptuous haves and the raging have nots (represented by a Spencean woman).

> *"AND pray what are the Rights of Infants?"* cry the haughty Aristocracy, sneering and tossing up their noses.
> Woman: Ask the she-bears, and every she-monster, and they will tell you what the rights of every species of young are. — They will tell you, in resolute language and actions too, that their rights extend to a full participation of the fruits of the earth. ...

Spence goes on to claim that women are the natural defenders not only of the

10 Most of Spence's pamphlets, and a full bibliography of their numerous editions, are available online at http://thomas-spence-society.co.uk

11 Cited in *The Life of Francis Place, 1771-1854*, by Graham Wallas (Longmans, Green, 1898), p. 61.

12 See, for example, http://en.wikipedia.org/wiki/Children%27s_rights_movement

rights of children but rights in general.

Spence saw his political ideas as inseparable from a wider programme of rational and popular improvement. Like many autodidacts, he had a passion for learning. He was frustrated by the fact that ordinary people were trapped in illiterate ignorance by the arcane rules of the English language. As we shall see in the chapters by Robert Rix and Joan Beal, Spence applied himself to systematic language reform and published many of his works in his own unique phonetic script.

In his later years Spence was plagued by ill health. An account from 1811 describes him as 'reduced by persecution' yet remaining a 'victim of publishing what he thought was right'. Spence also appears to have maintained his habit of having regular open meetings. A depiction of one such encounter is found in a jaunty song, 'Spence's Plan', by Mr. Porter.

> As I went forth one Morn
> For some Recreation,
> My thoughts did quickly turn,
> Upon a Reformation,
> But far I had not gone,
> Or could my thoughts recall, sir,
> Ere I spied Spence's Plan
> Wrote up against a wall sir.
>
> I star'd with open Eyes,
> And wonder'd what it meant sir,
> But found with great surprise
> As farther on I went, sir,
> Dispute it if you can,
> I spied within a Lane sir,
> Spence's Rights of Man,
> Wrote boldly up again sir.
>
> Determin'd in my mind,
> For to read his Plan, sir,
> I quickly went to find
> This enterprising man, sir,
> To the Swan I took my flight,
> Down in New-Street-Square sir,
> Where every Monday night,
> Friend Tommy Spence comes there sir.
>
> I purchased there a book,
> And by the powers above sir,
> When in it I did look,
> I quickly did approve sir.[13]

In 1814 Spence started a new news-sheet, *The Giant-Killer; or Anti-Landlord*. Only two issues were published. He died on the 1st September, after a stomach ailment. Over the next few years Spence's name emerged as a touchstone of

13 Cited by Ashraf, pp. 87-88.

English radicalism. In 1816 William Cobbett reported, 'We have all seen, for years past *written on the walls*, in and near London, these words 'Spence's Plan".[14] Soon after his death a Society of Spencean Philanthropists was formed. A report issued by a Government Secret Committee, in 1817, noted that,

> the doctrines of the Spencean clubs have been widely diffused through the country, either by extension of similar societies, or more frequently by the intervention of missionaries or delegates.[15]

The Spencean Philanthropists were described by contemporaries as poor artisans, the 'next to nobody and nothing'.[16] Amongst their ranks were shoemakers, ex-sailors and ex-soldiers. Spence's tavern radicalism was taken to new and violent extremes by the some of the Philanthropists.

Yet approaching Spence through the activities of his more desperate followers is a mistake. He was an angry man, a revolutionary and an insurrectionist but he was anchored by humanitarian concerns and a wide-ranging, omnivorous, interest in the betterment of his fellows. In this book we hope to go some way in retrieving Spence, of bringing him before a new generation. In the 200 years since he died, many revolutionary plans have come and gone. But the voice of ordinary men and women has rarely been to the fore. Some even imagine that 'a working-class hero is something to be'. The story of Thomas Spence tells us otherwise.

14 W. Cobbett, 'A letter to Henry Hunt', *Cobbett's Weekly Political Register*, December 14th, 1816: 737-768, 749.

15 *The Annual Register ... For the Year 1817*, (London: Baldwin, Cradock and Joy, 1818), p. 16.

16 Francis Place cited by E. P. Thompson, *The Making of the English Working Class*, (London: Penguin, 1991), p. 527.

1
Property in Land Every One's Right

Proved in a LECTURE Read at the Philosophical Society
in Newcastle, on the 8th of Nov. 1775

•

Thomas Spence

Th' invention all admir'd, and each, how he
To be the inventor miss'd; so easy it seem'd
Once found, which yet unfound most would have thought
Impossible. PAR. LOST

MR PRESIDENT,

As it is my turn to lecture, I chose to give some thoughts on this important question, viz. Whether mankind, in society, reap all the advantages from their natural and equal rights of property in land, and liberty, which in that state they possibly might and ought to expect? And as I take you, Mr President, and the good company here to be sincere friends to truth, I am under no apprehensions of giving offence by defending her cause with freedom.

That property in land and liberty among men, in a state of nature, ought to be equal, few, one would fain hope, would be foolish enough to deny. Therefore, taking this to be granted, the country of any people, in a native state, is properly their common, in which each of them has an equal property, with free liberty to sustain himself and connections with the animals, fruits and other products thereof. Thus such a people reap jointly the whole advantages of their country, or neighbourhood, without having their right in so doing called in question by any, not even by the most selfish and corrupted. For upon what must they live, if not upon the productions of the country in which they reside? Surely to deny them that right is, in effect, denying them a right to live. Methinks some are now ready to say. But is it lawful, reasonable and just for this people to sell, or make a present, even of the whole of their country, or common, to whom they will, to be held by them and their heirs, even for ever?

If their posterity require no grosser materials to live and move upon than air, it would, to be sure, be very ill-natured, to dispute their power of parting with what of their own, their posterity would never have occasion for; but if their posterity cannot live but as grossly as they do, the same gross materials must be left them to live upon. For a right to deprive anything of the means of living, supposes a right to deprive it of life; and this right ancestors are not supposed to have over their posterity.

Hence it is plain that the land or earth, in any country or neighbourhood, with everything in or on the same, or pertaining thereto, belongs at all times to the living inhabitants of the said country or neighbourhood in an equal manner. For as said before, there is no living but on land and its productions, consequently, what we cannot live without, we have the same property in as in our lives.

Now society being properly nothing but a mutual agreement among the inhabitants of a country, to maintain the natural rights and privileges of one another against all opposers, whether foreign or domestic, would lead one to expect to find those rights and privileges, no further infringed upon, among men pretending to be in that state, than necessity absolutely required. I say again, it would lead one to think so. But I am afraid whoever does will be mightily mistaken. However, as the truth here is of much importance to know, let it be fought out; in order to which, it may not be improper to trace the present method of holding land among men in society, from its original.

If we take a look back to the rise of the present nations, we shall see that the land with all its appurtenances was claimed by a few, and divided among themselves, in as assured a manner, as if they had manufactured it, and it had been the work of their own hands, and by being unquestioned, or not called to an account for such usurpations and unjust claims, they fell into a habit of thinking, or which is the same thing, to the rest of mankind, of acting as if the earth was made for or by them, and did not scruple to call it their own property, which they might dispose of without regard to any other living creature in the universe. Accordingly they did so, and neither a man, nor than any other creature, could claim a right to so much as a blade of grass, or a morsel of anything, though to save its life, without the permission of the proprietor; and not an inch of land, water, rock, or heath, but was claimed by one or other of these lords; so that all things, men as well as other creatures, who lived, were obliged to owe their lives to some or other's property, consequently they too were claimed, and as properly as the wood, herbs, etc., that were nourished by the soil. And so we find, that whether they lived, multiplied, worked or fought, it was all for their respective lords, and they most graciously accepted of all as their due. For by granting the means of life, they granted the life itself, and consequently they thought they had a right to all the services and advantages that the life or death of the creatures they gave life to could yield.

Thus the title of Gods seems suitably enough applied to such great beings: nor is it to be wondered at that no services could be thought too great by poor, dependent, needy wretches to such mighty and all-sufficient lords. Thus were the first land-holders usurpers and tyrants; and all who have since possessed their lands, have done so by right of inheritance, purchase, etc., from them; and the present proprietors, like their predecessors, are proud to own it; and like them too, they exclude all others from the least pretence to their respective properties. And any one of them still can by law oblige every living creature to remove off his property, (which, to the great distress of mankind, is too oft put in execution) so of consequence, were all the landholders to be of one mind, and determined to take their properties into their own hands, all the rest of mankind might go to heaven if they would, for there would be no place found for them here. Thus men may not live in any part of this world but by the permission of the pretender to the property thereof: which permission is for the most part paid extravagantly for, and they are still advancing the terms of permission though many people are so straitened to pay the present demands, that it is believed in a short time, if they hold on, there will be few to grant the favour to. And those Land-makers, as we shall call them, justify all this by the practice of other manufacturers, who take all they can get for the products of their hands, and because that every one ought to live by his business as well as he can, and consequently so ought the Land-makers. Now having before supposed it both proved and allowed, that mankind have as equal and just a property in land as they have in liberty, air, or the light and heat of the sun, and having also considered upon what hard conditions they enjoy those their privileges, it seems plain they do not reap all the advantages from them, which they might or ought to expect.

But lest it should be said, that a method whereby they might reap more advantages consistent with the nature of society cannot be proposed, I will attempt to show the outlines of such a method. Let it be supposed then, that the whole people in some country, after much reasoning, conclude, that each man has an equal property in the land in the neighbourhood where he resides. They therefore resolve, that if they live in society together, it shall only be with a view, that every one may reap all the benefits from their natural rights and privileges possible. Therefore a day is appointed on which the inhabitants of each parish meet, in their respective parishes, to form themselves into corporations. So then each parish becomes a corporation, and all the men who are inhabitants become members. The land, with all that appertains to it, is, in every parish, made the property of the corporation, with as ample power to let, repair, or alter all, or any part thereof, as a landlord enjoys over his lands, houses, etc. but the power of alienating the least morsel, in any manner, from the parish, either at this or any time hereafter, is denied. For it is solemnly agreed to, by the whole nation, that a parish that shall either sell, or give away, any part of its landed property, shall be looked upon with as much horror and detestation, and used by them as if they had sold all their children to be slaves, or massacred them with their own hands. Thus are there no more nor other landlords in the whole country than the parishes; and each of them is sovereign landlord of its own territories.

There you may behold the rent, which the people have paid into the parish boxes, employed by each parish in paying the government its share of the sum, which the parliament at any time grants; in maintaining and relieving its own poor, and people out of work; in paying its clergymen, schoolmasters and officers their salaries; in building, repairing and adorning its houses, bridges, and other structures; in making and maintaining convenient and delightful streets, highways, and passages both for foot and carriages; in making and maintaining canals, and other conveniences for trade and navigation; in planting and taking in waste grounds; in providing and keeping up a magazine of ammunition and all sorts of arms sufficient for all its inhabitants in case of danger from enemies; in premiums for the encouragement of agriculture, or any thing else thought worthy of encouragement; and, in a word, in doing whatever the people think proper; and not as formerly, to support and spread luxury, pride, and all manner of vice and corruption. Corruption has now no being or effect among them; for all affairs to be determined by voting either in a full meeting of a parish, its committees, or the house of parliament, are done by balloting. So that votings, or elections among them, occasion no animosities, for none need to let another know for which side he votes; all that can be done, therefore, in order to gain a majority of votes for any thing, is to make it appear in the best light possible by speaking or writing.

Among them government does not meddle in every trifle, but on the contrary, allows to each parish the power of putting the laws in force in all cases, even to the inflicting of death; and does not interfere, but when they act manifestly to the prejudice of society, and the rights and liberties of mankind as established in their glorious constitution and laws. For the judgment of a parish may be as much depended upon as that of a house of lords, because they have as little to fear from speaking or voting according to truth as they.

A certain number of neighbouring parishes have each an equal vote in the election of a person to represent them in parliament; and each of them pays equally towards his maintenance. He is chosen thus: all the candidates are proposed in every parish on the same day, when the election by balloting immediately proceeds, and he who has the majority in most of the parishes, is acknowledged to be their representative.

A man by dwelling a whole year in any parish becomes a parishioner, or member of its corporation; and retains that privilege, till he lives a full year in some other, when he becomes a member in that parish, and immediately loses all his right to the former for ever, unless he choose to go back and recover it, by dwelling again a full year there. Thus none can be a member of two parishes at once; and yet a man is always member of one, though he shift ever so oft.

Buildings, clergymen, etc. for the established religion of the country, are maintained by each parish out of its treasury; but dissenters, if they set up any other religion, must bear the expense of it themselves.

All the men in every parish, at times of their own choosing, repair together, to a field for that purpose, with their officers, arms, banners, and all sorts of martial music, in order to learn, or retain the complete art of war: there they become soldiers! Not to molest their neighbours unprovoked, but to be able to defend what none have a right to dispute, their title to the enjoyment of; and woe be to them who occasion them to do this! they would use them worse than highwaymen, or pirates, if they got them in their power.

There is no army kept in pay among them, in times of peace; as all have property alike to defend, they are alike ready to run to arms when their country is in danger; and when an army is to be sent abroad, it is soon raised, either by recruiting, or by casting lots in each parish for so many men.

Observe further: As each man has a vote in all the affairs of his parish, the land is let in very small farms, which makes employment for a greater number of hands; and makes more victualling of all kinds be raised.

There are no taxes of any kind paid among them, by native or foreigner, but the aforesaid rent, which every person pays to the parish, according to the quantity, quality, and conveniences of the land, housing, etc. which he occupies in it. The government, poor, roads, etc. etc. as said before, are all maintained, by the parishes with the rent; on which account all wares, manufactures, allowable trade, employments, or actions are entirely duty-free. Freedom to any thing whatever cannot there be bought; a thing is either entirely prohibited as theft or murder; or entirely free to every one without tax or price. And the rents are still not so high, notwithstanding all that is done with them, as they were formerly, for only the maintenance of a few haughty, unthankful landlords. For the government, which is the greatest mouth, having neither excisemen, customhouse men, collectors, army, pensioners, bribery, nor such like ruin-nation vermin to maintain, is soon satisfied; and, moreover, there are no more persons employed in offices, either about the government or parishes, than are absolutely necessary; and their salaries are but just sufficient to maintain them suitable to their offices. And as to the other charges, they are but trifles, and might be increased or diminished at pleasure.

But though the rents were obliged to be something raised, what then? All nations have a devouring landed interest to support besides those necessary expenses of the public; and they might be raised very high indeed before their burden would be as heavy as that of their neighbours. And it surely would be the same, for a person in any country to pay for instance five pounds taxes a year, at once upon one thing, as to do it by little and little upon every thing he gets. It would certainly save him a great deal of trouble and inconvenience, and government much expense.

And the final consequence of all this, all things that are allowed to be imported from abroad; or that are the growth, or manufacture of the country, are as cheap as possible; and living is so easy, that he must be a rogue in his heart that cannot honestly live there.

But what makes this prospect yet more glorious is, that after this empire is thus established, it will stand for ever. Force and corruption attempting its downfall, shall equally be baffled, and all other nations struck with wonder and admiration at its happiness and stability, shall follow the example; and thus the whole earth shall at last be happy, and live like brethren.

2
Paine, Spence, Chartism and 'The Real Rights of Man'

•

Malcolm Chase

His creed was – and Thomas Spence had taught it him – that 'the Land is the people's farm' and that it belongs to the entire nation, not to individuals or classes.[1]

Thus did George Harney, a pivotal figure in nineteenth-century radical politics, begin a speech to a Chartist meeting in south London in 1845. Born in 1817 on a troopship lying off Deptford, Harney was the son of a naval rating. Too sickly to follow his father to sea, he started his working life as a potboy in a London pub until, aged seventeen, he was taken on by the leading radical bookseller and publisher Henry Hetherington. The latter was at the height of his influence, publishing the great unstamped weekly *Poor Man's Guardian*, and the teenage Harney quickly absorbed his employer's politics. A few months later London's other great radical publisher at this time, Richard Carlile, faced financial ruin when his entire stock was confiscated after he refused to pay church rates. Harney's response was to decorate the window of his employer's shop with grotesque effigies of a Church of England bishop and the Devil.[2]

Harney was no milk and water radical, demonstrating but never fighting for his beliefs. In the same year as his vivid gesture of support for Carlile, he served the first of three prison sentences for selling unstamped newspapers. He was co-founder of what — in effect — was a Paineite club: the London Democratic Association, the largest and liveliest of the capital's Chartist organisations. From here Harney forged a reputation as one of the outstanding leaders of Chartism, the reform movement that dominated domestic politics during much of the early Victorian period. In 1843, Harney joined the staff of *Northern Star*, the mighty Chartist weekly that, at its peak, outsold even *The Times* (and was thus, by definition, the biggest selling newspaper in history up to that point). As editor of the *Star* paper, Harney commissioned Frederick Engels to contribute articles on German politics, and he became good friends with Engels and also Marx who, by 1847, was speaking at Harney's invitation at London Chartist meetings.

Despite the decline of Chartism, Harney's career as a campaigning journalist continued. He was still writing a regular column of political comment and

1 *Northern Star* 30 August 1845.

2 'George Julian Harney', in *Dictionary of Labour Biography*, vol. 10, ed. J. Bellamy and J. Saville, (Basingstoke: Macmillan, 2000), pp. 81-92.

reminiscence for the *Newcastle Weekly Chronicle* when he died, aged 80, in 1897. I detail Harney's political career because he was a pivotal figure in the history of British radical politics. In his youth he had been the friend of veterans from the London Corresponding Society of the 1790s; he outlived both Marx and Engels and was still writing newspaper columns into the late 1890s (some readers of which would have lived into the 1950s). One of the things that interests me as a historian is the transmission of political ideas — not so much through the intellectual analysis of the influence of one great writer upon another, but rather at the 'grassroots' level of day-to-day belief and conviction. Eloquent testimony to the importance of Thomas Paine in this sense is to be found in the words of the almost apoplectic Attorney General at Paine's trial for seditious libel in 1792: 'In all shapes and in all sizes, with an industry incredible, it [Paine's *Rights of Man* Part 2] was either totally or partially thrust into the hands of all persons in this country … even children's sweetmeats were wrapped in parts, and delivered into their hands, in the hope that they would read it'.[3]

It is therefore very significant that a leading political activist of Harney's stature should have nailed his political colours so firmly to the mast not of Paine but of the other great radical Tom of the 1790s, Thomas Spence. Harney even took this admiration so far as to call for the statue of Earl Grey to be removed from the famous monument in Newcastle and one of Spence to be placed there instead.[4] For Harney and the Chartists, Spence (not Paine) was the benchmark figure in the evolution of ideas about land reform. In this the Chartists were deferring to a position that Spence himself first advanced in 1795, in *The End of Oppression*, a dialogue 'between an old mechanic and a young one'. It was a theme to which he would return several times, that Paine for all his manifest merits did not go far enough in prescribing what the future shape of society should be.

> YOUNG MAN: I hear there is another RIGHTS OF MAN by *Spence* that goes farther than *Paine's*.
> OLD MAN: Yet it goes no farther than it ought.
> YOUNG MAN: I understand that it suffers *no* private property in land, but gives it all to the parishes.
> OLD MAN: In doing so it does right, the earth was not made for individuals …
> YOUNG MAN: It is amazing that Paine and other democrats should level all their artillery at kings, without striking like Spence at this root of every abuse and of every grievance.[5]

An uncritical deference to Paine's memory all-too-easily obscures the contribution of others among his contemporaries to radical political thought. Especially in the field of agrarian ideas, concerning the distribution and tenure of

3 From Archibald MacDonald's speech for the prosecution at Paine's seditious libel trial in 1792, reprinted in *Revolutions in Romantic Literature: An Anthology of Print Culture*, ed. Paul Keen, (Peterborough, ON: Broadview, 2004), p. 32.

4 *Northern Star* 31 August 1850; see also *Reynolds's Weekly News*, 1 September 1850.

5 Thomas Spence, *The End of Oppression, being a Dialogue between an Old Mechanic and a Young One, Concerning the Establishment of the Rights of Man*, 2nd edn (London: Spence, 1795), p. 3.

landed property, it was Spence not Paine whose influence was the more decisive. What follows considers Spence's criticisms of Paine's *Agrarian Justice* (1797) and traces their subsequent reception, notably by Richard Carlile, and their influence through to Chartism and beyond.

Unlike Paine, Spence was not a 'citizen of the world'. He seems not to have travelled beyond Northumberland and London, although he probably did meet the future French Revolutionary Jean Paul Marat during the latter's residence in Britain in 1765-77.[6] The formative influences on his distinctive brand of political radicalism were seventeenth-century and Enlightenment ideas, especially the neo-classical concept of natural law. The young Spence was also shaped by an iconoclastic Calvinism and until his death his political beliefs had a strongly millenarian tone. His critique of private property was qualitatively different from the customary eighteenth-century radical attack on land as inducing effeminate and corrupting luxury, or for having abrogated its reciprocal obligations to society at large. Private property in land, Spence argued, was a wholesale theft, for the loss of which there could be no act of reciprocity — certainly not the system of taxation and pensions proposed by Paine. In terms of the development of natural law theories of property he may not have made as decisive a break as Paine did; but this is, literally, an academic issue. Greater historical significance should be attached to the impact of political ideas on contemporary popular political practice and thinking.

For Spence the original state of nature was a simple axiom and therefore one to which he devoted comparatively little time:

> That property in land and liberty among men, in a state of nature, ought to be equal, few, one would fain hope, would be foolish enough to deny. Therefore, taking this to be granted, the country of any people, in a native state, is properly their common, in which each of them has an equal property, with free liberty to sustain himself and connexions with the animals, fruits and other products thereof.[7]

Spence's idea of an original state of nature owes a little — but only a little — to divine intervention: there are none of Paine's contortions in accepting this. In fact Spence does not seem to have been very interested in the issue, instead concentrating on building up moral and political arguments in favour of community of property (exactly what he means by community of property is a point to which we shall return). For Spence the true significance of the state of nature was wider than that advanced by Paine in *Agrarian Justice*. It is as much liberty as land which is important in the state of nature, which in Spence's thought is far from being notional. The biblical authority he emphasised was not Genesis, but the early Hebrew republic under Moses. Hence the state of nature

6 Malcolm Chase, *The People's Farm: English Radical Agrarianism, 1775-1840*, 2nd edition (London: Breviary Stuff, 2010 [first published by Oxford University Press, 1988]), pp. 23-4. The analysis of Spence's theories that follows is based on chapters 2 and 3 of this book.

7 Thomas Spence, *Property in Land Every One's Right, proved in a Lecture read at the Philosophical Society in Newcastle, on the 8th of Nov. 1775* (Newcastle upon Tyne: n.p., 1775), p. 1. This is the first edition of his key publication, published several subsequent times by Spence under the title *The Real Rights of Man*.

on which Spence mainly rested his arguments was not the Garden of Eden. Nor was it some kind of arcadian wilderness after the manner of John Locke. Rather, in the tradition of the civic humanists of the seventeenth century, it was an economic and social democracy in which an active civic life was possible for all: in the Spencean vision of how society should be, 'each parish is a little polished Athens'.[8]

Spence therefore rejected any notion of a social contract, arguing that private property in land was anathema. 'Our boasted civilisation is founded on conquest'; if the 'country of any people, in A NATIVE STATE is properly their common', then they jointly reap its fruits and advantages: 'for upon what must they live if not upon the productions of the country in which they reside? Surely to deny them that right is in effect denying them a right to live?' It follows from this that members of any one generation cannot, by personally appropriating the soil, deny rights to that soil to generations after them. 'For to deprive anything of the means of living, supposes a right to deprive it of life; and this right ancestors are not supposed to have over their posterity'.[9]

Here again Spence broke free from the prevailing conception — derived from Locke — of the development of private property in land. And here, too, lies the fundamental difference of his views from those of Paine, in the disavowal that time confers innocence upon private property in land. 'There is no living but on the land and its productions, consequently, what we cannot live without we have the same property in as our lives'. It should be noted though, that Spence followed Locke in using the term *property* to embrace selfhood ('what we cannot live without we have the same property in as our lives'). It is this property in one's own life that is the most important of all property rights, and upon which communal rights of ownership in land are contingent. The so-called 'right' of private property in land is no right at all, but its very antithesis: a pretence and usurpation sanctioned only by the apathy or ignorance of the population as a whole about their true rights. Any ascendancy over land is hence an ascendancy over people. Therefore in Spence's view the issue of land ownership lay at the root of all social inequality, economic exploitation and injustice.

In his early works, Spence advanced the argument that the power of education would suffice to secure universal assent to a system of agrarian equality. It was to be some time after he moved to London, and immersed himself in the radical maelstrom of the capital as it reacted to the French Revolution, that Spence sharpened his perception that more forceful means might be needed to persuade land-owners to yield up their property. His perception of the ends, however, was unchanging: a partnership in every community of the residents of all ages and both sexes, equally dividing between them the revenue from the lease of the land to those who actually cultivated it. Restrictions would be placed on the duration of leases and the size of holdings. Each community would be self-governing, but joined with others in a federation

8 Thomas Spence, *Supplement to the History of Robinson Crusoe* (Newcastle upon Tyne, Saint, 1782), p. 30.

9 Spence, *Property in Land Every One's Right*, p. 3.

to coordinate the defence of the nation by citizen militias.

Once in London, where he moved from Tyneside in 1788, Spence devoted himself full-time to radical politics, printing and writing and — his own unique contribution to popular political culture — the manufacture of copper token coins depicting radical icons and figures (including Paine) and inscribed with slogans. He also devoted much time to the affairs of the London Corresponding Society, as a member of its general executive committee and publisher of some of its publications. In 1793 he was one of a distinguished group of signatories to the *Declaration* of the Friends of the Liberty of the Press. He was arrested several times, including twice in December 1796 for selling Paine's *Rights of Man*. In 1794 Spence was detained without trial for seven months on suspicion of high treason. Imprisonment only had the effect of galvanising him more. Soon after his release he published the pamphlet *The End of Oppression*. Here Spence re-evaluated the means by which his reforms could be secured and conceded for the first time that compulsion would be necessary. It was at this point that he attacked other reformers (Paine included) for passing over the critical issue of agrarian reform. Not only did Spence now explicitly endorse the use of force to secure radical objectives, he was emphatic that the destruction of the economic basis of political power must be chief among those objectives. It was a controversial and far-reaching step, and it met with considerable opposition among metropolitan radicals. Spence answered with a biting *Recantation of the End of Oppression*, containing this barely-veiled satirical attack on Thomas Paine:

> Adieu then to striving against the stream, since the readiest way to get to port is to go with it. So here goes, my boys, for an estate and vassals to bow to me! Who would not be a gentleman and live without care! Especially a democratic gentleman without a king. Avaunt rights of man! I am henceforth a democrat, but no leveller.[10]

Spence further developed his critique of Paine in *The Rights of Infants* (1797), which also contained an extensive argument in favour of women's rights, including to the vote. This concern to widen the constituency of radical politics was also reflected in his continuing preoccupation with education and it was as an educator and author that he was mainly content to concentrate his energies. However from the beginning of the nineteenth century until his death in 1814, Spence attracted a small but loyal circle of followers, the Spencean Philanthropists. His book *The Restorer of Society to its Natural State*, published in 1801, the year the Spencean Philanthropists were founded, reiterated the justice of applying force to secure reform, invoking the examples of the American and French Revolutions and the British naval mutinies of 1797. For this Spence was arrested and tried for seditious libel. William Cobbett attended his trial: 'he had no counsel and insisted that his views were *pure* and *benevolent* ... He was a plain, unaffected, inoffensive–looking creature. He did not seem at all afraid of any punishment, and appeared much more anxious about the success

10 *Spence's Recantation of the End of Oppression* (London: Spence, 1795), p. 4.

of his *plan* than about the preservation of his life'.[11]

Spence was gaoled for a year. It ruined him financially. On his release he resumed bookselling from a barrow, usually stationed in Oxford Street and more enterprisingly sometimes in Parliament Street, Westminster. But the Spencean Philanthropists continued to meet and were responsible for a flurry of publications in which their leader's ideas were further refined to embrace forms of public ownership for 'Shipping, Collieries, Mines and Many other Great Concerns'.[12] It was they who organised Spence's funeral in 1814.

It is clear from the Spence's *Recantation of the End of Oppression*, that his very real admiration for Paine was tinged by envy — and this even before Paine's *Agrarian Justice* was published. The latter served only to strengthen Spence's conviction that republicanism alone would not suffice to secure real justice. The very name of its author secured for *Agrarian Justice* an audience far beyond Spence's vainest hopes. One senses a certain righteous indignation that Paine (for selling whose publications Spence had after all twice been imprisoned) should venture into agrarian reform entirely without reference to him. (We can only conjecture how far, if at all, Paine was acquainted with Spenceanism.)

Like Spence, Paine postulated the historical reality of the state of nature, in which the right of every individual to an equable share of the soil was absolute; both men believed that such a situation persisted among North America's indigenous peoples. In such a state, Paine points out, there were none of,

> those spectacles of human misery which poverty and want present to our eyes in all the towns and streets of Europe. Poverty therefore is a thing created by that which is called civilised life. It exists not in the natural state.[13]

Spence and Paine therefore shared their primary supposition: but thenceforward their proposals diverged. Paine does not countenance the real yet figurative state of nature that Spence sought to restore. On the contrary, he held that, 'it is never possible to go from the civilised to the natural state', because the latter was incapable of supporting the level of population that, through manufactures and commerce, it could in civilisation.[14]

The problem as Paine perceived it was therefore not really agrarian at all: it was one of poverty. 'I am', he declared, 'a friend to riches because they are capable of doing good. I care not how affluent some may be, provided that none be miserable in consequence of it'. Thus it was that he posited in *Agrarian Justice* that all landowners should pay 'to the community a ground-rent', to be accumulated in a national fund. From the latter every person reaching the age of 21 would receive a bounty of 'Fifteen Pounds Sterling, enabling him, or her, to begin in the World'; and all persons aged fifty and over would receive an annuity

11 *Political Register* 34: (14 December 1816), col. 634.

12 *Spence's Songs: Part the Third* (London: Spence, [1812?].

13 Thomas Paine, *Agrarian Justice Opposed to Agrarian Law, and to Agrarian Monopoly*, '2nd edition', (London: Watson, 1842?), p. 5.

14 Paine, *Agrarian Justice*, p. 5.

of £10, 'to enable them to live in Old Age without Wretchedness, and go decently out of the world'.[15] Having made this postulation, virtually the rest of *Agrarian Justice* is devoted to the arithmetic of the proposal. Paine's calculations were no more or less spurious than those which feature in the writings of other reformers, for example Cobbett arguing that the population of early nineteenth-century England was declining, or Robert Owen arguing that the soil would be much more productive if ploughs were abandoned in favour of spade husbandry.

Paine's proposals had sufficient in common with Spenceanism for Spence to feel perhaps that his ideas were in danger of being eclipsed. But mainly Spence was irked by Paine's refusal to return to first principles and disavow that the passing of time rendered private property in land morally innocent. Paine's *Agrarian Justice* would extend no democratic control over the land and no opportunity for the landless to return to it if they so wished. In Spence's view, Paine's plan would effectively reinforce the landed interest by incorporating it into a centralised state system of welfare payments.

> Under the system of Agrarian justice, the people will, as it were, sell their birthright for a mess of porridge [*sic*], by accepting a paltry consideration in lieu of their rights ... [T]he people will become supine and careless in respect of public affairs, knowing the utmost they can receive of the public money.[16]

This was a major issue for Spence, the latter-day civic humanist for whom in each 'little polished Athens' there would be extensive public participation in the processes of government. He was quick to argue that Paine's version of *Agrarian Justice* would give rise to 'the sneaking unmanly spirit of conscious dependence'.[17] In Spence's opinion, his own plan would be an incentive to vigilance over public expenditure, necessitating parliamentary democracy and stimulating education. His greatest fear was that Paine's vision would deteriorate into a placebo for social ills, masking the continuation of oppression. For Spence, the distribution of property, rather than political systems in themselves, determines the real character of a nation and the liberties it enjoys. 'What does it signify whether the form of government be monarchical or republican while [landed] estates can be acquired?', he demanded.

This critique of 'Paine and other democrats who level all their artillery at kings' is essentially a civic humanist one. Indeed, in his works Spence quotes James Harrington, the formative theorist of British civic humanism, more frequently than any other author.[18] If there is a pivotal transitional figure in the development of radical ideas about property it is Spence, not Paine. The latter's *Agrarian Justice* represents at most a fine-tuning of the secularisation of natural law arguments. It is doubtful what impact — if any — these actually had. In the nineteenth century *Agrarian Justice* received little attention other than as a coda to its author's earlier and more significant works. It was not reprinted after the

15 Paine, *Agrarian Justice*, pp. 11, 13.

16 Thomas Spence, *Rights of Infants* (London: Spence, 1797), p. 11.

17 Spence, *Rights of Infants*, p. 12.

18 Chase, *People's Farm*, pp. 29-39, 32, 49-50.

1790s until William Sherwin's edition in 1817; Carlile produced another (1819). It then lay dormant until the 1830s.

Why this neglect? Great as his reputation as a democrat and polemicist was, Paine's *Agrarian Justice* is deficient as an argument for land reform. Its most eye-catching proposal, for old age pensions, simply repeats without much elaboration remarks he had made in *Rights of Man* Part 2. Its fiscal proposals, concentrating as they do on death duties, are arguably less radical in scope and intent than the progressive taxation Paine had earlier proposed in *Rights of Man*. Paine's *Agrarian Justice* was markedly less innovative in character than the work of Thomas Spence, and it was less precise in identifying the roots of injustice — all this without the compensatory merit of being any more plausible or practicable. Arguably, it reveals an estrangement between Paine and English popular radicalism, the consequence perhaps of his years of exile.

Paine's so-called agrarian reform, doing nothing to reduce the power of the landed interest, attracted little attention other than on account of its author. It was Spence's agrarianism which more commonly informed theory and practice in the early labour and radical movements. This is evident even in the writings of Paine's indefatigable disciple Richard Carlile. For example in 1822 Carlile, in an extensive essay on tax reform, rejected the argument that financial investments should alone be subject to taxation, thus creating an equitable tax that would avoid discriminating against the poor while taxing only those able to pay.[19] Carlile was not opposed to a socially progressive tax regime; but he argued that to base a so-called 'equitable tax' on investments would concede the legal and moral right to such property. Carlile opposed this: 'land, and land only', he argued, was 'the only tangible property'. The only sensible, and morally defensible, equitable tax would be 'the Spencean plan ... certainly the most simple and most equitable system of society and government that can be imagined'.

The Spencean plan, Carlile continued, had been dismissed without proper examination. It was eminently suited to immediate adoption by the emerging republics of Latin America though it was futile 'to urge it against the prejudices of those who have established properties in this country' given the economic make-up of the Houses of Parliament. However, a reformed parliament should pursue, Carlile argued, a single equitable tax on land as the most effective social and financial strategy for social reform. The owners of large estates, much of them unproductive parks or shooting land, would be forced either to give them up or turn them over to productive cultivation in order to meet the burden of the tax. This incentive to full cultivation was in turn a guarantor of greater employment, which would in turn increase demand for goods and agricultural produce that — because no longer taxed — would be more affordable.

Thereafter the 'equitable tax' would be a recurrent feature of Carlile's political thinking. And whenever he returned to the land question, he would cite Thomas Spence as his prime authority, reiterating the merits of equitable taxation:

19 *Republican* 22 November 1822.

> The sentiment of Thomas Spence, that THE LAND IS THE PEOPLE'S FARM, is incontrovertible by any other argument than that of the sword. The land cannot be equitably divided among the people; but all rent raised from it may be made public revenue, and to save the people from taxation.[20]

The case against '[a]grarian monopoly and usury ... the two master evils of society' was one of the few economic arguments that Richard Carlile consistently advocated across his long and turbulent career. Indeed, this was the economic policy that sat alongside his advocacy of Paineite republicanism in the political arena. Criticising the early Chartist movement's preoccupation with parliamentary reform, Carlile declared in 1839 that the Spencean agenda was 'a subject worth thinking, worth talking, worth writing, worth printing ... Universal Suffrage, in the present state of mind, and church, and kings, and priests and lords, is all humbug and trickery compared to it'. The Chartists should be 'for getting the rent paid to the right landlord', and he concluded by repeating Spence's slogan 'the Land is the people's farm'.[21]

This is an instructive moment in the history of radicalism. Richard Carlile, perhaps Paine's foremost disciple, was urging the nascent Chartist movement to draw back from universal suffrage in favour Spencean land reform. Though he did reprint Paine's *Agrarian Justice*, Carlile clearly saw Spence as the more authoritative thinker on agrarian and fiscal reform. Spencean theories were central to the pedigree of radical ideas about property and taxation in a way that Paine's were not.

Carlile was not alone in arguing that 'the Land is the people's farm', as Harney's tribute to Spence that opened this chapter indicates.[22] Robert Owen recounted with pride in his autobiography how he was once mistaken for Spence.[23] Francis Place, architect of the repeal of the Combination Acts which had made trade unions illegal between 1798 and 1824, endorsed the views 'of my old and esteemed friend ... making the whole country the *people's farm*'.[24] The innovative thinking of Thomas Spence on land reform was a bench-mark to which subsequent radicals (and sometimes their opponents) often referred. Among opponents, for example, Thomas Malthus singled out Spence for specific criticism in the extensively revised 1817 edition of his *Essay on Population*.[25] Regency contemporaries also read earlier work by Malthus as targeting 'Spence's plan'.[26] In 1833, John Stuart Mill warned of the dangers of falling 'into the

20 *Gauntlet* 10 February 1833.

21 *Operative* 3 March 1839.

22 Other examples of Chartists using 'The People's Farm' formula can be found in *Northern Star* 26 July 1845, 4 July and 1 August 1846, 29 May and 20 November 1847, and 8 December 1849.

23 Robert Owen, *Life of Robert Owen, Written by Himself*, (London: Effingham Wilson, 1858), p. 389.

24 *London Dispatch* 18 June 1837.

25 Thomas Malthus, *Essay on the Principle of Population*, 5th edn (London: Murray, 1817), vol. 2, book 3, ch. 3, pp. 276-281.

26 Specifically his *Inquiry into the Nature and Progress of Rent* (London: Murray, 1815): see Anon., *An Inquiry into those Principles Respecting the Nature of Demand and the Necessity of Consumption* (London, 1821), p. 108. See also *A Brief Vindication of the Principles of Mr. Malthus, in a Letter to the Author of an Article in the Quarterly Review* (London,

vagaries of Spenceanism', whilst a decade late Marx enlisted Spence in his *German Ideology*.[27] Beyond Chartism, Spencean ideas became a point of reference for a variety of reformers, including the pioneer of the Garden City movement, Ebenezer Howard. The rediscovery of Spence by H. M. Hyndman was especially significant. In 1882, at the insistence of Henry George, Hyndman republished what he described as 'Spence's practical and thoroughly English proposal for nationalisation of the land'.[28] This was the first of three important late nineteenth-century reprints of Spence, the others being the initiatives of the English Land Restoration Society in 1896, and the Independent Labour Party *Labour Leader* in 1900.[29]

But it is within Chartism that Spence's influence was particularly influential. The Chartist movement was (as it remains) one of the high points in the history of British popular politics. It was in effect Britain's civil rights movement. Its foundation document, the People's Charter of 1838, concentrated upon the need to reform parliament, and for universal male suffrage in particular. This, however, should not be allowed to obscure the deeper and more-fundamental challenge that Chartism posed to the political establishment of early Victorian Britain; and that establishment, of course, was overwhelmingly still a landed one. Especially during the years after 1842, when Parliament rejected Chartism's greatest petition (mustering 3.3 million signatures), Chartists directed their energies to a broader social and economic reform agenda. It was here that Spence's ideas were particularly influential.

Throughout the years after Spence's death, former members of the Spencean Philanthropists were pivotal figures in London radical politics. For example, the London Democratic Association, the organisation that absorbed George Harney's earliest Chartist energies, counted among its members several influential Spenceans, including Spence's biographer, the poet and socialist Allen Davenport, and the Brick Lane tailor turned radical bookseller Charles Hodgson Neesom (who, in 1847, would also became a founding member of Britain's first ever Vegetarian Society).[30] The young Harney was profoundly influenced by the Spencean generation and in turn disseminated awareness of Spence through the *Northern Star*, especially promoting Davenport's writings about Spence.[31]

Studies of Chartist attitudes to landed property have overwhelmingly focused

---

1813), pp. 32-33.

27 [J. S. Mill], *Tait's Edinburgh Magazine*, vol. 3 (1833), p. 352; Karl Marx and Frederick Engels, *The German Ideology* vol. 2, ch. 1 (1846/7), reprinted in Karl Marx and Frederick Engels, *Collected Works*, vol. 5 (London: Lawrence & Wishart, 1976), pp. 460-461.

28 H. M. Hyndman, *Nationalisation of the Land in 1775 and 1882* (London: Allen, 1882).

29 Frederich Verinder, *Land for the Landless* (London: English Land Restoration League, 1896); J. M. Davidson, *Concerning Four Precursors of Henry George and the Single Tax* (Glasgow: *Labour Leader* Publishing Department, 1900).

30 See the entries for Davenport and Neesom in *Dictionary of Labour Biography*, vol. 8; *The Life and Literary Pursuits of Allen Davenport, with a Further Selection of the Author's Work*, ed. Malcolm Chase (Aldershot: Scolar Press, 1994); Malcolm Chase, *Chartism: A New History* (Manchester: Manchester University Press, 2007), esp. pp. 184-191.

31 Reviews of Davenport's life of Spence and of his own autobiography appeared in *Northern Star* 30 August 1845 and 27 June 1846. Other Spence material appearing under Harney's editorship can be found in these issues: 26 July 1845, 29 May, 27 June, 20 November 1847, 13-27 January 1849, 3-10 February and 31 March 1849.

upon its Land Plan, a remarkable (but sadly also remarkably flawed) initiative to settle its members on the land in cottage smallholdings. It speaks volumes for the extent of popular interest in agrarian reform that the Land Plan could mobilise well-over 70,000 subscribers in the teeth of the economic crisis of 1847-1848. However, the sheer scale of the Chartist Land Plan has obscured the extent to which agrarian ideas were central to other facets of the movement.[32] Furthermore, historians have traditionally had difficulty reconciling the sturdy possessive individualism of the Land Plan with other arguments within Chartism for public ownership of the soil. Chartists advanced arguments for, variously, forcible re-appropriation, land and building societies, a free market in landed property, deeply radical taxation regimes and, from 1850, 'the Charter and something more' (a social democratic programme with land nationalisation at its heart).

Yet three common elements underpinned them all. First was an outright hostility to *large* accumulations of landed property, irrespective of the legal form in which they might be held. Secondly, therefore, Chartism was suspicious of central government as the putative owner or manager of the national estate. Thirdly, all Chartist conceptions of land reform shared a 'way of seeing' land that was shaped by ideas of shared access, usage and control rather than by possessive individualism. These three elements very much encapsulate the essence of Spence's thinking.

A powerful adjunct to this perspective was that, of all methods of organising land holding, smallholding maximised the productivity return from working on the land. This in turn would alleviate poverty both by widening employment opportunities and increasing food production, countering the spectre of starvation that Whig Malthusians used to justify the draconian 1834 reform of the poor law. This perspective on land holding was also powerfully rooted in contemporary idealization of spade husbandry (just about the only principle held consistently and unanimously by three greatest figures of early nineteenth-century radicalism, William Cobbett, Robert Owen and Feargus O'Connor). Even Bronterre O'Brien, the Land Plan's fiercest critic from within the Chartist movement, eulogized smallholding.[33]

The development of arguments favouring large-scale collective farming was an ideological Rubicon that no Chartist ever crossed. Land nationalisers and Land Planners alike favoured small-scale cultivation. Support for land nationalization certainly did not equate with any interest in the collectivization of agriculture. For the Chartists, suspicion of centralizing state power was a *leitmotif*. This, like the promotion of the smallholding ideal, was one of the elements that bound together supporters of the Land Plan with its critics in the movement. And it was an element which acted to curtail enthusiasm for land nationalization, because the mechanism needed to administer the national estate

32 The paragraphs that follow draw on a much-more detailed analysis in Malcolm Chase, 'Chartism and the land: "The mighty people's question"', in *The Land Question in Britain, 1750-1950*, ed. Matthew Cragoe and Paul Readman, (Basingstoke: Palgrave Macmillan, 2010).

33 [Bronterre O'Brien], *A Brief Inquiry into the Natural Rights of Man* (London: Watson, 1852), p. 45; see also *Northern Star* 27 Nov 1841.

was essentially incompatible with the Chartist concept of light government nationally and significant local autonomy. The response of the main Chartist land nationaliser, Bronterre O'Brien, to this was to argue (just as Spence had done) in favour of local community control, once the nationalisation of property in soil had been secured by nationwide legislation. For O'Brien, Spence was a pioneering political thinker: 'Twenty years ago the doctrine of making land public property would subject the man who held it to the imputation of either being a fool or a rogue; and even Cobbett could find no better excuse for poor Spence than that he was half-cracked. But now, thank god, the doctrine had ceased to be considered either knavish or ridiculous'.[34]

For Chartists of every persuasion, the first duties of a reformed parliament would include land reform:

> Monopoly of land is the source of every social and political evil ... every law which 'grinds the face of the poor' has emanated from time to time from this anomalous monopoly ... our national debt, our standing army, our luscious law church, our large police force, our necessity for 'pauper' rates, our dead weight, our civil list, our glorious rag money, our unjust laws, our game laws, our impure magistracy, our prejudiced jury system, our pampered court, and the pampered menials thereunto belonging, are one and all so many fences thrown round the people's inheritance.[35]

The Land Plan's presiding genius and Chartism's greatest leader, Feargus O'Connor, specifically interweaved mechanisation into this catalogue of injustice:

> What is the loud demand of the working people for a plain, simple, and efficient PLAN for practical operations on THE LAND, but the effort of man to regain his natural position, from which he has been dislodged by the combined operations of high-taxation, paper-money, and an unduly-hot-bed-forced amount of manufacturing machinery?[36]

This abiding perception of history as a continuing decline in the people's fortunes echoes both Spence and William Cobbett and it had an important impact on Chartist ideology. It meant that even within the deepening economic difficulties of the 1840s, an agrarian analysis of contemporary problems — and an agrarian prescription for them — was not redundant. The key social problem that Chartists perceived was not so much a society that was rapidly industrialising, but a society that was increasingly divided (politically, socially and economically) between rich and poor. Therefore all Chartists agreed land reform must be a political, economic and social imperative for a reformed parliament. There was virtual unanimity that the basis on which land should be held for cultivation must be that of smallholdings and small farms. The emergence of arguments in favour of land nationalization was attenuated by suspicion of the State and its centralizing tendencies, as well as by a continued

34 *Northern Star* 8 December 1849.

35 *Northern Star* 22 March 1845.

36 *Northern Star* 26 August 1843.

disposition in favour of small-scale ownership (which in time meant ex-Chartists contributed significantly to the emergence of building societies).

Was there a single defining feature of the various Chartist positions on land reform? There was and it can be described as neo-Spencean. The ostensibly Janus-headed stance of the Chartists, at once critical of private ownership of the soil and yet zealous in promoting smallholdings, ceases to be problematic once we register that the key issue for all Chartist land reformers was access to — rather than direct ownership of — the land.

Concluding a lengthy account (spread over three weeks) of Spence's life and trial, *Northern Star* commented: 'As yet no stone or other memorial marks the spot where this persecuted friend of mankind at length found rest. When will the gratitude of the working classes raise a fitting monument to commemorate the virtues, and martyr-like sacrifices, of this model man of their "order"?'[37] Thomas Spence mattered to Chartism. When Spence spoke of 'the real rights', or 'the whole rights' of man, he was signalling that the radical political agenda for which Paine argued had to become more radical still. Republicanism, even accompanied by progressive taxation, would not alone suffice to restore humanity to the natural state Spence believed necessary and possible. In Chartism's emphatic drive for radical parliamentary reform, we can see the working out of Paineite thinking. And in the same movement's impulse towards agrarian reform, we can see the working out of Spencean thinking.

37 *Northern Star* 13, 20 and 27 January 1849.

3

Four Roads from 'Genesis': Spence, Paine and Rights to Property

•

Gregory Claeys

> YOUNG MAN: I hear there is another RIGHTS OF MAN by Spence, that goes farther than Paine's.
> OLD MAN: Yet it goes no farther than it ought.
> YOUNG MAN: I understand it suffers no private property in land, but gives it all to the parishes.
> OLD MAN: In so doing it does right, the earth was not made for individuals.[1]

The careers of Thomas Paine (1737-1809) and Thomas Spence (1750-1814) parallel and intertwine with each other in a variety of interesting ways. Both were of plebeian origin and had Dissenting backgrounds, though Spence's precise affiliations are unclear. Spence probably having been influenced by his father's Sandemanianism, while Paine was raised as a Quaker and was for a time a Methodist preacher. Both would die in relative obscurity, martyrs to the cause of the 'rights of nature' whose historians today in their construction of genealogies of 'human rights' still occasionally pay homage. The 'unfed advocate of the disinherited seed of Adam', as he described himself at his trial, Spence would be remembered as a forerunner of Marxism and the later nineteenth century land nationalisation movement led by Alfred Russel Wallace and others. After much controversy, Paine would become a failed Founding Father and radical American alter ego. Cited without being named in Barack Obama's first inaugural address, he would be reincarnated once again by the libertarian right of the Tea Party.

Whether the two ever met is unknown though unlikely.[2] For a time their paths crossed in London. We do not know when exactly Spence arrived in the metropolis, the first information about him there being dated at the time of his arrest on 6 December 1792 for selling Paine's *Rights of Man*.[3] But Paine had fled to France in September that year and they may have overlapped for several years if Spence's purported arrival in London in 1787 or 1788 is correct. Their

1 Thomas Spence. *The End of Oppression* (1795), p. 1.

2 None of Paine's biographers has found a connection. Spence has been described as 'very friendly' with Paine, however: Richard Gimbel, 'Thomas Paine Fights for Freedom in Three Worlds', *American Antiquarian Society Proceedings*, 70 (1960), p. 477.

3 Both Francis Place and William Hone met him first in this year (P. M. Ashraf. *The Life and Times of Thomas Spence*, (Newcastle upon Tyne: Frank Graham, 1983), p. 41).

starting-points as public figures were distant. Spence's first lecture in Newcastle in 1775 laid the foundations for the 'Plan for Parochial Partnerships' he thereafter adhered to. Paine burst forth upon the public stage with *Common Sense*, which appeared in early 1776 after his emigration to the American colonies in 1774, and was instrumental in turning the colonists towards a complete breach with Britain. Paine would go on to both international fame and infamy, becoming a figure of immense controversy in Britain over *Rights of Man*. Then, after the *Age of Reason* (1794) appeared, he became increasingly unpopular in the United States in particular. Spence suffered imprisonment several times, and, after a brief meteoric ascent into public view would sink, comparatively, into relative obscurity, reviving chiefly when his name was linked to the Cato Street Conspiracy to assassinate the prime minister, Lord Liverpool.

Yet in the intellectual history of radicalism and the labour movement both figures remain of interest. Their intellectual engagement, such as it was, culminated with Spence fulminating in The *Rights of Infants* (1797) at Paine's unwillingness in *Agrarian Justice* (1796) to take further steps towards greater equality of property through parish ownership of land and management of rents. To Spence this was the only logical outcome of the entire revolutionary epoch, the extension of rights without which other rights claims were hollow protests. In his view it was much superior to ancient modes of agrarian law, which 'could never establish complete equality in Estates'.[4] Paine thus in Spence's words 'aimed only at kings', while his own plan solved the problem of inequality once and for all. Paine and his followers seemingly reduced the question of poverty to one of the oppressive expenses of government. Spence felt that he alone had found the true cause, in landed monopoly. Spence's reputation would emerge once again only when a new generation of reformers reached a similar conclusion. Thus his views were taken up again with the emergence of a strand of Chartism which held equally radical views of property, and then again with the late nineteenth and early twentieth century land reform and socialist movements, which rightly saw him as an important forerunner.[5]

The contrast between Paine and Spence which this confrontation revealed illustrates a number of interesting points about British and Anglo-American radicalism in the late eighteenth century. The first relates to the legacy of Harringtonian republicanism after 1776. From the ancient world onwards a rich critical tradition associated, amongst others, with the Spartan model in Greece, the Roman Republic, and the Italian city-states of the Renaissance, had contended that luxury and inequality of property in particular threatened the longevity of states by concentrating political power in the hands of the wealthy. The device of an agrarian law had been introduced in 133BC in Rome by Tiberius Sempronius Gracchus to attempt to limit the private appropriation of

4 Spence's Trial, Letter 5, Sept. 20th, 1800, in A. W. Waters, *Trial of Thomas Spence* (Leamington Spa: Courier Press, 1917), p. 49.

5 Firstly in H. M. Hyndman, *Nationalization of Land in 1775 and 1882* (1882). On Spence's legacies see Malcolm Chase, *The People's Farm. English Agrarian Radicalism 1775-1840*, 2nd edition (London: Breviary Stuff, 2010 [first published by Oxford University Press, 1988]), and Iain McCalman, *Radical Underworld: Prophets, Revolutionaries and Pornographers in London, 1795-1840* (Cambridge: Cambridge University Press, 1988).

public lands. The holding of all lands in common was a much more radical variant on this, and came to be associated from the Renaissance onwards with the scheme projected in Thomas More's *Utopia* (1516). James Harrington's more limited 'agrarian' was described in fictional utopia, *Oceana* (1656), and thereafter was often referred to by reformers anxious to set a limit on landed property. (Spence excerpted Harrington's writings in *Pigs' Meat*.)[6]

In the later eighteenth century James Burgh, William Ogilvie, and Robert Wallace explored the ground between More and Harrington. A number of these, like Burgh and Spence, would also project such schemes in utopian fictional form (and Spence was a great admirer of both *Robinson Crusoe* and *Gulliver's Travels*). These utopian republicans were the forerunners of much of the later nineteenth and twentieth century socialism. Many were communitarians who stressed the necessity for organising humanity in small groups in the first instance. Often they were inspired by Christian experiments, such as the Shakers and Moravians, in the American colonies, who were also a chief source for Owen's famous 'Plan'.[7] This trend in the Morean inheritance remained ambivalent about cities (like William Godwin, another important contributor to the debate during the 1790s). It was also generally hostile to commerce, and especially the luxury trade, as again was Godwin. Neither Paine nor Spence, however, were communitarians of this type. Neither wished to take the utopian road towards community of goods charted by Thomas More. But both wanted a considerably more equal society. And both drew upon a Biblical and philosophical inheritance which described the first state of mankind as one of equality. What then divided them?

Spence's starting-point in 1775 was the original equality of property which characterised the state of nature.[8] (One of his later pamphlets was *The Restorer of Society to Its Natural State*, 1801.) Over the generations natural property had come to be treated by the rich 'in as assured a manner as if they had manufactured it and it had been the work of their own hands.' What was required was the recognition that 'every man has an equal property in the land in the neighbourhood where he resides'. This was, however, not to be accomplished by returning to the original position, which was the use of the earth as a common hunting and grazing ground, like the Indians (Spence imagined) of North America. Instead, a second historical stage, letting out the land as farms and tenements, 'but reserving the Rents to the People of the District in lieu of their Rights of Pasturage, and Hunting', was to be preferred. Thus parishes, organised like corporations, would rent the land out and all common expenses would be met from the proceeds.[9] Spence wished to prohibit all commerce in land, as 'the

6 Thomas Spence, *Pigs' Meat; or, Lessons for the Swinish Multitude* (3 vols, 1793-5), vol. 1, pp. 80-85, 126-128, 272-274.

7 For a restatement of this theme see my "The Only Man of Nature That Ever Appeared in the World': 'Walking' John Stewart and the Trajectories of Social Radicalism, 1790-1822', *Journal of British Studies*, 53 (2014) (forthcoming). Some of Spence's followers moved in this direction, notably Thomas Evans, in *Christian Policy the Salvation of the Empire* (1816), p. 9, and *Christian Policy in Full Practice Among the People of Harmony* (1818).

8 A good start for the background to this theme is Helen Thornton, *State of Nature or Eden? Thomas Hobbes and His Contemporaries on the Natural Condition of Human Beings* (New York: University of Rochester Press, 2005).

9 A. W. Waters, *Trial of Thomas Spence* (Leamington Spa: Courier Press, 1917), p. 57. G. I. Gallop, ed. *Pigs' Meat: The*

Root of all the other Branches of injurious Trade.'[10] Though he occasionally railed at 'luxury, pride, and all manner of vice,' the 'abominations of luxury and dissipation,' and 'Extravagance and Luxury' and the 'cursed spirit of trade',[11] he was not hostile to trade as such. Nor was he averse, like many republicans, to cities as such. In Spence's *A Supplement to the History of Robinson Crusoe* (1782), for instance, a city of fifty thousand is described which exudes 'order, industry, wealth, and the most pleasing magnificence'.[12] The chief source here was the Bible, supplemented by John Locke, Samuel Pufendorf and others. Thus Spence quoted Leviticus 25 on the inalienability of land and the Jubilee scheme for redistributing land every fifty years, 'Locke on government' and Pufendorf's *Whole Duty of Man*, as reinforcing the case for common rights.[13] Spence knew, of course, that these authors had not described common ownership as practicable. But that was beside the point.

The inheritance upon which both Paine and Spence drew thus included many variations in its interpretations of many issues. The starting-point most were agreed upon. A state of nature had once existed in which humankind were relatively equal and land was not owned at all but was used in common. The problem was interpreting what had happened thereafter, and how far the benefits of private appropriation outweighed the disadvantages. Most eighteenth century commentators on these issues agreed that the earth had originally been given by God to all as common property, which explained its original condition. Thereafter it had evolved gradually into private ownership. The key question here was whether this accorded with divine intention or not, and whether it suited humanity as a whole or only those landowners who most profited from the arrangement. Many natural law writers, like Pufendorf, contended that property was intended to be common only negatively, that is, to be developed as population in particular expanded.[14] Against this dominant view a small number of utopian republicans inspired chiefly by Thomas More contended that a positive community of goods had been intended by God, 'a very notorious leveller' (in Spence's phrase), and best suited humanity's needs. In the 1790s this view would be associated with some of William Godwin's followers in particular.[15] In the early nineteenth century it would be the Spenceans and Owenites who would inherit and develop this perspective, then the later socialists and advocates of land nationalisation.

We see, thus, that there were metaphorically four interpretative roads from the assertion in 'Genesis' that God had given the world to humanity in common. In the first interpretation, this was merely the original state of things, and

Selected Writings of Thomas Spence (Nottingham: Spokesman, 1982), pp. 55, 60.

10 G. I. Gallop, ed. *Pigs' Meat: The Selected Writings of Thomas Spence* (Nottingham: Spokesman, 1982), p. 131.

11 Gallop, ed. pp. 63, 75, 151; *The Important Trial of Thomas Spence* (2nd edn, 1803), p. 16.

12 Reprinted in G. Claeys, ed. *Modern British Utopias 1700-1850* (8 vols), (London: Pickering and Chatto, 1997), vol. 4, p. 110.

13 Gallop, ed. *Spence*, pp. 69-70.

14 See generally Istvan Hont, *Jealousy of Trade. International Competition and the Nation-State in Historical Perspective* (Cambridge, MA: Harvard University Press, 2005), pp. 159-184.

15 For the context here see my *Utopias of the British Enlightenment* (Cambridge : Cambridge University Press, 1994), pp. vii-xxviii.

mankind had evolved onwards thereafter, chiefly through the pressure of population growth. This was usually conceived in this period as a progression through four stages (hunting and gathering, pasturage, agriculture and commerce) to the present. The advantage of private ownership here was defended in terms of the vast wealth it had created. This view is usually associated with Adam Smith and the origins of liberal political economy. In the second variation, rights of common ownership could still be recognised, but the utilitarian advantages of private ownership were also conceded. Some balance between the two thus had to be struck. This was broadly Paine's position. In the third variation, such rights were claimed, but the utilitarian advantages of private ownership of land were denied. This was Spence's position. And in the fourth variation, common ownership was combined with common living. This was utopian republicanism.

Spence clearly felt that Paine's position was deficient from the first publication of *Rights of Man* (1791-2). He only fully confronted Paine's views, however, in *The Rights of Infants* (1797). Paine had completed the second part of *Rights of Man* (1792) by arguing that a graduated income tax scheme would effectively rectify the injustices of the existing property system. By 1795, however, he argued that stronger measures needed to be taken to secure the position of the poor. Paine's *Agrarian Justice* (1796) thus offered a series of new claims partly based upon natural rights arguments about God's intentions. Here he argued that 'the earth, in its natural, uncultivated state was, and ever would have continued to be, *the common property of the human race*. In that state every man would have been born to property. He would have been a joint life proprietor with the rest in the property of the soil, and in all its natural productions, vegetable and animal.'[16]

Paine's argument was thus based upon divine intention. Land was 'the free gift of the Creator to the human race'. Man had not made the earth, and 'though he had a natural right to occupy it, he had no right to locate as his property in perpetuity any part of it; neither did the Creator of the earth open a land-office, from whence the first title-deeds should issue.' *Agrarian Justice* thus argued that the dispossessed should be compensated by being granted £15 at age 21 (about half a year's wage for an agricultural labourer), and a further £10 annually from the age of 50 onwards. The result would be a 'revolution in the state of civilization' which would extend a republican revolution in government.[17] Paine was insistent about not being able to extend this argument further. 'I have', he wrote

> entitled this tract Agrarian Justice, to distinguish it from Agrarian Law. Nothing could be more unjust than Agrarian Law in a country improved by cultivation; for though every man, as an inhabitant of the earth, is a

16 *The Writings of Thomas Paine*, ed. Moncure Conway (4 vols), (New York, 1908), vol. 3, p. 329. The stress here is on 'would have'. Ashraf assumed that Paine stated that the earth 'is common property', while his point was precisely that it once had been but was no longer (P. M. Ashraf. *The Life and Times of Thomas Spence*, (Newcastle upon Tyne: Frank Graham, 1983), p. 172). But this is also how Spence described Paine's position.

17 *The Writings of Thomas Paine*, ed. Moncure Conway (4 vols), (New York, 1908), vol. 3, pp. 330-331.

> joint proprietor of it in its natural state, it does not follow that he is a joint proprietor of cultivated earth. The additional value made by cultivation, after the system was admitted, became the property of those who did it, or who inherited it from them, or who purchased it. It had originally no owner. Whilst, therefore, I advocate the right, and interest myself in the hard case of all those who have been thrown out of their natural inheritance by the introduction of the system of landed property, I equally defend the right of the possessor to the part which is his.[18]

Paine thus regarded the natural right of property as fundamentally modified by subsequent cultivation. An historical right had accrued which needed to be factored into an accounting of the rights of the cultivators. This represented a compromise position. Yet it was a solution Spence regarded as half-hearted at best, and could not concede. The 'real' rights of man, in Spence's phrase, always implied the insistence that the rights of the cultivators remained unaltered. But it was perhaps hardly fair to charge 'Paine and the other democrats' with having only levelled 'all their artillery at kings', since Paine too sought to reduce social inequality through his scheme of redistributive taxation.[19]

In *The Rights of Infants* (1797) Spence thus attacked *Agrarian Justice* for having surrendered far too much to 'compromissory expediency'. Spence thanked Paine for having finally 'thought fit to own, with the Psalmist, and with Mr. Locke, that 'God hath given the earth to the children of men, given it to mankind in common". But he rejected the 'poor, beggarly stipends', based upon ten per cent of land values, which Paine had proposed by way of restitution. Most improvements in landed property were owed to the 'labouring classes', and the remaining ninety per cent were thus also theirs by right. Spence insisted once again that 'a landed interest is incompatible with the happiness and independence of the world.' Spence too wanted, like Paine, to ensure that free public education and the provision of public assistance for the 'unfortunate' take place.[20] Both authors aimed at the maintenance of some variation on the relief provided by the poor law, albeit on new foundations. The division between them lay in how this was to be funded, whether through taxation on landed value, as Paine proposed, or through the common scheme of rents, which was Spence's plan. Spence also conceived that Paine's plan, often understood as heralding the modern welfare state, would 'require a great number of placemen of various descriptions to manage it, and who being chosen, as they must be, by the ministry and their friends, will very much increase the already enormous influence of governments.'[21] Neither author, moreover, conceived of any plan for taxing commerce effectively, a point Charles Hall took up with Spence in correspondence. But Spence in turn thought Hall was 'sliding into the System of Sir Thomas More's *Utopia* wherein he makes every kind of Property the Property of the Nation and the People obliged to work under Gang Masters as you hint at,' adding that 'I don't think you will find many desirous to go into such

18 *The Writings of Thomas Paine*, ed. Moncure Conway (4 vols), (New York, 1908), vol. 3, pp. 330-331.

19 Gallop, ed. *Spence*, p. 93.

20 *The Important Trial of Thomas Spence* (2nd edn, 1803), p. 74.

21 Gallop, ed. *Spence*, p. 126.

a State of Barbarism and Slavery'.[22]

A second area of interest which a contrast of Spence and Paine indicates relates to how rights doctrines were understood in this period. Neither Spence nor Paine originated the phrase 'rights of man', though both did much to popularise it in this period.[23] As is well known, the modern language of 'human' rights was emerging gradually in this period out of natural rights arguments which had been reshaped in the early modern period by Hobbes, Locke, Pufendorf, Grotius and many other writers. Much of this debate was still embedded in a Christian framework in which divine intention was still important. Rights were usually not understood 'secular', and not derived from the fact of one's humanity as such, as they are normally now considered. They were still embedded in a theological framework, and seen as derived from the description of God's intentions in creating the earth as presented in 'Genesis', in particular. This was Paine's famous starting-point in *Rights of Man* (1791-2). And his restatement of it can be seen in quasi-religious terms, as an almost evangelical restatement of rights from a new, egalitarian perspective.[24] The religious context of many such claims in this period thus needs to be underscored.

Spence's use of the Bible was however somewhat different from Paine's. Spence rejected that interpretation of Christianity which would 'not allow of equality or rights'. He put into the hands of a fictional Indian the view: 'Their God, they tell us, has ordained that there shall be many sorts and conditions of men, and that some few shall have the lordship and disposal of the earth, whilst the far greater part must be reduced to supplicate to become their tributaries and vassals. This has always made us hate your God and your religion.'[25] We know that Spence was deeply religious in the moral sense, while scornful of much of Christian practice which did not recognise an equality of rights. It was, he insisted, 'only by good Laws and Constitutions that we must hope to amend our deplorable State, and not by our addressing ourselves to the Religion, Generosity, and Feelings of the Rich and Powerful, for their humiliating Charity.'[26] The Sandemanian sect in which he had been raised gave a special priority to serving the poor, and clearly guided him in some respects. But he was convinced that what 'religious people look for ... under the Notion of a Millennium, Philosophers in an Age of Reason, and Poets in a future Golden Age', he had found in a scheme of land management, 'the Constitution of the future Golden Age'.[27] Spence's basic point in this respect was that rights had been widely understood in the context of political reform. In *The Meridian Sun of Liberty* (1796) the dialogue runs:

22 'Four Letters between Thomas Spence and Charles Hall', *Notes and Queries*, 28 (1981), pp. 318, 320.

23 On this language see Peter De Bolla, *The Architecture of Concepts. The Historical Formation of Human Rights* (New York: Fordham University Press, 2013).

24 See my 'Paine and the Religiosity of Rights,' in Rachel Hammersley, ed. *Revolutionary Moments* (London: Bloomsbury, 2014, forthcoming).

25 Gallop, ed. *Spence*, pp. 80-81.

26 Gallop, ed. *Spence*, p. 154.

27 Waters, p. 65.

> *Reader.* Does not the whole Rights of Man consist in a fair, equal, and impartial representation of the People in Parliament?
> *Author.* No. Nobody ought to have right of suffrage or representation in a society wherein they have no property. As more are suffered to meddle in the affairs of a benefit society or corporation, but those who are members, by having a property therein, so none have a right to vote or interfere in the affairs of the government of a country who have no right to the soil; because such are and ought to be accounted strangers.[28]

Spence's point was that political rights without rights to land were meaningless. He accepted the view that only the propertied should vote, the 'poor' as such having no stake in the nation in the traditional view. If all had a stake, however, a commensurate political right followed.

A third issue which the contrast of Spence to Paine indicates relates to the development of the revolutionary debate during the 1790s. I have argued elsewhere that the reason the Paineites steered clear of arguments which implied a 'levelling' of property were integral to the way the revolution debate evolved in Britain. Thomas Cooper was unusual in referring to William Ogilvie's *Essay on the Right of Property in Land* (1781) as 'a very important book too little noticed' insofar as it discussed distributing commons and waste lands amongst the poor.[29] (Spence probably read it around 1793.)[30] Otherwise the Paineites were scrupulously cautious in avoiding the inference that proclaiming an equality of rights implied an equality of property claims. This, they rightly reasoned, would prove fatal to the political argument by shifting the ground from the reform of the system of representation to hints at the expropriation of large landed estates. And so it proved. Once the debate commenced in earnest, in the course of 1792-3 in particular, loyalists successfully contended that the thrust of Paine's arguments were in favour of levelling. This was evidently one of the chief reasons for the loyalist victory in the war of ideas of the mid-1790s. Paine was already too radical for his epoch: Spence was far more so. It would be the better part of a century before these forms of reckoning with poverty would be brought once again to the centre of British political life. And then many socialists, and even more the communists, would find Spence a more appealing forerunner than the more moderate Paine.

28 Gallop, ed. *Spence*, p. 107.

29 Cited in my *Thomas Paine: Social and Political Thought* (London: Unwin Hyman, 1989), p. 124.

30 Olive Rudkin. *Thomas Spence and His Connections* (London: George Allen & Unwin, 1927), p. 17.

4

Spence's *Property in Land Every One's Right*: Problems and Solutions

•

Rachel Hammersley

This volume sees the publication for the first time since the eighteenth century of the original version of Spence's lecture 'Property in Land Every One's Right', the first statement of his controversial system, which he delivered to the Newcastle Philosophical Society on 8 November 1775. Though copies of the version of the lecture that Spence published in the 1790s did survive, it had long been thought that no copies of the original (1775) edition remained, until one was discovered, appropriately enough in the Newcastle Literary and Philosophical Society, in 2005.[1] The differences between the original and later editions are fairly small and primarily stylistic, but this discovery should perhaps prompt us to focus again on the context within which the original lecture was produced and the purpose (or purposes) it was designed to fulfil.

Though it gained a national reputation, particularly after Spence's move to London in late 1787 or early 1788,[2] the lecture was very much a Newcastle creation, born out of the particular circumstances that existed in the city in the early 1770s. Indeed, it could even be argued that Spence's land plan was designed as a deliberate response to the specific problems facing the Newcastle freemen in the mid-1770s. Yet, in seeking to address those problems, Spence did not simply look to local ideas, but rather he drew on earlier political theories, and in particular the ideas of the English republican writer James Harrington, to construct his distinctive solution.

The Problems: Newcastle in the 1770s

The election of 1774 was the first contested election in Newcastle for many years. Since 1747 the choosing of the city's MPs had been a compromise, with the Tory Sir Walter Calverley Blackett and the Whig Matthew Ridley sharing power. In 1774 Blackett stood again alongside Ridley's son, Sir Matthew White

1 Both Olive Rudkin and Mary Ashraf believed that no copies of the original edition of the lecture had survived. O. D. Rudkin, *Thomas Spence and his connections* (New York: Augustus M. Kelley, 1966 — first published 1927), p. 37 and P. M. Ashraf, *The Life and Times of Thomas Spence* (Newcastle upon Tyne: Frank Graham, 1983), p. 146. However, the existence of the 1775 edition was still known to people in Newcastle in the late nineteenth century, since James Clephan cites extensively from the 1775 edition in his article on Spence in the *Monthly Chronicle of North-Country Lore and Legend*. J. Clephan, 'Thomas Spence', *The Monthly Chronicle of North-Country Lore and Legend* (Newcastle upon Tyne, 1887), I, pp. 296-302.

2 M. Chase, *The People's Farm: English Radical Agrarianism 1775-1840* 2nd edition (London: Breviary Stuff, 2010 [first published by Oxford University Press, 1988]), pp. 41-42.

Ridley, but in addition there were two further candidates: Constantine John Phipps, who had distinguished himself in the navy and was MP for Lincoln from 1768-1774, and Thomas Delaval, the younger brother of Sir Francis Delaval (who had died in 1771) and John Hussey Delaval of Seaton Delaval Hall. In the end, the newcomers proved unsuccessful, but they did gain considerable support from some of the town guilds. The Joiners and Butchers gave the majority of their votes to Phipps and Delaval and the Bricklayers not only did this, but also admitted them to the freedom of their incorporation and presented them with silver trowels and mahogany hods. At the root of this contest were two related controversies, one national and the other local, that for several years had plagued relations between the freemen, on one side, and the Common Council and MPs, on the other. First, there was the national controversy surrounding the journalist and politician John Wilkes. Secondly, there was the locally focused Town Moor Affair, which came to a head in 1773.

The Wilkes Controversy actually comprised three distinct issues.[3] The first, which was prompted by the publication of the forty-fifth issue of Wilkes's newspaper *The North Briton* on 23 April 1763, concerned the use of general warrants to arrest individuals. In that issue of his paper Wilkes had attacked the new Prime Minister, George Grenville, for his commendation of the Peace of Paris and had, by implication, cast aspersions against the King, George III. In response the government issued a general warrant for the arrest of the authors, printers and publishers involved. In total forty-nine people were arrested and Wilkes himself lost his seat as an MP and eventually served time in prison for his involvement. However, the case prompted public indignation, brought an end to the use of general warrants to arrest individuals, and gave birth to the cry 'Wilkes and liberty!' The second issue, which was perhaps the one of greatest concern to the Newcastle freemen, was that surrounding Wilkes's election as MP for Middlesex. He was first elected in March 1768, but because of his past actions and reputation the Commons used various means to expel him, eventually succeeding in early February 1769 on the grounds of his allegedly libellous suggestion that the Massacre on St George's Field, which had taken place on 10 May 1768, had been premeditated. Following this decision, fresh elections were held and Wilkes was twice re-elected unopposed, but each time the Commons immediately expelled him. In the third election, in April 1769, Parliament put up its own candidate, Henry Lawes Luttrell to stand against Wilkes. Despite the fact that Wilkes defeated Luttrell by 1,143 votes to 296, the Commons reversed the decision and voted to admit Luttrell as MP for Middlesex. The third issue was Wilkes's campaign, launched in 1771, to overturn Parliament's prohibition on the reporting of parliamentary debates in

3 For a more detailed account of the Wilkite controversies see R. Hammersley, *The English Republican Tradition and Eighteenth-Century France: Between the Ancients and the Moderns* (Manchester: Manchester University Press, 2010), pp. 101-102 and also G. Rudé, *Wilkes and Liberty: A Social Study of 1763 to 1774* (Oxford: Clarendon Press, 1962); P. D. G. Thomas, *John Wilkes: A Friend to Liberty* (Oxford: Oxford University Press, 1996); P. D. G. Thomas, 'Wilkes, John (1725-1797),' *Oxford Dictionary of National Biography* (Oxford: Oxford University Press, 2004; online edition, May 2008), www.oxforddnb.com/view/article/29410, accessed 4 April 2014; and A. H. Cash, *John Wilkes: The Scandalous Father of Civil Liberty* (Newhaven and London: Yale University Press, 2006).

the press. Following Parliament's issuing of legal proceedings against two printers in February 1771, Wilkes sought to pit the authority of the City of London (where he was then an alderman) against that of Parliament. Since the City had the exclusive right of arrest within its boundaries, he and his associates encouraged any printer who was facing prosecution for reporting parliamentary debates to take refuge there.

Wilkes's activities and the issues with which he was concerned, seemed to strike a particular chord with the Newcastle freemen.[4] Like many others across the country, they responded to Wilkes's ejection from Parliament by appointing a committee to draw up a list of instructions to send to their MPs.[5] The Newcastle instructions covered legal issues (the importance of protecting habeas corpus and trial by jury, and of opposing new and unusual punishments) as well as political ones (preserving the privileges of parliament and rights of electors, and supporting a bill for shorter parliaments and an end to places and pensions) and made explicit reference to the Wilkes affair and in particular his expulsion from Parliament: 'and that at this time you exert yourselves in supporting this right to the freeholders of *Middlesex*, which we have observed of late repeatedly violated.'[6] The rather dismissive response offered by Blackett and Ridley — in which they expressed their thanks, but insisted on their freedom to judge these issues for themselves — angered the freemen.[7] They responded by drawing up a petition to the King asking him to dissolve Parliament. Since Blackett had declared that he would 'sooner have that right hand cut off, than sign such a petition' and Ridley refused either to attend a meeting himself or to allow his son to do so (though both he and Blackett did subsequently attend) the freemen invited Sir Francis Delaval of Seaton Delaval Hall to chair their meeting. He obliged and was subsequently invited to present the petition to the King in place of their sitting MPs.[8] When that petition failed to prompt a response it was followed up with a remonstrance, which was also presented by Sir Francis (though his brother Thomas had chaired the meeting at which it was signed).[9]

As the election of 1774 approached, a number of publications appeared that were designed to remind electors of this episode. Two of the key publications in this campaign were *The Contest* and *The Freemen's Magazine, or the Constitutional Repository*, both of which were probably the work of the Rev. James Murray. The former, as the subtitle made clear, offered a straightforward account of '*the Matter in Dispute between the Magistrates and Burgesses, and an*

---

4 On this subject see also: T. R. Knox, 'Wilkism and the Newcastle Election of 1774', *Durham University Journal*, 72 (1979), pp. 23-37. For more general accounts of Newcastle politics in this period see: T. R. Knox, 'Popular Politics and Provincial Radicalism: Newcastle Upon Tyne, 1769-1785', *Albion* (1979), pp. 224-241; H. T. Dickinson, *Radical Politics in the North-East of England in the Later Eighteenth Century* (Durham: Durham County Local History Society, 1979); and K. Wilson, *The Sense of the People: Politics, Culture and Imperialism in England, 1715-1785* (Cambridge: Cambridge University Press, 1995), pp. 315-373.

5 *The Freemen's Magazine, or the Constitutional Repository* (Newcastle upon Tyne, 1774), pp. 1-2.

6 Ibid., p. 2.

7 Ibid., p. 5. The response of the Common Council members was also negative, with only the Mayor, John Baker, agreeing to sign the instructions.

8 Ibid., pp. 41-3, 45-50, 89, 91-94; Murray, *The Contest*, p. 23.

9 *The Freemen's Magazine*, p. 139.

examination of the merit and conduct of the Candidates in the present election for Newcastle upon Tyne'.[10] The latter, however, was a more subtle work. As its title suggests, it was a periodical which juxtaposed poems praising liberty with accounts of recent episodes in North East politics, essays on constitutional theory, and letters from readers. While the editor explicitly stated that the intention was to give both sides a hearing in order to allow the public to come to their own decision on these issues,[11] the overall thrust of the magazine was clear. In the 'Ode to Liberty' which opened the work and in the Preface that followed, much emphasis was placed on the current threat to liberty. The poem described 'Liberty' as having been 'banish'd from *Britannia's* court', while in the Preface the current situation was compared to that during the mid-seventeenth century. While it was acknowledged that the tyranny of Charles I was more overt, it was asserted that the current tyranny was in some ways more dangerous precisely because it was less obvious. At its heart lay the use of bribery, venality and corruption by the Government to pursue its own interests, and those of individual ministers, against the wishes and interests of the public. The Wilkes affairs were seen as revealing this hidden tyranny, and in the Preface the editors made reference both to the *North Britain* and general warrants and to the Middlesex election: 'A member was admitted into the house of commons, in opposition to Mr Wilkes, and the voices of three-fourths of the freeholders of that county, and determined to be the legal representative of *Middlesex*. By this new authority, the representatives of the people have taken upon them, both to elect members, and determine elections.'[12] Moreover, as the *Freemen's Magazine* made clear, Newcastle residents were concerned by these events and engaged directly with them. The *Magazine* reprinted an 'Ode for the Day of Mr Wilkes's Enlargement' which had supposedly been performed in Liberty Hall Newcastle on 6 April 1770 and had subsequently been published in the *London Evening Post*.[13] Similarly, the 'Ode to Liberty' that opened the magazine emphasised the expectation that the men of Northumbria would be at the forefront of the struggle to save liberty:

> But hark! what grateful sounds salute my ear?
> Behold *Northumbria's* freeborn sons appear.
> Their souls with inward greatness soar on high,
> And bear bright freedom's banners to the sky.
> They know the wish'd-for crisis is at hand,
> When *Britons* ought to make a glorious stand;
> With virtuous zeal to check oppression's rage,
> And *slew* the *venal torrent of the age*.[14]

All of this was, of course, designed to urge the Newcastle freemen to do the

10 James Murray, *The Contest*.

11 *The Freemen's Magazine*, p. vii.

12 Ibid., p. v.

13 Ibid., pp. 38-40.

14 *The Freemen's Magazine*, 'Ode to Liberty'.

'right thing' at the forthcoming election.[15] To this end, there was specific discussion of the sitting MPs and their recent conduct, particularly that of Sir Walter Blackett. While letters to the periodical included some that were more positive about his conduct, (in *An Advice to Patriots*, for example, it was noted that he had at least remained independent having never accepted a pension),[16] the general tone of the magazine was critical. Similarly, *The Contest* emphasised and detailed Blackett's fall from favour among the Newcastle freemen and the reasons behind it.[17] In particular, his support for general warrants and his slipperiness on key issues was noted. It was asserted that in 1740 he had acted as though he thought septennial parliaments were wrong, and yet in 1774 he supported them. Even more controversial was his behaviour over Wilkes's expulsion as MP for Middlesex. Blackett had initially opposed that decision, but he subsequently changed his mind and actually apologised publicly in parliament for supporting the wrong side. In addition, Blackett's central role in the other key controversy of the early 1770s — the Town Moor Affair — was also emphasised.[18]

The Town Moor had traditionally been used by the freemen for grazing cattle. Two issues relating to the Moor brought the freemen and magistrates into conflict. One of these concerned the attempt by the Common Council to grant a local inhabitant the right to build a carriage road over part of the Moor.[19] The burgesses would have been happy with a bridleway, but were not willing to allow a more substantial road to be built. The affair went to law and the burgesses lost, leaving many out of pocket. Blackett took the part of the magistrates and Common Council on this issue. The other issue involved the decision by the Common Council to let out part of the land for cultivation and improvement.[20] Though the suggestion had originally come from the freemen, there was anger over the Common Council's attempt to impose the scheme without the consent or involvement of the freemen. Direct conflict on the land ensued, and Blackett once again supported the magistrate's cause. A charge of trespass was eventually brought against the freemen, for destroying property on the land that had been enclosed, and the case eventually came to court. According to the account in *The Contest*, the freemen feared that by this means: 'every part of the moor might be inclosed and granted to worthless individuals, and the poor freemen and their widows, stand entirely stripped of the ONLY BENEFIT, THEY ENJOYED, out of TWENTY THOUSAND POUNDS REVENUE, A YEAR — the rest being swallowed up in offices.'[21] Blackett supposedly promised that the suit would be amicable, but in the end nothing was 'spared which power, money, quirks, quibbles, and cunning could afford, to render it as hostile and

15 On this, see in particular, *The Freemen's Magazine*, pp. 106-8 and Murray, *The Contest*, pp. 5-6.

16 *The Freemen's Magazine*, p. 33.

17 Murray, *The Contest*, especially pp. 2-4 and 19-22.

18 Ibid. pp. 22-9.

19 Ibid., p. 22.

20 Ibid., pp. 24-9.

21 Ibid., p. 26.

oppressive as possible'.[22] The magistrates even sought to influence local lawyers such that the freemen could not find anyone locally to represent them. In the end they enlisted George Grieve, a Northumberland man who was also a friend of Wilkes, to ask Serjeant John Glynn (who had defended Wilkes and his supporters) to plead their cause. Glynn ultimately proved successful, the magistrates were required to pay £300 costs and it was agreed that an Act of Parliament would be sought 'to enable them to enclose, let, and the rent to be divided by the stewards of the respective companies, among their poor brethren and widows'.[23] According to Murray the magistrates still sought to get their own way and produce an Act more favourable to them, but Glynn continued to act on behalf of the freemen and thus secured favourable terms in the Act of Parliament which was passed in 1774. Following this, another set of instructions were drawn up by the freemen, again asking their MPs to urge the Commons to recognise that they had acted wrongly in expelling Wilkes, and calling for shorter parliaments, a reduction in placemen and pensioners in the commons, and a more equal representation. They were offered to Blackett and Ridley, both of whom refused to support them, which was why the freemen approached Phipps and Delaval to act as their candidates, both agreed to submit to the articles if elected.[24]

The Freemen's Magazine and *The Contest* reminded their readers of Blackett's direct involvement in the Town Moor Affair: 'The worthy man with all the pious pretensions to charity and benevolence, with the arbitrary domination of a feudal tyrant, had the assurance to put in a claim of lordship over your inalienable rights and possessions, and as far as arbitrary power, contrary to law, could proceed, had in farm let, by the aid of his common-council, the property of the freemen of *Newcastle*.'[25] Moreover, in doing so it was clear that Blackett and his associates were seeking to usurp the rights of the freemen: 'The bringing of this matter to an issue at law, loudly declared that some persons were serious in their intentions of having the Town-moor into their own hands, that they might parve out the perquisites among their obedient creatures, who were ready to bow down to the dagon of their arbitrary authority.'[26] In contrast to Blackett, Ridley and White Ridley, Phipps and Delaval were described in much more positive terms. Phipps was praised for his previous behaviour in Parliament and though Delaval had not sat as an MP before his actions locally were seen as giving good grounds for trust: 'Mr Delaval's character stands as unimpeached, as a man; and any one may know it, by enquiring in the neighbourhood of his native place, where the suffrages of his inferiors in fortune, do him more honour in being graced with the highest titles which sovereignty itself could bestow.'[27]

22 Ibid., p. 27.

23 Ibid., p. 28.

24 Ibid., p. 30.

25 *The Freemen's Magazine*, p. 27. See also Murray, *The Contest*, p. 14.

26 *The Freemen's Magazine*, p. 29.

27 Murray, *The Contest*, p. 18. Delaval was no doubt chosen partly because he was the brother of Sir Francis, who had already helped the freemen in their cause, but his positive reputation locally was perhaps also due to his role in improving the sluice at Seaton Sluice and building a glassworks in the area.

Both the contested election and the Town Moor Affair attracted attention beyond the North East (no doubt partly because of the Wilkes connection). Copies of a pamphlet by the future French revolutionary Jean-Paul Marat entitled *The Chains of Slavery* were sent to various Newcastle guilds, and proved particularly popular with those that were involved in the Town Moor Affair, and those who supported the opposition candidates at the election.[28] The pamphlet pre-figured Marat's later writings in offering a vociferous attack on despotism of all kinds (indeed Marat published a French translation of the work in 1793). Like *The Freemen's Magazine* it too stressed the rise of corruption and venality and the threat posed by this hidden form of despotism. Marat's pamphlet also included a preface entitled 'Address to the Electors of Great Britain' which emphasised the importance of the role to be played by the electors, and offered detailed advice on the kinds of men they should choose and those they should reject. It was, thus, ideally suited to the circumstances of Newcastle's contested election. The editors of *The Freemen's Magazine* appear to have been aware of this, since they reprinted the 'Address to the Electors of Great Britain' in their publication.[29] In the minds of certain freemen the pamphlet also appears to have been relevant to the Town Moor Affair, since a copy of the Town Moor Act was bound in at the back of the copy of *The Chains of Slavery* owned by the Company of Butchers.[30]

Thus, the concerns of the Newcastle freemen in the mid-1770s centred on several key issues: the control of electors over their representatives (at both a local and a national level); the rise of venality, places and pensions in national politics; corruption at elections; and the rights of freemen over common land. These issues also lie at the heart of Spence's lecture, but before considering how he sought to address these problems it is necessary to consider the circumstances in which that lecture was presented and Spence's association with the Newcastle Philosophical Society.

The Newcastle Philosophical Society

On 15 March 1775 a new Society was established in Newcastle. Described as a Philosophical Society it was an example of a breed that became increasingly popular in Britain during the course of the eighteenth century. John Locke's Dry Club, which met during the 1690s, and the Edinburgh Select Society established by Allan Ramsay in 1754, are more famous examples of gatherings of this

28 A notice announcing the arrival of the pamphlets in Newcastle appeared in the *Newcastle Chronicle*, 28 May 1774, p. 2. Moreover, several of these copies are still held among the guild records at the Tyne and Wear Archives. Tyne and Wear Archives Service (TWAS): GU/BR/15, GU/BU/28 and GU/CW/61. A copy also appears to have been sent to the company of House Carpenters, since their book of Orders refers to the rules concerning the loaning out of the work to Company members. TWAS: GU/HMT/3, p. 18. Copies can also still be found in the Special Collections Department of the Robinson Library at Newcastle University (Bradshaw 321.6MAR and W321.6MAR). See also J. Clephan, 'Jean-Paul Marat in Newcastle', *Monthly Chronicle of North-Country Lore and Legend* 1:2 (1887), pp. 1-53, and especially p. 49 and R. Hammersley, 'Jean-Paul Marat's *The Chains of Slavery* in Britain and France, 1774-1883', *The Historical Journal*, 43: 3 (2005), pp. 641-660.

29 *The Freemen's Magazine*, pp. 95-99.

30 Tyne and Wear Archives Service (TWAS): GU/BU/28.

kind,[31] but by the second half of the eighteenth century they were by no means confined to the intellectual elite.[32] The rules of the Newcastle Society (drawn up in 1777) give a good sense of the intentions of those involved. The idea was that members would be given the opportunity to speak 'with Facility' on every subject and that through discussing issues in this way they would come to a better understanding of the topic and would thereby establish their own views on it.[33] Indeed the question selected for debate at the first meeting was:

> Which of two persons, equally qualified, is most likely to attain first to a distinct knowledge of any intricate subject, he who searches into it by contemplation and the help of books only, or he who attends a well-regulated society, where the subject is freely debated as a question, on both sides, or demonstrated by the joint endeavours of the members?[34]

It is perhaps not surprising that after two hours of discussion the meeting found in favour of the second proposition. The topics discussed by the Society were wide ranging and, unlike many other societies of this time, they did not shy away from potentially controversial religious or political topics. On 5 July 1775 they considered 'Whether the pulpit or the stage in their present depraved states is most detrimental to our morals?' The decision, by just one vote, was that the pulpit posed the greatest threat. On 27 September of the same year they discussed 'Whether the Civil War in the reign of Charles I and the present contest with America be similar?', unanimously agreeing that they were. And on 25 October they debated 'Which is the better form of government, a limited monarch as in Great Britain, or a republic?', with the republicans coming out on top by a majority of two.[35]

It was just after the debate on republicanism, on 8 November 1775, that Spence delivered his lecture to the Society. He claimed that it was his 'turn' to lecture and chose to address the 'important question': 'Whether mankind in society, reap all the advantages from their natural and equal right of property in land, and liberty, which in that state they possibly might and ought to expect?'[36] Spence subsequently published it as an eight-page pamphlet which sold for a penny. It appears to have been the fact that it was printed (and that the Society was explicitly referred to in that publication) that caused particular upset among

31 On Locke's Dry Club see Oxford: Bodleian Library, Locke Manuscripts, c.25, folios 56-7, 'Rules of the Dry Club: For the Amicable Improvement of Mixed Conversation'. See also Locke's correspondence with William Popple c.17, 201-8 and Benjamin Furly to John Locke, 7/17 November 1692', *The Correspondence of John Locke*, ed. E. S. de Beer (Oxford: Oxford University Press, 1979), IV, pp. 571-576. On the Edinburgh Select Society see R. L. Emerson, 'Select Society (*act.* 1754-1764)', *Oxford Dictionary of National Biography* (Oxford: Oxford University Press, 2004; online edition, May 2006) http://www.oxforddnb.com/view/article/73614, accessed 7 April 2014.

32 Donna Andrew's extensive study of London debating societies in 1780 reveals a wide social mix and also the regular presence and participation of women at debates. D. T. Andrew, 'Popular Culture and Public Debate: London 1780', *The Historical Journal*, 39:2 (1996), pp. 405-423.

33 *The Reports, Papers, Catalogues, &c. Of the Literary and Philosophical Society of Newcastle Upon Tyne, collected by Anthony Hedley*.

34 Quoted in Clephan, 'Thomas Spence', p. 297.

35 *Newcastle Chronicle*, 8 July 1775, p. 2; 30 September 1775, p. 2; and 28 October 1775, p. 2.

36 Thomas Spence, 'Property in Land Every One's Right, proved in a lecture read at the Philosophical Society in Newcastle, on the 8th of Nov. 1775', reprinted in this volume, pp. 7-11.

the Society's members. According to the account in the *Newcastle Chronicle* of the meeting held on 22 November they:

> expelled Mr Tho. Spence, for publishing, without and against the approbation of the Society, a lecture with the title of 'Property in Land, every Man's Right,' which he had delivered at a former meeting, of which they disclaim patronage; being informed that he had, previous to the delivery of the lecture, read it in different public-houses; and become a member, apparently, for the purpose of obtruding upon the world, the ERRONEOUS and *dangerous levelling principles*, with which this lecture is replete, under the sanction of the Society.[37]

It is clear, however, that not all the Society's members were happy with this decision. On 23 December 1775 the Rev. James Murray, the editor of the *Freemen's Magazine* and a known friend of Spence, sent a series of questions to the Society challenging their censuring of Spence and asking them to return '*pertinent* answers' to him.[38] Murray's questions explored the relationship between natural law, divine law, and reason and what they had to say with regard to property; they drew attention to the Biblical notion of jubilee (by which land was redistributed approximately every half century); and generally implied that the Philosophical Society ought to have taken Spence's system more seriously.

It would appear that the Newcastle Philosophical Society was not the only forum in which Spence sought to promote his system. Thomas Bewick's *Memoirs* include a well-known account of a fight that allegedly occurred between Bewick and his friend Spence over the latter's promotion of his plan at another debating society. The account is interesting, not least for the reference to Sir Walter Blackett, clearly a by-word among Newcastle's politically active citizens for a traitor:

> For the purpose, chiefly I believe, of making converts to his way of thinking, about "property in land being every ones right" — he got a number of young men gathered together & formed into a debating society, which was held in the evenings, at his first School Room, in the Broad-garth, Newcastle — One night, when his favourite question was to be debated — he reckoned upon me as one of his *backers* — in this however he was mistaken for notwithstanding my tacitly assenting, in a certain degree to his plan ... yet I could not at all agree with him in thinking it right to upset the present state of society ... The question being given against him, without my having said a word in its defence, he

37 *Newcastle Chronicle*, 25 November 1775, p. 2.

38 The questions were appended to Spence's 1793 edition of his lecture. Thomas Spence, *The Rights of Man, as exhibited in a lecture, read at the Philosophical Society in Newcastle*, fourth edition (London 1793), pp. 36-38. Interestingly, however (and contrary to what Ashraf suggests, Ashraf, *The Life and Times of Thomas Spence*, p. 13) controversial political topics continued to be debated by the Society including those typical of the concerns expressed in *The Freemen's Magazine*. On 27 March 1776 they discussed: 'If in the present context between the mother country and America, the latter should be declared free and more independent, would it be an advantage to other nations?' and voted yes. On 18 July they debated: 'Whether a nation under a free government, or one under tyranny and absolute monarchy, is likely to be the better neighbour?', deciding in favour of the former. And on 27 March 1777 (another election year) they debated whether an MP should vote according to his own wishes or those of his constituents and decided in favour of the constituents. *Newcastle Chronicle*, 30 March 1776, p. 2; 20 July 1776, p. 2; and 29 March 1777, p. 2.

> became swollen with indignation which, after all the Company were gone, he vented upon me, to reason with him was useless — he began by calling me (from my silence) a Sir Walter Blackett, and adding "if I had been as stout as you are I would have thrashed you" — indeed! Said I "it is a great pity you are not" — but said he, "there is another way in which I can do the business", and have at you! — He then produced a pair of cudgels — & to work we fell.[39]

However, members of the Newcastle Literary and Philosophical Society were keen to distance their institution from the earlier gathering and in particular from Spence and his lecture. Following an article in the *Annual Register* for 1792, which quoted an extract from Spence's lecture and suggested that it had been read at the Newcastle Literary and Philosophical Society, the Society drafted an advertisement, which was published in the *Newcastle Chronicle*, in which they reaffirmed that their Society had only been established in February 1793 and had nothing to do with the earlier Philosophical Society with which Spence was associated.[40]

The Solutions: Spence's Land Plan and James Harrington's *The Commonwealth of Oceana*

If the conflicts between the Newcastle freemen and their representatives at both a local and national level provided the problems that inspired Spence's plan, and the Newcastle Philosophical Society (and Spence's own debating society) provided the forum for its expression, what about the inspiration behind the solutions it offered? On this it is worth noting the striking similarities that exist between Spence's ideas and those set out in *The Commonwealth of Oceana*, which was published by James Harrington in 1656. Once again, the key to the connection is undoubtedly James Murray, who was himself a convinced Harringtonian and is known to have educated and supported the young Spence as he grew to maturity in Newcastle. While the influence of Harrington on Spence has been noted by scholars before, this has tended to be asserted rather than demonstrated.[41] What will be offered here is a careful analysis of the particular elements of Spence's plan that can be seen to have been derived from Harrington's work, and it will be suggested that Harrington appears to have provided solutions to precisely the problems that the Newcastle freemen were grappling with in the mid-1770s.[42]

Before delving into the similarities in the details of the plans put forward by Spence and Harrington, it is worth noting the interesting parallels in the mode of operation of the two writers. While both produced works of political theory, the plans that they developed were directly inspired by the concerns circulating at

---

39 Thomas Bewick, *A Memoir*, ed. I. Bain (Oxford: Oxford University Press, 1979), pp. 52-53.

40 *The Reports, Papers, Catalogues, &c. Of the Literary and Philosophical Society of Newcastle Upon Tyne, collected by Anthony Hedley*. See also, Clephan, 'Thomas Spence', *Monthly Chronicle*, pp. 299-300.

41 Rudkin, *Thomas Spence and his connections*, p. 19; T. R. Knox, 'Thomas Spence: The Trumpet of Jubilee', *Past and Present*, 76 (1977), p. 79 n8; and Ashraf, *The Life and Times of Thomas Spence*, pp. 24-25 and 125.

42 Of course, Spence also cited Harrington extensively both in *Pigs' Meat* and at his trial.

the time in which they lived and both worked tirelessly to disseminate their ideas and to put their plan into action. Moreover, both used the twin strategy of publishing and political clubs in an attempt to achieve these ends. In addition to the basic account of their systems ('Property in Land Every One's Right' and *The Commonwealth of Oceana* respectively), both men produced numerous other publications that repeated the ideas expressed there or adapted them for new audiences and circumstances. Both clearly sought to develop interest in their system by producing a wealth of publications, and both were evidently frustrated when their works did not generate the kind of interest they sought. More specifically, Spence's debating society, as described by Bewick; his use of the Newcastle Philosophical Society to promote his ideas; and his establishment of a society in London for the promotion of his plan, echo Harrington's creation of the Rota Club in 1659 which, like Spence's organisation, was deliberately designed as a forum for discussing and promoting his own system.[43] The two schemes themselves also share two general features. First, despite the pretence of their authors that they were not proposing a new system of government for England, it was apparent that that was precisely what they intended. Harrington dressed his proposal in utopian garb by using invented names for the countries and individuals depicted, but the fact that he was presenting an alternative constitution for England in the 1650s was implicit in *The Commonwealth of Oceana* itself and was made explicit in his publications and other activities in 1659.[44] Similarly, Spence appeared to deny his present-centred intentions in his use of a quote from Jonathan Swift in the Preface to the 1793 edition of his lecture: 'What the celebrated Dean Swift said upon another Occasion, do I say upon this: viz. "I hope the Reader need not be told, that I do not in the least intend my own Country in what I say upon this Occasion."'[45] The validity of this claim is belied by Bewick's account of his confrontation with Spence and by Spence's activities once he moved to London, not least the activities of his club. Secondly, both men appear to have been intent on establishing a system of government that would last and would not be overcome by the vagaries of human action. As subsequent commentators have noted Harrington's intention was to create a system that would prove immortal.[46] Similarly, Spence ended his lecture by declaring: 'But what makes this prospect yet more glorious is, that after this empire of right and reason is thus established, it will stand forever. Force and corruption attempting its downfall, shall equally be baffled, and all other nations struck with wonder and admiration at its happiness and stability, shall follow the example; and thus the whole earth shall at last be happy, and live like brethren.'[47]

43 On the Rota Club see James Harrington, *The Rota, or, a Model of a Free State or Equal Commonwealth* (London, 1660); John Aubrey, *Aubrey's Brief Lives*, ed. Oliver Lawson Dick (Harmondsworth, 1949), pp. 282-285; Samuel Pepys, *The Diary of Samuel Pepys*, edited by R. C. Latham and William Matthews, 11 vols (London, 1970, 1983), I, 13, 14, 17, 20, 24, 61.

44 On Harrington's activities in 1659 see R. Hammersley, 'Rethinking the Political Thought of James Harrington: Royalism, Republicanism and Democracy' *The History of European Ideas*, 39:3 (2013), pp. 354-370.

45 Spence, *The Rights of Man*, p. iii.

46 C. Blitzer, *An Immortal Commonwealth: The Political Thought of James Harrington* (New Haven: Yale University Press, 1960).

47 Spence, 'Property in Land Every One's Right', p. 11.

It is, however, the more specific similarities between the two plans that are most striking. These similarities can be grouped into three themes. First, those measures designed to make elections fair and effective, secondly those relating to the nature and practice of citizenship, and finally those concerning the ownership and organisation of land. Significantly, each of these themes is directly pertinent to the concerns of the Newcastle freemen in the 1770s.

Part of the reason why Harrington's system was said to be immortal was that instead of depending on the virtue of those in positions of power, (as most other republican proposals of the 1650s tended to do), Harrington explicitly sought to create a system in which by acting in their own interests individuals would produce a virtuous outcome. This idea lay at the heart of Harrington's key proposal to separate debating from resolving within the political system, which was reflected in his story of two girls dividing a cake:

> But that such orders may be established as may, nay must, give the upper hand in all cases unto common right or interest, notwithstanding the nearness of that which sticks unto every man in private, and this in a way of equal certainty and facility, is known even unto girls, being no other than those that are of common practice with them in divers cases. For example, two of them have a cake yet undivided, which was given between them. That each of them therefore may have that which is due, "Divide", says one unto the other, "and I will choose; or let me divide, and you shall choose." If this be but once agreed upon, it is enough; for the dividend dividing unequally loses, in regard that the other takes the better half; wherefore she divides equally, and so both have right.[48]

Harrington equated dividing the cake to the debating and proposing of legislation (which was to be undertaken by the Senate) and choosing which piece to have to voting for or against the legislative proposals put before them (which was the task of the lower house).[49] His reasoning was that since the members of the Senate would know that their proposals would only become law if approved by the popular assembly, they would not make laws contrary to the public good. At the same time, the people (or their representatives) while not wise enough to decide upon good laws, would be perfectly able to judge what was and what was not in the public interest and would act accordingly. While Spence did not adopt Harrington's complex bicameral system in his plan, he too seems to have had the idea that a system would work better if it were to utilise rather than deny self-interest and he appeared to see his system as doing precisely that: 'For the judgment of a parish may be as much depended upon as that of a house of lords, because they have as little to fear from speaking or voting according to truth, as they.'[50]

Both authors were also greatly preoccupied with the question of how elections could be made fair, given the human tendency towards corruption. Both

48 James Harrington, *The Commonwealth of Oceana*, ed. J. G. A. Pocock (Cambridge: Cambridge University Press, 1992), p. 22.

49 Ibid., p. 24.

50 Spence, 'Property in Land Every One's Right', p. 10.

insisted that elections take place on a named day in all the parishes. And both advocated the use of a secret ballot as a means of avoiding corruption. The fourteenth order of Harrington's constitution dictated that 'the ballot of Venice, as it is fitted by several alterations, and appointed unto every assembly, … be the constant and only way of giving suffrage in this commonwealth'.[51] As the label suggests, Harrington claimed to have derived his balloting system from the Republic of Venice. It involved a combination of lot and election with secret voting (by placing coloured balls into a ballot box) as a means of overcoming the problems of corruption and bribery that plagued the alternatives.[52] As Harrington's character Lord Archon explained: 'Men are naturally subject unto all kinds of passion; some you have that are not able to withstand the brow of an enemy, and others that make nothing of this are less of proof against that of a friend. So that if your suffrage be barefaced, I dare say you shall not have one fair cast in twenty. But whatever a man's fortune be at the box, he neither knoweth whom to thank nor whom to challenge. Wherefore … there is in this way of suffrage no less than a demonstration that it is the most pure; and the purity of the suffrage in a popular government is the health if not the life of it'.[53] Spence was equally keen to bring an end to corrupt elections. Though once again he did not advocate such a complex system as that proposed by Harrington, he did identify a secret ballot as the obvious solution to the problem: 'Corruption has now no being or effect among them; for all affairs to be determined by voting either in a full meeting of a parish, its committees, or the house of parliament, are done by balloting. So that voting's, or elections among them, occasion no animosities, for none need to let another know for which side he votes; all that can be done, therefore, in order to gain a majority of votes for any thing, is to make it appear in the best light possibly by speaking or writing'.[54]

Behind the issue of elections and the ballot was, of course, the question of citizenship. Both Harrington and Spence appear to have envisaged a much more extensive franchise than that which was in operation in England in their own times. In Harrington's system citizenship extended to all adult men who were not servants but 'live of themselves'.[55] Similarly, Spence asserted that any adult male who had lived in a parish for a year would become a parishioner and member of the corporation. Moreover, both men identified two sides to citizenship, the civil and the military, with the former involving both a local and a national element. Harrington distinguished the citizens of Oceana according to age, with those aged 18 to 30 forming the marching army while those aged over 30 would make up the standing garrisons and would also have the right to participate in the election of one fifth of their number to serve as deputies of the parish, and in the selection of parish officers including overseers, constables and churchwardens

51 Harrington, *Oceana*, p. 114.

52 Harrington saw the Venetian ballot as so crucial that he even produced a diagram entitled *The Manner and Life of the Ballot*, which was then incorporated by Toland into his 1700 edition of Harrington's works.

53 Harrington, *Oceana*, p. 118.

54 Spence, 'Property in Land Every One's Right', p. 10.

55 Harrington, *Oceana*, p. 75.

(again from among their number).[56] Significantly, when the deputies of each parish then gathered at the level of the hundred the following month they did so 'in arms' in order to elect further local officers (a JP, jurymen, a captain an ensign, a crowner (coroner) and a high constable).[57] The same was true of their gathering the following month, this time at the level of the tribe, to elect further officers (Lord High Sheriff or commander in chief, Lord lieutenant, muster master, quartermaster-general and two censors).[58] Once again, Spence's system was considerably simpler than that of Harrington, but incorporated many of the same elements. The inhabitants of each parish would gather in their parish on a set day and would thereby form a corporation. That corporation was then responsible for local affairs and for the implementation of the laws of the land.[59] Several parishes together would then have the right to elect an MP: 'He is chosen thus: all the candidates are proposed in every parish on the same day, when the election by balloting immediately proceeds, and he who has the majority in most of the parishes, is acknowledged to be their representative.'[60] The militia too would be organised via the parish: 'All the men in every parish, at times of their own choosing, repair together, to a field for that purpose, with their officers, arms, banners, and all sorts of martial music, in order to learn, or retain the complete art of war: there they become soldiers! Not to molest their neighbours unprovoked, but to be able to defend what none have a right to dispute'.[61] Moreover, Spence even seems to have acknowledged that following the principle of self-interest a citizen militia could be a very effective defensive force: 'There is no army kept in pay among them, in times of peace; as all have property alike to defend, they are alike ready to run to arms when their country is in danger'.[62]

While elections and citizenship were clearly of great importance to both Harrington and Spence it was land that lay at the heart of both of their systems. Harrington was widely credited with being the first to have noted the connection between land and power. As the Harringtonian Walter Moyle acknowledged in his *Essay Upon the Constitution of the Roman Government*:

> Thus it appears that Land is the true Center of Power, and that the Balance of Dominion changes with the Balance of Property; as the Needle in the Compass shifts its Points just as the great Magnet in the Earth changes its Place. This is an eternal Truth, and confirm'd by the Experience of all Ages and Governments; and so fully demonstrated by the Great HARRINGTON in his OCEANA, that 'tis as difficult to find out new Arguments for it, as to resist the Cogency of the old.[63]

Harrington's explanation as to why, as he put it, 'dominion follows the

56 Ibid., pp. 78-79.

57 Ibid., pp. 83-85.

58 Ibid., pp. 90-91.

59 Spence, 'Property in Land Every One's Right', p. 9-10.

60 Ibid., p. 10.

61 Ibid.

62 Ibid.

63 W. Moyle, *An Essay Upon the Constitution of the Roman Government*, in *The Works of Walter Moyle Esq* (London: Darby &c., 1726), p. 73.

balance of property' centred on the fact that land is required in order to sustain soldiers and therefore those who held the land would have the means to gather an army to enforce their will. Harrington therefore asserted that if the land within a country was owned by just one man, then the nation would be best suited to absolute monarchy; if it was shared among a few, then it would be ideal for a mixed monarchy; and if it was shared by the majority (as he believed was the case in England from the late sixteenth century) then it would be fitted for a commonwealth.[64] Moreover, he insisted that if the form of government was not in line with the balance of property, then it would prove unstable and short-lived. On this basis Harrington proposed the use of an agrarian law, which was designed to establish and then preserve the appropriate balance of property for the system of government.[65] This law, which was set out in the thirteenth order of the commonwealth, effectively placed a cap of £2,000 per year in revenue on estates in England (£500 in Scotland and £2,000 in Ireland), which was deliberately calculated to divide the whole territory of Oceana into 5,000 lots, which was presumably deemed to provide a sufficient balance.[66] Anyone with an estate worth more than £5,000 per year in revenue who had more than one son would be required to divide his lands more or less equally among his male children. At the same time, anyone who already had lands worth more than £2,000 per year in revenue would not be allowed to purchase more land. In addition, dowries were limited to a maximum of £1,500 in land, goods, or money, though interestingly Harrington had a relatively liberal attitude to female inheritance, insisting on the right of women to their just inheritance on the death of their father or husband and not ruling out inheritance to female as well as male heirs.

While Spence's plan was again less complex than Harrington's and while his concerns focused on the poor, where Harrington's lay with the gentry, some of the underlying principles were very similar. Like Harrington, Spence challenged and sought to transform the conventional system of land transmission, albeit having less respect for the existing distribution of land: 'The land, with all that appertains to it, is, in every parish, made the property of the corporation, with as ample power to let, repair, or alter all, or any part thereof, as a lord of the manor enjoys over his lands, houses etc. But the power of alienating the least morsel, in any manner, from the parish, either at this or any time hereafter, is denied. ... Thus there are no more nor other landlords in the whole country than the parishes; and each of them is sovereign landlord of its own territories.'[67] Moreover, Spence too appears to have acknowledged the connection between ownership of land and political rights: 'As each man has a vote in all the affairs of his parish, the land is let in very small farms, which makes employment for a greater number of hands; and makes more victualling of all kinds be raised.'[68]

Significantly it is also precisely these themes which appear to dominate in the

64 Harrington, *Oceana*, pp. 11-12.

65 Ibid., p. 101.

66 Ibid., p. 108.

67 Spence, 'Property in Land Every One's Right', p. 9.

68 Ibid., p. 11.

passages that Spence cited from Harrington's works in his *Pigs' Meat* volumes. In the first volume he cites a passage from *Aphorisms Political* which includes various points about the need to create a system that produces virtuous results even while the people continue to act out of their own self-interest, and concludes that: 'Commonwealths, of all other governments, are more especially for the preservation, not for the destruction, of mankind.'[69] The tendency for those in power to become corrupt is also noted. In the third volume Spence includes an extract from *The Prerogative of Popular Government* which he entitles 'The Danger of Suffering the too long continuance of the public servants in office'. It considers the causes of the dissolution of the Roman commonwealth demonstrating: '*how dangerous it is to states that would enjoy their liberty, to suffer magistracy* (how deservedly soever conferred) *to remain long in the possession of the same men*.'[70] The concern with citizenship is also evident from the passages cited. For instance, the first volume includes a passage which Spence claims is from *Oceana*, but which actually comes from *The Prerogative of Popular Government*, which he gives the title: 'A Government of Citizens is Invulnerable'. In that passage Harrington asserts that a commonwealth will be a government of citizens and that it is the hardest to be conquered and the hardest to hold. He also notes the advantages of using a citizen militia as a defensive force.[71] Finally, the centrality of land and the use of an agrarian law also feature in the passages that Spence quotes from Harrington. For instance, in the first volume of *Pigs' Meat* he includes a passage, which he entitles 'Whether the Balance of Dominion in Land be the Natural Cause of Empire?', which is taken from *The Prerogative of Popular Government* and which sets out Harrington's theory on the relationship between land ownership and the possession of power.[72] Similarly in the third volume he includes a passage entitled 'God Intended a Commonwealth among the Israelites by Dividing the Land Among all the People'.[73]

Conclusion

It has been suggested here that the problems Spence was seeking to solve in 'Property in Land Every One's Right' were at least partly sparked by the events that had coloured politics in Newcastle in the early 1770s, and the concerns that were preoccupying the freemen at that time. The Wilkes controversies and the Town Moor Affair had both struck a particular chord with the politically active members of the town, and had raised questions surrounding the control that local citizens could exercise both over their representatives at a local and national level and over the land within their vicinity. As well as providing issues for Spence to grapple with, Newcastle also provided him with a public forum in which to present and discuss his ideas, in the form of the Newcastle Philosophical Society

69 Thomas Spence, *One Pennyworth of Pigs' Meat; or, Lessons for the Swinish Multitude* (London, 1793), I, pp. 272-274.

70 Thomas Spence, *Pigs' Meat; or, Lessons for the Swinish Multitude* (London, 1794-5), III, pp. 280-282.

71 Spence, *Pigs' Meat*, I, pp. 126-128.

72 Ibid., pp. 114-118.

73 Spence, *Pigs' Meat*, III, pp. 279-280.

— though the members (and even some of his close friends, such as Bewick) proved less amenable to his proposals than Spence had perhaps hoped. It has also been argued here that in terms of the solutions that he put forward to the issues raised by contemporary affairs in Newcastle, Spence's main source of inspiration was the political theory of the English republican writer of the previous century, James Harrington. Both men were intent on rooting out corruption within the political and electoral system that was the result of flawed human nature, while yet believing that this nature could be harnessed to serve the common good; both developed and linked the twin aspects of citizenship — political and military; and both placed land at the foundation of their system and insisted on the significance of the ownership of land to the possession of political power.

Of course, the figure who links all of these things is the Rev. James Murray.[74] Murray was himself deeply interested in and concerned about the issues facing the Newcastle freemen in the 1770s. He was probably behind both *The Freemen's Magazine* and *The Contest*, in which he discussed the controversies in which Wilkes was engaged and the Town Moor Affair, and sought to encourage the Newcastle electors — in the light of these events and of Sir Walter Blackett's involvement in them — to vote for Phipps and Delaval in the contested election of 1774. After that bid failed, Murray wrote on American affairs and campaigned in favour of the revolutionaries and was perhaps also involved in the establishment of the Newcastle Philosophical Society in 1775, which was perhaps intended as another vehicle for educating the local population and ensuring that important ideas and issues were discussed rather than ignored.[75] Murray was also a keen Harringtonian who drew on the English republican's ideas in his own works and who perhaps introduced them to the young Spence, inspiring his lifelong devotion to Harrington.

It is also interesting to set both Murray and Spence in the wider context of eighteenth-century Harringtonianism, since they arguably hold a unique position. Harrington's name was certainly reasonably well known in the eighteenth century and a number of authors drew directly on his ideas and produced works inspired by his constitutional plan. However, the vast majority of these figures, at least in Britain, were if anything more conservative in their politics than their mentor. Thus, in John Toland's 1700 edition of his works Harrington's ideas were used in support of monarchy, and in the journalistic writings of Henry St John, viscount Bolingbroke his ideas were associated with the upholding of aristocracy. In the later eighteenth century David Hume drew directly on *The Commonwealth of Oceana* in his essay 'A Perfect Commonwealth', describing it as 'the only valuable model of a commonwealth, that has yet been offered to the public.'[76]

74 For more detail on Murray see Rudkin, *Thomas Spence*, pp. 21-22 and Ashraf, *The Life and Times of Thomas Spence*, pp. 17-29.

75 Murray was clearly a member of the society by the time Spence gave his lecture and he remained a member long after. Around the same time Murray also put on a series of philosophical lectures for both male and female Newcastle residents, which presumably had a similar purpose. *Newcastle Chronicle*, 11 March 1775, p. 2.

76 D. Hume, 'The Idea of a Perfect Commonwealth', in *Essays, Moral, Political and Literary* (Indianapolis: Liberty Fund, 1987), p. 514.

Yet, he was critical of both the system of regular rotation of office and the agrarian law in ways that reflected a more conservative orientation than Harrington. Spence (and Murray), however, bucked this trend, appropriating Harrington's ideas for radical rather than conservative ends, and developing some of the implications of his theories and ideas to extreme conclusions. Yet, while Spence's appropriation of Harrington may have been against the grain from a British perspective he was not completely alone. Just a decade after Spence had delivered his controversial lecture to the Newcastle Philosophical Society, a Frenchman announced his own discovery of Harrington and his interesting ideas in a periodical entitled *Calypso, ou les Babillards*.[77] Like Spence, Jean-Jacques Rutledge was concerned about land and the political rights of the poor, and his interest in Harrington's writings was premised on his belief that they provided the basis for 'the most equal and the most durable democratic constitution' possible.[78] In the early 1790s, at precisely the time that Spence was republishing his lecture as *The Rights of Man*, Rutledge and his associates in the radical Paris-based 'Société des amis des droits de l'homme et du citoyen' or Cordeliers Club were drafting, publishing and defending a model constitution for France that drew directly on Harrington's *Commonwealth of Oceana*, adapting it for radical democratic ends.[79]

77 J. J. Rutledge (ed.), *Calypso, ou les Babillards* (Paris, 1784-5), III, pp. 217-225 and 313-359.

78 Rutledge, *Calypso*, III, p. 221. The translation is my own.

79 J. J. Rutledge, *Idées sur l'espèce de government popular qui pourrait convenir à un pays de l'étendue et de la population présumée de la France* (Paris, 1792). For a more detailed discussion of Rutledge, the Cordeliers and their use of the ideas of Harrington and other seventeenth-century English republicans see R. Hammersley, *French Revolutionaries and English Republicans: The Cordeliers Club, 1790-1794* (Woodbridge: Boydell and Brewer, 2005).

5

Thomas Spence and the London Corresponding Society, 1792-1795

•

Jon Mee

Thomas Spence is rightly primarily known for his radical land plan. Malcolm Chase's essay in this volume shows that Spence's plan inspired generations of radical thinking about the redistribution of property. As part of its demonstration that the private ownership of land was at the heart of social inequality, Spence's thinking, at least after 1795, also contained a powerful critique of the ideas of his fellow radical Thomas Paine. Spence's plan itself had its origins in the lecture 'Property in Land Every One's Right', reproduced for the first time in this volume. Nevertheless for much of his early period in London, Spence was deeply involved with the work of the London Corresponding Society, founded in 1792, on what might be called a broad popular front for parliamentary reform based on annual parliaments and universal manhood suffrage. This essay looks at Spence's role in the early years of the LCS from 1792-5, that is, up until its activities were sharply curtailed by the Convention Bills passed at the of 1795. For most of this period, Spence worked creatively alongside radicals in London inspired by Paine's *Rights of Man*, who believed they could bring about radical change through the distribution of political knowledge via print, debate, and other forms of political organization. They imagined a world of reader-citizens where meeting in discussion was understood to be a form of direct democratic participation, a constitutive part of the political process, not just a means of collecting public opinion.

The LCS was founded in January 1792 by a group of workingmen already used to meeting after work to discuss the affairs of the day. There is no doubt they were encouraged by the first part of Paine's *Rights of Man*, published the previous year, but there were other influences. Several of the earliest members, for instance, including the founder Thomas Hardy, seem to have been Scots Presbyterians. Hardy had come to London in the late 1770s. He shared with Spence a religious inheritance critical of any form of church governance that took power away from the congregation as well a broader tradition of struggle against the tyranny of Church and King.[1] The LCS program crystallised around the Duke of Richmond's plan of annual parliaments and universal manhood

1 See Hardy's account of the disputes about the right to appoint a minister that he explicitly related to the development of his political consciousness in Thomas Hardy, *The Memoir of Thomas Hardy, Founder of, and Secretary to, the London Corresponding Society*, p. 7.

suffrage, first mooted in the gentry reform movement of the 1780s, although the government always attempted to identify the LCS with French republicanism and more radical levelling schemes. The LCS was not just limited to a narrow interest in the ballot box, however. Hardy had a genuine interest in the abolition of slavery and there were always parts of the movement that looked beyond the Duke's plan both in moral terms and in relation to their ultimate political goals. Maurice Margarot, another important early leader in the LCS, until he was transported to Botany Bay in 1794, urged the societies forming in other parts of the country not to dwell on 'trifling' differences among them, but to concentrate on the Duke's plan as 'the ground-work of every necessary reform.' At Thomas Hardy's trial for treason late in 1794, the prosecution chose to read this letter as pointing towards an ultimate goal of 'pure democracy'. The construction put upon the letter was certainly part of a government conspiracy to manufacture a guilty verdict against Hardy and others, including Spence, arrested soon after Hardy, but it does point to the way some LCS members at least imagined the Duke of Richmond's plan as a staging post to larger changes, without necessarily agreeing what those should be. Spence almost certainly engaged with the LCS on this basis too, although, in his case, with a definite plan of what his ultimate aims were.[2]

To this extent, the LCS might be thought of as an umbrella organization primarily concerned with the diffusion of political knowledge to the people. 'Indeed their object was publicity', as Thomas Hardy later put it, 'the more public the better.'[3] Spence played a key role in disseminating political ideas in this period, not only his own ideas on land reform, as part of an attempt to educate the people at large. In this scenario, it was imagined that a society of reader-citizens, meeting to discuss texts that the LCS had circulated, could represent the will of the people and determine their own futures. The role of printer and bookseller was, potentially at least, as important as writer and thinker in this situation. By the winter of 1792 at the latest, Spence seems to have begun selling books, pamphlets, and the drink known as saloop from a stall on Chancery Lane, leased from a John Harrington, an operation that was obviously very cheap in terms of operating costs. Custom for his stock of books and pamphlets was undoubtedly stimulated by the great public interest in the events of the French Revolution, as France became a republic, and their significance for British politics. Spence seems to have sold copies of *Rights of Man*, a version by Paine and another that was probably the third edition of his 1775 lecture, as well as Burke's conservative diatribe *Reflections on the Revolution in France* (1790). He seems to have been left relatively unmolested until the loyalist zealot John Reeves formed his Society for Protecting Liberty and Property against

2 Margarot's letter of 26 November 1792 TS 11/958, National Archive, Kew, was produced at Hardy's trial. See John Barrell and Jon Mee, eds., *Trials for Treason and Sedition, 1792-1794*, 8 vols (London: Pickering & Chatto, 2006-7), 2: pp. 234-235 and the prosecution's opinion, given at 5: p. 232. There is an analysis of the courtroom discussion in John Barrell, *Imagining the King's Death: Figurative Treason, Fantasies of Regicide 1793-1796* (Oxford: Oxford University Press, 2000), pp. 146-147.

3 Hardy, 'Introductory letter to a Friend' (1799), British Library Additional Manuscripts 27817, f. 62.

Republicans and Levellers in November.[4]

From this time onwards, the campaign of harrying radical booksellers that had started with the indictment of Paine back in May 1792 intensified to a new pitch of harassment. Spence claims he was frequently surrounded and insulted by members of the Association, with 'uncommon violence and persecution', until he was taken before the magistrate at Hatton Gardens for selling seditious tracts on 6 December. The magistrate turned his accusers away; taking the view that Spence had committed no crime in selling political pamphlets. Then two Bow Street runners turned up on 10 December, Spence believed at the instigation of Reeves, and had him thrown into Clerkenwell prison while it was decided whether a grand jury would find the true bill against him needed for a prosecution to proceed. When Spence returned to his stall a few days later, after the grand jury had proved the bill against him, he found that Harrington had served notice on him to quite the stall. He was forced to take up the shop at No. 8 Little Turnstile, on Holborn, which was his base for most of this period.

A rough single-sheet handbill, issued from the new premises, survives in the Treasury Solicitor's depository of seized papers at the National Archive, which gives some sense of the financial upheaval involved for Spence. He addresses 'Friends in general of Free Investigation and the Liberty of the Press', asking for their custom, 'having been precipitated into a Shop before he was prepared for it'. He promises to stock 'particularly ... periodical publications of every kind, whether weekly or monthly' but needs help to pay his increased rent.[5] Luckily for Spence, the case against him for selling *Rights of Man* collapsed in February 1793 because of a mistake on the indictment, a legal technicality, common to every kind of criminal case, to do with the accused having the right to know exactly what charge was being brought against him or her. Spence seems to have used the brief respite to launch his famous periodical *One Pennyworth of Pigs' Meat*, later simply *Pigs' Meat*, issued in weekly parts until 1795, and reprinted in two multi-volume editions. The first definite signs of Spence's involvement with the LCS come in March and April 1793, when his shop was being used as a place where people could sign a petition in support of a parliamentary reform.[6]

The content of *Pigs' Meat* is a good illustration of the LCS's commitment to the circulation of political information, although it should be remembered that it was never an official publication of the society, however much its members read it. Spence published excerpts from political classics in the tradition of English liberty, like Milton and Locke, together with contemporary songs and satires; some he had written, some were sent in by readers, and some culled from other

---

4 The details of the events described in this and the next paragraph can be found in *The Case of Thomas Spence, Bookseller, the Corner of Chancery Lane* (London, 1792). A slightly different edition appeared early in the following year. Both sold for three pence.

5 The handbill is at TS 11/953, National Archive, Kew.

6 See Mary Thale, ed., *Selections from the Papers of the London Corresponding Society 1792-1799* (Cambridge: Cambridge University Press, 1983), pp. 57 and 60-61. Spence's name is often given as 'Spencer' in the minutes and spy reports of 1793, but the Holborn address usually indicates that it is Spence. For instance, the spy Lynam reported division 12 meeting at 'Spencer's Little turnstile Holborn' on 12 November 1793. See Thale, *Selections*, p. 92. By early 1794, Spence seems to have been the delegate for division 30 and involved in the various disputes about the society's constitution. See Thale, *Selections*, pp. 116 and 118.

sources. Quite possibly, Spence was already beginning to think about putting together the periodical when he was arrested in December, as he complained that the officers had confiscated from his pocket book excerpts from Locke, Pope, Swift, the legal theorist Pufendorf, and More's *Utopia*, as well as Leviticus 25. The last provided him with the text one of his most ubiquitous songs 'Hark how the trumpets Sound,' celebrating the Spencean 'Jubilee', which he claimed had originally appeared in his 1782 *Rights of Man*:

Hark! How the trumpets sound
Proclaims the land around
The Jubillee!
Tells all the poor oppress'd,
No more they shall be cess'd,
Nor the landlords more molest
Their property.[7]

Like some other radical songs, as we shall see, Spence took over 'God save the King' as the tune for his song, implying that his was the more authentic national anthem, in the sense of really representing the voice of the nation.

Although the song celebrated his land reform plan, there was no obvious political program connecting the mixture of texts in *Pigs' Meat*, although some of his key influences, like James Harrington's *Oceana*, were reprinted there. Much of the politics was in the confidence that the common people had as much right to read and debate these classic and contemporary texts as the elite. Spence like many other members of the LCS at this stage at least had great faith in the power of print to bring freedom. He was one of several LCS booksellers, for instance, who sold the copy of Lord Stanhope's speech celebrating the acquittals at the treason trials at the end of 1794:

> The invaluable ART OF PRINTING has dispelled that former Darkness; and like a new *Luminary* enlightens the whole Horizon. The *gloomy Night of Ignorance* is past. The pure unsullied *Light of Reason* is NOW much diffused, that it is no longer in the power of *Tyranny* to destroy it. And I believe, and hope, that glorious *intellectual Light* will, shortly, shine forth on Europe, with *meridian* Splendor.[8]

Spence himself was among those arrested and eventually released after eight months, but he was not quite as complacent about the power of print to deliver freedom as the noble earl, a matter I'll return to at the end of this essay.

If some within the LCS, at times anyway, seem to have believed with William Godwin that it was enough for the truth to be printed for it to triumph, then the engagement of men like Spence with print more often took the form of hand-to-hand combat with John Reeves and his gang. They used whatever

7 See *Pigs' Meat* (1795), 1: pp. 42-43 . The song was also printed in *Supplement to the History of Robinson Crusoe* (1782), pp. 8-9; *The End of Oppression; being a Dialogue between an Old Mechanic and a Young one*. (1795), pp. 11-12; *Spence's Songs: Part the First*, (1811?) iii. There is also an undated broadside version.

8 *Substance of Earl Stanhope's speech, delivered from the chair, at a meeting of citizens, at the Crown and Anchor* (London: 1795), p. 8.

weapons lay at hand in the armoury of print, including taking up the satirical methods of earlier participants in the struggle over the freedom of the press, including Pope, Swift, and the many others who came after them, almost regardless of the actual political sympathies of the original text. Prosecutions for seditious libel, as I have noted, had to say exactly what was seditious about words printed or spoken. In this context, irony and other forms of figurative speech provided a cover that could at least be exploited by an able defence attorney. In November 1793, Daniel Isaac Eaton, publisher of the other great radical periodical at this time, *Politics for the People* (1793-95) was acquitted for publishing an allegory of a tyrannical gamecock decapitated by a farmer, because the prosecution could not readily prove it referred to George III.[9] Spence always had a gift with allegory and irony. Within days of Eaton's acquittal, widely celebrated in the LCS, Spence published two pages under the title 'Examples of Safe Printing' in *Pigs' Meat*. The text was mainly made up of a passage from Edmund Spenser's *The Faerie Queene* glossed by bogus innuendoes, mimicking the form of court indictment, pretending to distance the poem from any malicious intent. So the poem's reference to a 'savage tiger' is glossed in square brackets, exactly as in a formal indictment, as 'Not meaning our most gracious sovereign Lord the King, or the Government of this country'.[10] Spence followed the example with the first of a series of animal fables, where the innuendoes ironically denied any application to contemporary affairs. Fundamentally, Spence is alerting his readers to the possibilities of the medium and what can be said by not saying what one means:

> Let us, O ye humble Britons be careful to shew what we do not mean, that the Attorney General may not, in his Indictments, do it for us.

This sly exploitation of the slipperiness of language and the formalities of the courtroom is a long way from any simple faith that it was enough to print the truth to bring about reform. Spence knew he had to operate in the cracks and fissures of the system to get his message across.

Apart from sly satire and extracts from political classics, songs were an important part of *Pigs' Meat* as they were of the culture of the LCS and the tavern sociability that surrounded it. In the first year of the movement's existence, the Scotsman Robert Thomson secured a reputation for himself as the bard of the society, even being dispatched to divisions where enthusiasm for the cause seemed to be waning. His most famous song was 'A New Song' sung to the tune of 'God Save the King', which remained in demand long after he was forced to flee to France as part of the same crackdown that saw Spence driven from his stall. Thomson's songs were collected in *A Tribute to Liberty* (1793), which includes a song 'To the London Corresponding Society,' obviously intended to cement a sense of identity in new divisions as they formed by

9 See my discussion of the Eaton case in Jon Mee, "Examples of Safe Printing': Censorship and Popular Radical Literature in the 1790s', in *Literature and Censorship*, Essays and Studies 1993, ed. Nigel Smith (Cambridge: D. S. Brewer, 1993), pp. 81-95.

10 *Pigs' Meat*, 2: p. 14, followed by 'The Lion and Other Beasts', pp. 14-15.

'dividing' from earlier ones:

> See our numbers how they grow!
> Crowding and dividing;
> Eager all their Rights to know,
> Reason still presiding.

A note glosses 'crowding and dividing' as a reference 'to the affiliated divisions which file off every night of meeting to different parts of the town'. For those singing the song at a meeting, it would have provided a sense of unity both 'here' within the particular division and with those 'dividing' meetings imagined as going on as the same time:

> Boldly all with heart and hand,
> Meet we here united,
> By each other firmly stand,
> To see our Country righted.[11]

Presumably, like Thomson's 'A New Song' or 'God Save the Rights of Man', as it was often called, this song had first existed as a slip song that could be passed around at meetings for others to join in with. Others gathered in the collection were also in circulation as broadsides, including 'Whitehall Alarmed!' and 'Burke's Address to the Swinish Multitude'. Songs were certainly a very malleable cultural form, easily adapted to circumstances, and capable of being produced as song slips, printed in newspapers, or gathered in anthologies. Spence reprinted Thomson's 'God Save the Rights of Man' and 'Burke's Address to the Swinish Multitude' in *Pigs' Meat.*[12] Available in cheap weekly numbers, Spence's periodical was effectively providing a kind of script for the divisional meetings out of songs to be sung and prose extracts to be read and discussed.

Preparing the evidence for the treason trials and softening up public opinion for a guilty verdict, the *Second Report of the Committee of Secrecy* noted with alarm the use 'of play bills and songs, seditious toasts; and a studied selection of the tunes which have been in use since the revolution' as a means to 'seduce and corrupt the thoughtless and uninformed': 'The appearance of insignificance and levity, which belongs at first sight to his part of the system, is, in truth, only an additional proof of the art and industry with which it has been pursued.'[13] But some elements within the LCS itself were not without qualms about the political theatre of toasts and songs. In its 'History of the Society' (1796), the LCS's *Moral and Political Magazine* recalled Thomson as one of those early members who were 'indefatigable in visiting and instructing new divisions', but then went on to describe him as 'possessed [of] a lively poetical genius, which did not exactly accord with the calm prudential principles on which the Society was

---

11 [Robert Thomson], *A Tribute to Liberty, or, A New Collection of Patriotic Songs* (London, 1793), p. 52. Two versions of Thomson's collection were published.

12 See *Pigs' Meat*, 2: pp. 91-93 and 'Burke's Address to the Swinish Multitude' 1: p. 250. There is a different song with the same title at 2: pp. 29-30.

13 *Second Report of the Committee of Secrecy*, p. 26.

instituted'.[14] 'The fervent desire for moral reform, educational improvement, and rational debate,' James Epstein and David Karr have suggested, 'was at odds with the norms of plebeian sociability'.[15] Perhaps this overstates the case. Reading, discussion, and singing co-existed as activities within the LCS; even if for some members they were two very different forms of print sociability, the last too likely to degenerate, as Godwin put it, from 'the conviviality of the feast to the depredations of a riot'.[16] Not everyone, though, feared this outcome for LCS sociability. John Thelwall, for instance, took over something of Thomson's role as LCS songwriter and his songs seem to have circulated rapidly around the divisions in 1794, some of them printed three to a sheet to ease circulation, as the prosecution disapprovingly remarked at Hardy's trial.[17] Whatever his skills as a songwriter, Thelwall certainly also encouraged reading and debate as part of LCS activities.

For Spence, Eaton, Thelwall and plenty of others, there was no necessary contradiction between reading and singing at political meetings, but the great archivist of the LCS, Francis Place, certainly seems to have felt the tension between the moral aspect of the movement and plebeian culture, but then his entire account of the organization is notoriously marked by a concern with respectability, as he saw it. Place's unpublished *Autobiography* strongly favours the idea that reading and debate were the key activities of the LCS and represented the key achievement of the LCS as bringing of sobriety and usefulness to working-class culture. Songs did appear in his accounts of the older plebeian culture he remembered from his childhood before he joined the LCS in 1794:

> Some of these songs sung by the respectable tradesmen who spent their evenings in my fathers [*sic*] parlour, were very gross, yet I have known the parlour door thrown open, that whoever was in the bar and the Tap room might hear every word.

Place's attitude to this material was complex. He was fascinated enough by it to collect it. If he placed the material within a narrative of respectability, then he also identified it with a lost world not entirely unmourned. These songs, he recalled, 'were sung with considerable humour by men who were very much excited'.[18] Place's primary concern here is with lewdness rather than politics, which he represents as a question of prosaic reason, but his account for the causes of the disappearance of songs invokes the political context of late 1792, precisely when Spence was being harassed on his stall and Thomson fled to France:

> John Reeves and his associates together with the magistrates extinguished

14 'History of the Society,' *Moral and Political Magazine of the London Corresponding Society*, August 1796, 1: p. 221.

15 James and David Karr, "Playing at Revolution: British 'Jacobin' Performance,' *Journal of Modern History* 79 (2007), p. 515.

16 William Godwin, *An Enquiry into Political Justice* (1793), 1: p. 208.

17 See the copies of 'News from Toulon,' 'The Sheepshearing Song', 'Britons Glory' printed three to a sheet at TS 11/953 and Barrell and Mee, *Trials*, 4: p. 312.

18 Place, *Autobiography*, pp. 57-8.

> them. The association printed a large number of what they called loyal songs, and gave them to ballad singers, if any one was found singing any but loyal songs he or she was carried before the magistrate who admonished and dismissed him or her, they were then told they might have loyal songs for nothing and that they would not be molested while singing them. Thus the bawdy songs, and those in praise of thieving and getting drunk were pushed out of existence.[19]

Place has little room for political songs in the account that precedes this paragraph, perhaps because the category didn't make sense for him, just as his account of LCS meetings and even their parties is dominated by reading and nowhere mentions the singing fed by the songs of Thomson and those who took his place after he went to France. As it happens, Place was fascinated by Spence, but regarded many of those he associated with after 1795 as representatives of an old 'unrespectable' culture that he thought had been replaced by the new world of 'rational' reading and debate promoted by the LCS. In fact, as we have seen, in its heyday between 1792 and 1795, political songs were intrinsic to the LCS culture of reading and discussion.[20]

With the acquittal of Eaton and the emergence of John Thelwall as a political writer and lecturer of note over the winter of 1793-4, the government became increasingly alarmed at the upsurge in radical activity around the LCS in association with the older Society for Constitutional Information. Pitt and his colleagues were particularly alarmed — or at least claimed to be at the treason trials — that plans for a convention were an attempt to form a rival to parliament that could claim to represent the will of the people. At the end of 1793, when the British Convention gathered in Edinburgh, with delegates from London, Maurice Margarot and the gentleman firebrand Joseph Gerrald, in attendance, the government moved in to arrest them. In the early months of 1794, the LCS, by now well and truly infiltrated by spies and informers, met with the SCI and consulted with other radical societies around the country with a view to calling a meeting to determine the best way forward. Disputes arose within the movement as to whether this meeting should be understood as a 'convention'. SCI members, especially, feared that the word implied an intention to install a popular assembly that would claim to have more authority than parliament. The issue was key to the government's decision to begin rounding up Hardy and the other leaders of the reform movement in May 1794.

Prior to the arrests, Reeves prepared a long report for the government, dated 29 April 1794, on the topography of London radicalism, including a description of the key booksellers.[21] He included samples of the works doing mischief, including copies of *Politics for the People* and *Pigs' Meat*, 'instances of those

19 See Place's 'Notes on grossness in publications and street songs: 1705-1795', British Library Additional Manuscripts 27825, f. 144r.

20 See the discussion of Place's attitude to Spence and his associates in Malcolm Chase, *The People's Farm: English Radical Agrarianism 1775-1840*, 2nd edition (London: Breviary Stuff, 2010 [first published by Oxford University Press, 1988]) and Iain McCalman, *Radical Underworld: Prophets, Revolutionaries and Pornographers in London, 1795-1840* (Cambridge: Cambridge University Press, 1988).

21 John Reeves, 'Report on Sedition' at TS 11/965, National Archive, Kew.

inferior publications that are the most cheap and the most mischievious'. He identifies Eaton's shop as the most successful and 'most frequented'. Then the report comes to Spence, described as living 'in the dirtiest poverty, but his shop is decorated with lines in verse and prose expressing a determination to carry on this traffic in spite of Laws and Magistrates'. It was above Spence's shop, Reeves claimed, that some members trained to arms, a claim made much of at the trials. Prompted by Reeves and other spy reports, the government swooped and arrested Hardy and Daniel Adams, the secretary of the SCI, on 12 May. A spy informed them that men gathered anxiously in Spence's shop, by now a major LCS resort, to discuss their fate and what they should do about it. On 13 May, Thelwall was arrested and the others, including the gentleman radical Horne Tooke, were soon taken into custody. Spence was arrested on 20 May. The trials did not come on until 5 November, when Hardy appeared in court. In the intervening six months, the government used the time provided by the suspension of habeas corpus to prepare the people for a guilty verdict with a barrage of negative propaganda in the press, including stories of the LCS arming. At the trials, the government did what it could to twist the law of treason, pushing for an understanding of 'imagining the king's death', the key term in the statutes, as setting in train a series of events that could conceivably lead to the king being deposed. In the process, they tried to shift the burden of proof away from the need to prove that the LCS were actively plotting the overthrow of the King.[22]

The last of the defendants, Thelwall, was finally acquitted on 5 December, but many of those who had been imprisoned by the government were not quickly released and spent days languishing in prison. John Richter and John Baxter remained there until mid-December; John Martin until September 1795. Spence was finally released on 22 December, after over 200 days in prison without trial. He announced that he had been restored to his shop by taking out an ad in the *Morning Chronicle* for 3 January and started up *Pigs' Meat* again. He published songs that had been written for the various dinners celebrating the acquittals in *Pigs' Meat* and helped distribute Stanhope's speech, quoted earlier, praising the verdicts as an affirmation of the liberty of the press. Nevertheless, the experience seems to have been something of a watershed for Spence, and he also printed an acerbic poetic commentary on the celebrations of genteel friends of liberty, 'On the late Barren Patriotic meetings':

> If half the wealth, and half the wind,
> That there was spent to no great end,
> Had been employ'd for to relieve
> The wants of patr'ots that now grieve,
> Who blushing for a nation's crimes,
> Dare yield to truth the homage due?
> Justice demands, &c.[23]

---

22 See the account of the strain put on the traditional understanding of the statute in Barrell's *Imagining the King's Death*.

23 *Pigs' Meat*, 3: pp. 57-58.

Others in the movement seem to have been developing similar feelings about fellow travellers from the elite. Horne Tooke's conduct at the trials, where he has compared Paine to the peasant poet Stephen Duck and equivocated in his testimony at Thelwall's, were subjected to scathing attack in the anonymous pamphlet *John Horne Tooke Stripped Naked and Dissected, and his Political Anatomy Exposed*. Published for sixpence, this bitter satire presented the veteran reformer as someone willing to accept only very partial reform:

> After adhering like a buzzing and teizing gnat, for so many years, to the buttocks of the Aristocracy, you now in the period of the grand climacteric, apologise for the annoyance, by the forfeiture of your admitted principle.[24]

The spirit within the debates of the LCS itself was hardly less rancorous as arguments over their own constitution flared between February and May 1795. Several divisions left to form independent societies like the Friends of Liberty and the London Reforming Society. The fight was primarily to do with the autonomy of the divisions from the central committee and whether rules and regulations ought to govern the activities of individual divisions. Conflict also seems to have raged about religious principles, resulting in Richard 'Citizen' Lee, whose millenarian poetry Spence published in *Pigs' Meat*, either leaving or being thrown out. The minutes don't give any clue as to Spence's involvement in either of these disputes, but he doesn't seem to have seceded. Given Spence's commitment to parish associations in his land plan, it seems likely he was among those who pushed against too much power for the executive, while his writing always breathed the millenarian spirit found in Lee's poems.[25]

Despite these schisms, a large degree of co-operation continued between the different groups in London over 1795. John Bone of the London Reforming Society proposed a programme of cheap publications that was accepted in principle by the LCS, although implementation was halted by the urgency of the struggle against the Convention Bills, once it became clear that in the wake of its defeat at the treason trials the government was going to legislate against traditional rights of freedom of association and expression. Spence joined in this struggle, selling tickets from his shop for the general meeting held at St. George's Field on 29 June, and collecting signatures there against the Convention Bills later in the year.[26] At the same time, Spence seems to have started to see the limits of what could be achieved by this culture of reading, debate, and discussion in the face of a government determined to close it down. *The End of Oppression*, probably published anonymously just as the new legislation was passing into law, places more emphasis on the right of resistance without explicitly condoning violence, a note that was being struck at the same time by other committed radicals like John Baxter, of the Friends of Liberty. Given the role Baxter gives to parish associations in his plan, it's not surprising he ended up

24 *John Horne Tooke Stripped Named and Dissected, and his Political Anatomy Exposed to the Electors of Westminster* [1795?], p. 13.

25 On Spence's millenarianism, see Chase, *The People's Farm*, pp. 41-51.

26 Thale, *Selections*, 252n and 325n.

associated with Speanceans in the United Englishmen and other underground radical groups after 1795.[27] Although the LCS limped on until it was officially proscribed in 1799, its vision of a co-ordinated universe of citizen-readers inspired by the diffusion of political knowledge was proving harder and harder to imagine as a way of bringing about the 'Jubillee' celebrated by Spence and the Spenceans.

27 McCalman, *Radical Underworld*, p. 19, places Baxter on his list of 'LCS and United movement notables who associated more or less regularly with Spence from at least 1811-12 onwards'.

6
The Economic Ideas of Thomas Spence: The Right to Subsistence

•

John Marangos

During the period of the industrial revolution, there is no doubt that the standard of living of the working class fell sharply in relation to the standards of the other classes. The working class lived near the subsistence level in 1750 and their standard of living was further deteriorating. It was no accident that Thomas Spence was advocating 'the right to subsistence' in the 1790s, which was a decade of great turbulence. The final quarter of the eighteenth century was a period of very rapid economic transformation in Britain, but the benefits trickled down only very slowly to the poor. Average real wages rose by five or six per cent in the 1790s,[1] but employment was precarious and periodic harvest failures sparked food riots and provoked intense debate over the poor person's right to subsistence.[2] Consequently, the rise of capitalism and the establishment of markets entailed the co-development of a class of the poor: 'those persons ... who, though willing to work, cannot subsist by labor' as explained by Richard Woodward an eighteenth-century exponent of the rights of the poor in his 1768 pamphlet, *An Argument in Support of the Right of the Poor in the Kingdom of Ireland, to a National Provision*.[3]

During the life of Thomas Spence (1750-1814) supporters of *laissez-faire* competitive capitalism campaigned vigorously for the abolition of the Speenhamland system of poor relief. Until the 16th century Protestant Reformation in England, virtually all of welfare was the responsibility of the Catholic Church. With the breakdown of feudal relations and the reduction of the influence of Catholicism in England, the Tudor monarchs experimented for half a century with providing assistance to the poor. At the end, during the reign of Queen Elizabeth I in 1601, a firm fiscal base for poor relief was established. The Elizabethan Statute of Artificers, the result of the Christian paternalistic ethic, sought to fix prices. Following, the 'Speenhamland Law' was initiated in 1795, the law was an amendment to the Elizabethan Poor Law, according to

1 Frank Geary and Tom Stark, 'Trends in real wages during the industrial revolution: a view from across the Irish Sea', *The Economic History Review* 57.2 (2004), pp. 362-395. Charles H. Feinstein, 'Pessimism perpetuated: real wages and the standard of living in Britain during and after the Industrial Revolution', *The Journal of Economic History* 58.03 (1998), pp. 625-658.

2 Dean, Mitchell, *The Constitution of Poverty: Toward a Genealogy of Liberal Governance* (London: Routledge, 1991), pp. 119-120.

3 Geoffrey Gilbert, 'Toward the Welfare State: Some British Views on the 'Right to Subsistence', 1768-1834', *Review of Social Economy* 46.2 (1988), pp. 145-146.

which 'subsidies in aid of wages should be granted on a scale dependent upon the price of bread, so that a minimum income should be granted to the poor *irrespective of their earning*'.[4] It held that unfortunates would be entitled to a certain minimum living standard whether employed or not. However, the subsidy depressed wages below the relief level in many cases (with the parish subsidies making up the difference) and severely limited labour mobility. But most of the arguments against the Speenhamland system were not confined to these negative features. The critique of the Speenhamland system dominated the writings of the new political economy discipline.[5] Classical economists from Adam Smith and David Ricardo to John Stuart Mill approached the poor laws with resentment.[6]

Classical economists were opposed to any government aid to the poor and many of their arguments were based on the ideas of Malthus.[7] Malthus rejected all schemes that would redistribute wealth or income. This is because in his view such redistribution would merely increase the number of poor and thus in the long run return them to the subsistence level. As such, redistribution would not raise the poor's standard of living in the long run, since redistribution would encourage the poor to have more children. Malthus together with the other classical economists tried to convince policy makers of the time that poverty is inevitable; that very little or nothing can be done about it since poverty is due to the weakness or moral inferiority of the poor.[8] Malthus said 'half the population of the country received relief'. According to Malthus, the 'evils of the poor laws seem to be irremediable'.[9] In the first edition of his *Essay*, Malthus advocated 'the total abolition of all the present parish laws'.[10] David Ricardo gave unqualified support to Malthus' position on poor laws and entitlements. In 1818 Ricardo wrote to a friend: 'Great evils result from the idea which the Poor Laws inculcate that the poor have a right to relief'.[11] Thus, at the time, public opinion associated classical political economy with a resolute denial of the right to subsistence to the poor and vigorous opposition to the English Poor Law.[12]

Anti-Malthusians believed that poor laws could be structured in such a way as to satisfy the concerns of classical political economists. Forthright critics of the Malthusian population theory argued that even the able-bodied poor might be granted assistance without danger of over-population, if the relief were

---

4 Karl Polanyi, *The Great Transformation: The Political and Economic Origins of Our Time* (Boston: Beacon Press, 2002), pp. 77-78.

5 Joseph Persky, 'Retrospectives: classical family values: ending the poor laws as they knew them', *Journal of Economic Perspectives* 11.1 (1997), p. 179.

6 Ibid., 182.

7 Emery Kay Hunt, *History of Economic Thought: A Critical Perspective* (New York: Harper Collins Publishers 1992), p. 85.

8 Ibid., p. 96.

9 Thomas Robert Malthus, *An Essay on the Principle of Population* (Sixth Edition), (London: William Pickering, 1826), pp. 355, 381, 367.

10 Thomas Robert Malthus, *An Essay on the Principle of Population* (First Edition), (London: William Pickering, 1798), pp. 36-37.

11 David Ricardo, *Letters 1816-1818*. In *Works and Correspondence of David Ricardo*, edited Piero Sraffa, Vol. VII (Cambridge: Cambridge University Press, 1952), p. 248.

12 Geoffrey Gilbert, 'Toward the Welfare State: Some British Views on the 'Right to Subsistence', 1768–1834,' *Review of Social Economy* 46.2 (1988), p. 153.

cautiously administered.[13] Richard Woodward, Michael Sadler, Samuel Read, Poulett Scrope, William F. Lloyd and Mountifort Longfield argued that the poor have a 'right to subsistence' as a matter of justice and/or argued for the advantages of poor relief either for the economy or its usefulness in maintaining political stability.[14] Anti-Malthusianism aimed to reposition labour capability in its traditional role of releasing and enhancing nature. Those who rejected Malthus' ideas, in fact, rejected an untouched, unsubdued and untamed 'natural' nature in favour of emphasizing cultivation and productivity. Unproductive nature was unnatural as 'the whole earth [should] be as the Garden of Eden' Spence declared.[15]

There was also a political crisis during the life of Thomas Spence (1750-1814), with the example of the French Revolution encouraging the spread of republicanism, democracy and radical egalitarianism among the lower orders, causing alarm, verging on panic, higher up the social scale and inducing unprecedented political repression by the agencies of the state.[16] The Revolution had asserted the universal rights of the people. But what did this entail for economic and social relations? How could the right to property be reconciled with the 'right to life', that is, to a decent minimum standard of living? How in particular could the massively unequal distribution of landed property be justified, in terms of either divine law or human reason? These were the profound issues that confronted Spence and an entire generation of radical thinkers. Underneath them, of course, lay even deeper questions about social and economic justice in a rapidly expanding capitalist market economy, and the connection between economic progress and political and social democracy.[17]

The radical ideas of Thomas Spence are well known, but his support for 'the right to subsistence' has received relatively little attention. The case for 'the right to subsistence' can be traced back to eighteenth-century France, beginning with Montesqieu and Mably and running through to Babeuf, Condorcet and Robespierre in the early years of the Revolution. Spence was a far more radical exponent of the rights of the poor. His version of the 'right to subsistence' places him at a considerable distance from the doctrine of Malthus and the classical political economists, and from the Anti-Malthusians.

In this chapter I set out Spence's arguments concerning 'right to subsistence' in his *The Rights of Infants* (published, largely in response to Paine's 'Agrarian Justice', in 1797). We show that natural rights arguments played an important, but by no means exclusive, role in his advocacy of the 'right to subsistence'.

13 Ibid., 154.

14 Ibid., 144.

15 Malcolm Chase, *The People's Farm: English Radical Agrarianism, 1775-1840*, 2nd edition (London: Breviary Stuff, 2010 [first published by Oxford University Press, 1988]), p. 158.

16 E. P. Thompson, *The Making of the English Working Class* (Harmondsworth: Penguin, 1968 [1963]), Ch. 5.

17 Noel W. Thompson, *The Real Rights of Man: Political Economies for the Working Class, 1775-1850* (London: Pluto Press, 1998).

Thomas Spence's Right to Subsistence

Thomas Spence's 'The Rights of Infants; or, the Imprescriptable RIGHT of MOTHERS to such share of the Elements as is sufficient to enable them to suckle and bring up their Young' is the title of a pamphlet written in response to Paine's 'Agrarian Justice'. In the Preface Spence states that he was very happy that Paine, even though late, acknowledged the indisputable truth of vast importance to humankind that 'God hath given the earth to the children of men, given it to mankind in common'.[18] He seems to have hoped that Paine's celebrity status would encourage readers to investigate this fundamental truth. Spence's appreciation of Paine always carried a hint of envy, as the popularity of the author of the 'Agrarian Justice' ensured an audience far beyond Spence's expectations.

Paine wrote the 'Agrarian Justice' in the winter of 1795-6 after his release from imprisonment in France. The complete title is 'Agrarian Justice. Opposed to Agrarian Law and to Agrarian Monopoly Being a Plan for Meliorating the Conditions of Man' published in 1797. For Paine every proprietor of cultivated land owes to society a ground-rent for the non-improved land which the person holds because it is common property. This ground rent would take the form of a tax of 10% on inheritances as the best alternative to the sharing of the land by the members of society. The rent would be deposited in the Natural Fund, which would provide to every person, when arrived at the age of twenty-one years, the amount of fifteen pounds sterling and the sum of ten pounds per annum, during life, to every person of the age of fifty years and over. Thus, for people between the ages of twenty-two to forty-nine and below nineteen no income would be provided from the Natural Fund. In the 'Agrarian Justice' Paine proposed:

> To create a Natural Fund, out of which there shall be paid to every person, when arrived at the age of twenty-one years, the sum of Fifteen Pounds sterling, as a compensation in part for the loss of his natural inheritance by the introduction of the system of landed property. AND ALSO, The sum of Ten Pounds per annum, during life, to every person now living of the age of fifty years, and to all others as they arrive at that age.[19]

The plan that Paine advocated, Spence argued, did not appear to be just or satisfactory. The 'poor, beggarly stipends' that Paine proposes are 'contemptible and insulting'.[20] Spence is convinced that landed interest is incompatible with the happiness and independence of the people because landlords raise the rents to the point where they get the 'whole fat' of the produce of hard working people. For Spence, Paine's proposal was merely the thief returning to the victims a part of what had been stolen and he condemned Paine's failure to envisage the

---

18 Thomas Spence, 'The Rights of Infants', (1797). In *The Political Works of Thomas Spence*, edited by H. T. Dickinson (Newcastle upon Tyne: Avero, 1982), p. 46.

19 Thomas Paine, 'Agrarian Justice'. In *Thomas Paine Collected Writings*, edited by Eric Foner, (New York: The Library of America, 1797), p. 400.

20 Thomas Spence, 'The Rights of Infants', (1797). In *The Political Works of Thomas Spence*, edited by H. T. Dickinson (Newcastle upon Tyne: Avero, 1982), p. 46.

transformation of private property into common property.[21] Spence found it strange that Paine, the famous democrat, would suggest agrarian reforms which were undemocratic and unlikely to root out injustice. Spence viewed his own proposals as being more plausible and practical.[22]

Spence's pamphlet was written in the form of a dialogue between a woman and an aristocrat. The main character takes the form of a woman, as she notes that men are not to be depended on.[23] She is also, therefore, a mouthpiece for Spence's advocacy of the rights of women. The woman states 'that mothers have a right, at the peril of all opposers, to provide from the elements the proper nourishments of their young'.[24] This right is not only known to women but they also have the courage and spirit to defend it, 'to the downfall of you [aristocracy] and all tyrants ... and throw you [aristocracy] and all your panyers in the dirt'.[25] It is made clear that the exercise of women's rights to feed, nurse, clean, cloth and lodge their children requires the abolition of the aristocracy, abolition of 'the bloody landed interest", the 'band of robbers', and the 'beasts of prey'. It is in the interest of the aristocracy to submit peacefully and give up their land for the sake of achieving a fair system. Otherwise, if the aristocracy resist the change 'by foolish and wicked opposition' then their total wealth would be confiscated, they will be cut off and 'then let your blood be upon your own heads, for we shall be guiltless'.[26] So Spence advocates the violent overthrow of the aristocracy, in case the aristocracy did not voluntarily give up their wealth. Unlike most land reformers — including Paine who believed that the aristocracy would adopt his proposal voluntary as a result of self-interest — Spence's plan appropriates land, industrial establishments and equipment.[27] For Spence the power and the 'drinking of the blood of infants' by the aristocracy and landlords, would end by dispossessing then instantaneously, 'as by an electric shock' all revenue from lands, with ownership given to parishes to administer and to make land available for use by all inhabitants. Gradualism was rejected by Spence.

Spence, in the dialogue between the woman and the aristocrat, states through the voice of the woman that nobody expects the fruits of labour for nothing. There would be equal right to land but unequal reward for labour. What hard working people are 'sick' of is labouring for an insatiable aristocracy. The abolition of the aristocracy would not hurt production rather it would be for the better, as rents would not be accrued to the landlords but rather to the people. In this context, the right of work would be guaranteed through the parish system, as property would be administered in such a way as to provide work to the unemployed though public works, or to provide tools and machinery for self-

21 John Keane, *Tom Paine: A Political Life* (Boston: Little, Brown and Company, 1995), p. 427. Noel W. Thompson, *The Real Rights of Man: Political Economies for the Working Class, 1775-1850* (London: Pluto Press, 1998), p. 137.

22 Malcolm Chase, *The People's Farm: English Radical Agrarianism, 1775-1840*, 2nd edition (London: Breviary Stuff, 2010 [first published by Oxford University Press, 1988]), p. 59.

23 Thomas Spence, 'The Rights of Infants', (1797). In *The Political Works of Thomas Spence*, edited by H. T. Dickinson (Newcastle Upon Tyne: Avero, 1982), p. 51.

24 Ibid., p. 48.

25 Ibid., p. 49.

26 Ibid., p. 52.

27 Phyllis Mary Ashraf, *The Life and Times of Thomas Spence* (Newcastle upon Tyne: Frank Graham, 1983), p. 120.

employment and land for cultivation. The parish system proposed was an alternative to the nationalization of land. Spence, like other radicals of the time, distrusted remote government, and was in favour of self-government and democracy. The numerous benefit clubs and societies — a thriving experience of the common people as voluntary associations administered on democratic principles without friction — provided a prototype for self-government. Spence instructs that women will appoint in every parish a committee of their own sex to receive the rents from houses and land and also lease vacant properties to the highest bidders for seven years. In addition, large scale industry will become common property, managed by the parish or by 'corporations' of work collectives.[28] Spence used the example of joint stockholding from shipping, mining and commerce to demonstrate the feasibility of communal land ownership and industrial equality.[29] The action of one parish would soon be mimicked by other parishes, thus in a short time the land, houses and industrial structures would become common property, owned by the parish system of corporations. The income derived would pay state taxes (so there would be no need for taxes and tax-collectors) and finance public goods (such as to clean and light the streets, pay public officers and build and repair houses). The remaining income, which should be around the two-thirds of the total amount of rents collected:

> shall be divided fairly and equally among all the living souls in the parish, whether male or female; married or single; legitimate or illegitimate; from a day old to the extremest age; making no distinction between families of rich farmers and merchants, who pay much rents for their extensive farms or premises, and the families of poor labourers and mechanics who pay but little for their small apartments, cottages and gardens, but giving to the head of every family a full and equal share for every name under his roof.[30]

Hence, Spence's proposal was truly universal and independent of age, in contrast to Paine's age-based plan. The justification for the equal distribution of net rents was based on the imprescriptible right of every member of a civilized society to the natural fruits of the earth. This right was set in contrast to the landlords' implicit claim, 'as if they had manufactured land'.[31] However, by giving up the right to the common property by allowing it to be rented for the sake of cultivation, members of the civilized society are deprived from the natural fruits of earth. Consequently, they have to be compensated. Spence wished for to make everybody 'landlords of property that they did not occupy, the owners of

28 Ibid., p. 120. Terence M. Parssinen, 'Thomas Spence and the origins of English land nationalization', *Journal of the History of Ideas* (1973), p. 136.

29 Malcolm Chase, *The People's Farm: English Radical Agrarianism, 1775-1840*, 2nd edition (London: Breviary Stuff, 2010 [first published by Oxford University Press, 1988]), p. 26.

30 Interesting enough, the income would be given to the head of every family who Spence took for granted is a male — 'his roof'. Thomas Spence, 'The Rights of Infants', (1797). In *The Political Works of Thomas Spence*, edited by H. T. Dickinson (Newcastle Upon Tyne: Avero, 1982), p. 51.

31 Phyllis Mary Ashraf, *The Life and Times of Thomas Spence* (Newcastle upon Tyne: Frank Graham, 1983): p. 122.

land-capital and the recipient of rent interest'.[32]

In the society proposed by Spence people will not need to work all hours: there will be a 5-day work week, holidays and feasts, people will be able to enjoy the fruit of their own-labour, be hospitable, dress decently and bring up their children in a proper manner. But the radical agrarianism of Spence is not a return to nature; rather it was the establishment of a society based on economic and social democracy: 'Thus each parish is a little polished Athens'.[33]

At the end of the dialogue between the woman and the aristocrat and before the conclusion Spence inserts an appendix with the title 'A Contrast between Paine's Agrarian Justice and Spence's End of Oppression, Both being built on the same indisputable Principle viz. That the land is the common Property of Mankind'. Here Spence contrasts the two proposals by creating a table of two columns and twenty rows, one column for 'Under the system of Agrarian Justice' and the other 'Under the system of End of Oppression'. The twenty rows compare one by one each element of the contrasting proposals. The original text is inserted in the appendix of this book.

Based on the comparison of the two proposals, Spence directly attacks Paine for providing only a tenth of the value of land to the people (due to the improvements in the land from the natural state expended by the landlords). For Spence, the definition of land is not restricted to its natural state; it also includes all human-made improvements and permanent structures. Spence reminds us that these improvements in land and the erection of permanent structures were the result of the work and the consumption of the labouring classes. 'Therefore, let us not in weak commiseration be biased by the pretended philanthropy of the great, to the resignation of our dearest rights'.[34] Spence's proposal is a process of 'recovering our rights'. The purpose was to make the sources of wealth, and thus of primary subsistence, common property.[35]

In this context, Spence attacks Paine for expecting that people should give up their birth-rights 'for a mess of porridge'; a loss that would only encourage people to "become supine and careless' in public affairs and be 'like pensioned emigrants and French priests'. As well, he argues that people cannot derive their right of suffrage from Paine's stipends and that his proposal is consistent with a non-democratic government, while enhancing the non-accountability nature of 'public establishments'. In addition, Paine's proposal is inconsistent with the spirit of a free state, at it maintains and increases the dependency of the poor, maintains and increases taxes, maintains the perception that children are a burden, maintains the dependence of the education of the poor on charity-schools and maintains in times of scarcity substitutes for bread. People would have to compromise with their 'conquerors and oppressors' under Paine's proposal and all the benefits of international and domestic trade would be accrued to the landed interests; likewise monopolies and privileges would be

32 Ibid., p. 124.

33 Thomas Spence, 'The Rights of Infants', (1797). In *The Political Works of Thomas Spence*, edited by H. T. Dickinson (Newcastle Upon Tyne: Avero, 1982), pp. 64-65.

34 Ibid., p. 53.

35 Phyllis Mary Ashraf, *The Life and Times of Thomas Spence* (Newcastle upon Tyne: Frank Graham, 1983), p. 120.

maintained, and as a result there would be a 'dissimilarity between their natural rights and enjoyments'. In addition, actual domestic trade would always be lower than its potential level, due to the maintenance of a poor class of people. Also, Paine's proposal increases the influence of government and, due to its provision of stipends, the government expressing the interest of the rich will use the stipends as an excuse to abolish hospitals, charitable funds, and parochial provision for the poor.

Paine wanted to reform the political system; Spence wanted to substitute the whole system with an entirely different one. For Paine, annual parliaments, proportional representation, universal suffrage and the secret ballot were adequate. But for Spence a republican government espoused by Paine is not a substitute to any real social equality, since the landlords would control the parliament and government. The ownership of land, he tells us, gives rise to economic and political power. It is 'the distribution of landed property, rather than political systems, dictates the real character of a nation and its liberties'.[36] For Paine and the republicans hereditary government was based on conquest but, for Spence, conquest was interpreted as the expropriation of the people's natural rights. 'Natural rights, since they arise at birth and are inalienable, cannot be bartered for civil rights nor mortgaged for future generations'.[37] For Spence it is natural, then, to dismiss the ideas of a new 'social contract,' as there cannot be any legitimate contract between those who are unequal. Society cannot change by preaching and/or peaceful tactics (as the example of the French Revolution demonstrates) or by advocating 'enlightened self-interest,' for the defence of 'natural and universal interest' demands collective interest, solidarity and mutuality. For Spence, people, especially the working class, do not need any 'transformation' other than to a state where they may regain their natural rights.

Conclusion

For Spence, ownership of land should be removed from the aristocrats (either peacefully or violently) and appropriated by the parishes, which would make land available for use by all inhabitants. Parishes would receive the rents from houses and land and also lease vacant properties to the highest bidders for a seven year lease. The income derived would pay state taxes, so there would be no need for taxes, and finance public goods. The remaining income would be divided equally among all the members of the parish and granted to the head of household.

Spence's proposal overall would result in the following: people would receive their common inheritance in full; people would be watchful over public expenditure; people would be concerned with improving their parishes; universal suffrage will be derived from common property; government would be democratic; fewer public officers with moderate salaries; robust spirit of independence; a progressive society; no taxes; industrious and decent modes of

36 Malcolm Chase, *The People's Farm: English Radical Agrarianism, 1775-1840* , 2nd edition (London: Breviary Stuff, 2010 [first published by Oxford University Press, 1988]), p. 27.

37 Phyllis Mary Ashraf, *The Life and Times of Thomas Spence* (Newcastle upon Tyne: Frank Graham, 1983), p. 126.

life would be promoted; children would be treated equally; education would be available; there would be no need to substitute for bread; oppressors must submit to the general mass of citizens; any increases in commodities would increase rents and they revert back to the people by increasing quarterly dividends; no monopolies; justice would prevail; no poor; the government would have little influence and no need for public charities.

Spence did not contribute anything more after the publication of *The Rights of Infants*, to the case of the 'right to subsistence'. Spence had moved from Newcastle to London in December 1787 or early 1788 and continued to agitate for political and social reform before dying in relative obscurity in 1814. The British radicals of the 1820s and early 1830s drew on new and different ideas, especially those of the so-called Ricardian socialists and the Owenites,[38] and after 1837 the Chartist movement gave priority to the campaign for political democracy as the essential prerequisite for social and economic reform. But Spence's 'right of subsistence' remained as one important theme in the broader working-class movement, as can be seen from the huge appeal of Feargus O'Connor's ill-fated Land Plan.[39] The popular slogan, 'The Land is the People's Farm', testifies to the enduring significance of Spence, reflected, for example, in William Cobbett's insistence on the poor man's right to a living.[40] Owenites like Allen Davenport, Thomas Preston and Samuel Waddington continued to acknowledge the merits of Spence's proposals, and it is not difficult to discern Spencean themes in the Anti-Poor Law Movement of the 1830s.[41]

38 Noel W. Thompson, *The Real Rights of Man: Political Economies for the Working Class, 1775-1850* (London: Pluto Press, 1998)

39 Alice Mary Hadfield, *The Chartist Land Company* (Newton Abbot: David & Charles, 1970).

40 Malcolm Chase, *The People's Farm: English Radical Agrarianism, 1775-1840*, 2nd edition (London: Breviary Stuff, 2010 [first published by Oxford University Press, 1988]), pp. 156-157.

41 Nicholas C. Edsall, *The Anti-Poor Law Movement, 1834-44* (Manchester: Manchester University Press, 1971).

7
Spence and the Politics of Nostalgia

•

Alastair Bonnett

We cannot see Spence directly. We peer at something that resembles him through two centuries of revolutionary history. And it is hard, most likely impossible, to talk about Spence without using words that would have meant nothing to him. Words like 'socialist', 'working class', 'communist', 'proletarian' are all creations of the nineteenth century. Spence was a product of an earlier period: he had his own vocabulary and his own traditions, some of which can seem very remote today.

It's ironic. Spence has been covered over by nearly two hundred years of Marxism, Bolshevism, Maoism, *et al.* But today it is these 'isms', not Spence, that seem wheezy and grey with age. To read Spence is to be reminded of the earthy, ever fertile, roots of radicalism. It is also to be confronted with the stark fact that Spence was a mortal enemy of tyranny and 'giantism' of all kinds. Later left-wing ideologies fitfully claimed him as an eccentric forefather. But Spence is awkward. He doesn't fit our stereotypes; and he still has the power to break our moulds.

This chapter does three things. First, it establishes that issues of loss and attachments to the past emerged as a chronic problem within English socialist history. The pertinence of this discussion to Spence is explained in the second section. Here I show that Spence offered a vision of radical change rooted in his attachments to the land and the popular culture of the people. Third, I illustrate, using the example of Marxism, how this 'rooted radicalism' was set aside by later progressivist and 'anti-nostalgic' ideologies which tried to lay claim to Spence. To trace the misappropriation of Spence is to take an increasingly uncomfortable journey. It starts well, with creative intellectuals, like Marx himself. But it soon takes us into the territory of those wishing to carve out new bureaucracies, totalitarian states in which Spence, who always prided himself on being 'as free as a cat', would have surely spent even more years locked up than he did in England.

The Politics of the Past in English Socialist History

> The history of nostalgia might allow us to look back at modern history not solely searching for newness and technological progress but for unrealised potentialities, unpredictable turns and crossroads.[1]

Svetlana Boym's aspiration offers a familiar message. In Britain the search for

1 Svetlana Boym, *The Future of Nostalgia*, (New York: Basic Books, 2001), p. xvi.

'unrealised potentialities' grew to prominence with the rediscovery of the diverse political heritage of the working class, associated with E. P. Thompson and kindred historians. 'In some of the lost causes of the people of the Industrial Revolution', Thompson explained, 'we may discover insights into social evils which we have yet to cure'.[2] However, to evoke Thompson's exploration of the birth of class consciousness, in the late eighteenth century and the first three decades of the nineteenth century, is also to invite further refinement of my argument that a rupture in the politics of the past can be identified later in the nineteenth century. In celebrating early English radicals, Thompson offers them as attractive, yet primal, figures at the beginning of a story which concludes with the accomplishment of a recognisably modern socialist identity. Nostalgia, if admitted at all — for even Cobbett is said by Thompson to be only 'seemingly "nostalgic"' — becomes a strategic device; the weapon of memory against capitalism.[3]

The progressivism found (but also sometimes questioned) in Thompson has much bolder expression in Hobsbawm, for whom 'primitive rebels' are

> *pre-political* people who have not yet found, or have only begun to find a specific language in which to express their aspirations about the world. Though their movements are thus in many respects blind and groping, by the standards of modern ones, they are neither unimportant nor marginal.[4]

The attempt to locate *transitions* towards class identity, and of people and periods which represent *turning points* in the achievement of authentic class struggle, is still characteristic of much socialist history.[5] This effort is usually assisted by the expectation that capitalist processes of social dispossession are naturally followed by political processes of affiliation around antagonistic class identities. Although often connected with Marx, one can find intimations of this chain of association throughout nineteenth century radical thought. In the 1850s, the Chartist leader, Ernest Jones, repeatedly wrote about the emergence of class conflict in the context of the fact that the 'intervening classes are melting away'.[6] Although Jones's repetition of the point suggests he believed it to be a novel one, it had in fact been observed decades earlier. Indeed, Thompson finds comparable ideas being voiced from the last decades of the eighteenth century, as connections were forged between 'the clamour of the mill' and a new population amongst whom 'levelling systems are the discourse; and rebellion may be near at hand'.[7]

By 1869, when John Stuart Mill started planning his major study of

---

2 E. P. Thompson, *The Making of the English Working Class*, (Harmondsworth: Penguin Books, 1968), p. 13.

3 Ibid., p. 836.

4 E. Hobsbawm, *Primitive Rebels*, (Manchester: Manchester University Press, 1959), p. 2.

5 Dated by Hobsbawm to 1880-1900. Hobsbawm, *Labour's Turning Point: Extracts from Contemporary Sources* (London: Lawrence & Wishart, 1948).

6 E. Jones, *Notes to the People: Volume I*, (London: J. Pavey, 1851), p. 245.

7 'An aristocrat traveller who visited the Yorkshire Dales in 1792', cited by Thompson, *The Making of the English Working Class*, p. 207. Thompson asserts that 'the outstanding fact of the period between 1790 and 1830 is the formation of "the working class"', p. 212.

socialism, the term had been in circulation for over four decades.[8] It was clear to Mill that, 'the fundamental doctrines which were assumed as incontestable by former generations, are now put again on their trial'.[9] Moreover, that a new dispossessed and alienated class had emerged that was the agent of a new 'standpoint':

> classes who have next to no property of their own ... will not allow anything to be taken for granted — certainly not the principle of private property, the legitimacy and utility of which are denied by many of the reasoners who look out from the standpoint of the working classes.[10]

Mill's analysis suggests that feelings of loss and attachment can best be described as residual. In placing nostalgia as a dying form, his narrative both problematises and marginalises it within the bigger story of a maturing class movement. Thus the persistent desire voiced by the radical poor, especially in the turbulent decades at the start of the nineteenth century (but echoed many times in later years), to see a transition, in the words of the *Poor Man's Guardian* (of November, 1831), back 'from a state worse than slavery to the old system of old England',[11] is rendered anachronistic.

A key figure in the expression of such supposedly anachronistic attitudes is William Cobbett (1763-1835). In the 1810s and 1820s, Cobbett was the most widely-read and influential radical in English politics. His *Political Register* campaigned against the immerisation of the labouring population as well as the corrupt nature of the new commercial society Cobbett saw growing around him. Cobbett also made it crystal clear that,

> we want *nothing new*. We have great constitutional laws and principles, to which we are immovably attached. We want *great alteration*, but we want nothing new ... the great principles ought to be, and must be the same, or else confusion will follow.[12]

It was on this basis that Cobbett denounced the new 'race of merchants and manufacturers, and bankers and loan-jobbers and contractors' which he saw as destroying the well-being and fine traditions of rural life.[13] 'Unnatural changes' are Cobbett's target throughout his *Rural Rides*. He foresees with horror 'the long oak-table' of village life disposed of at the 'bottom of a bridge that some stock-jobber will stick up over an artificial river in his cockney garden'.

'Nowadays the limits of Cobbett's outlook are obvious', John Derry confidently informed us in 1967: 'he idealised the England of his youth'.[14] This verdict accords with the widespread late modern assumption that Cobbett is part of an inherently conservative tradition of rural and national mythology. The fact

---

8 Max Beer identifies its first use with Robert Owen: the word 'socialism', he notes, 'is found for the first time in *The Co-operative Magazine* of November, 1827'. M. Beer, *A History of British Socialism*, (New York: Arno Press, 1979), p. 187.

9 J. Mill, *Socialism*, (New York: John B. Alden, 1886), p. 260.

10 Ibid.

11 *Poor Man's Guardian*, (November 19th, 1831), p. 174.

12 W. Cobbett, 'To the Blanketteers', *Cobbett's Weekly Political Register*, (March 27th, 1819), pp. 830-831.

13 W. Cobbett, *Rural Rides*, Volume 1, (London: J.M. Dent, 1917), p. 6.

14 J. Derry, *The Radical Tradition: Tom Paine to Lloyd George*, (London, Macmillan, 1967), p. 46.

that 'Cobbett most always had in mind the village labourer or small farmer', explains Richard Johnson, means that 'his prescriptions have an old-fashioned or "Tory" ring'.[15] More boldly, Linda Colley finds in Cobbett's nostalgic evocations of popular solidarity a precursor of fascism: he was, she suggests, a 'forerunner ... ultimately of the National Front'.[16]

Ian Dyck has effectively challenged many of these associations by making the case that, by 1805, Cobbett was 'an unqualified Radical'.[17] Dyck links the modern difficulty in accepting this political identity to the fact that 'folk tradition and cottage politics ... have become increasingly estranged from the theory and practice of left-wing radicalism'.[18] Dyck opens out Cobbett's nostalgia to show that, idealised as it undoubtedly was, it nevertheless referred to concrete experiences and specific memories. 'It was not country workers but middle-class rural writers', Dyck argues,

> who lapsed into vague and romantic effusions about the past. Cobbett and the labourers were not vague: their sense of the eighteenth-century past was grounded in experience and oral traditions rather than in a chronic and wistful impulse to recover the past for the past's sake.[19]

Surveying the evidence for generational differences in living standards between 1790-1840 E. P. Thompson found that 'there was a slight improvement in average material standards'.[20] However, looking beyond the statistics of income and prices, he comes down on the same side as Dyck.

> Over the same period there was intensified exploitation, greater insecurity, and increasing human misery. By 1840 most people were 'better off' then their forerunners had been fifty years before, but they had suffered and continued to suffer this slight improvement as a catastrophic experience.[21]

Dyck's argument also finds support in the portrait of Thomas Spence I offer in this chapter. He too had 'grounded' experience to draw on when he criticised the changes he saw around him. However, in turning to Spence we can also make a broader attempt to challenge the identification of early nostalgic radicalism with the right. For unlike Cobbett, whose thumping rhetoric and ruddy farmer's demeanour allow him to be easily rendered as 'really a Tory', Spence is the poorest and most determined militant in English history; an unassailable icon of revolutionary integrity.

To identify and understand the role of nostalgia in Spence's politics might seem, then, a disquieting prospect. However, as Dyck's intervention suggests, over recent years the history of socialism in Britain has become far more

---

15 R. Johnson, '"Really useful knowledge": radical education and working-class culture', in J. Clarke, C. Critcher and R. Johnson (eds) *Working-Class Culture: Studies in History and Theory* (London: Hutchinson, 1979), p. 89.

16 L. Colley, 'I am the Watchman', *London Review of Books*, (20 November, 2003), p. 17.

17 Dyck, *William Cobbett*, p. 214.

18 Ibid.

19 Ibid., p. 147.

20 Thompson, *The Making of the English Working Class*, p. 231.

21 Ibid., p. 231.

receptive to the complexity of radical identity. One of the most influential interdisciplinary contributions to this new mood was Craig Calhoun's *The Question of Class Struggle*.[22] Calhoun unpicks the fabric of Marxist analysis by arguing that it was not the factory worker but the artisan, deeply embedded in locality and tradition and rebelling against the destruction of his whole way of life, that provided the most active revolutionary agent.[23] The 'reactionary radicalism' of such workers, best exemplified for Calhoun by the Luddite movement of the 1810-20 period, was a fight for survival: 'what they sought could not be granted except by fundamentally altering the structure of power and rewards in English society'.[24] Hence such 'workers were not fighting for control of the industrial revolution as much as against that revolution itself'.[25] Contrary to Mill and Marx's idea that radicalism emerged from deracination (when people have 'nothing but their chains' to lose), Calhoun suggests that 'revolutionary and other radical mobilisations take place when people do have something to defend'.[26]

Turning one of the assumptions of class history on its head, Calhoun goes on to conclude that 'reformism is the characteristic stance of the working class'. For the 'new working class could gain an indefinite range of ameliorative reforms without fundamentally altering its collective existence.[27] Although Calhoun's assessment of defensive radicalism is compelling his notion that the proletariat are essentially reformist is less convincing. Whilst the former argument captures the specific social experience of artisan radicals in the early nineteenth century, the latter is sweeping. Moreover, it makes it difficult to understand why the proletariat in Britain were later to play a central role in non-reformist radicalism. Nevertheless, Calhoun's wider thesis opens up the question of whether later working class radicalism emerged in spite of, or because of, the diminution of cultural ties and traditional attachments. *The Question of Class Struggle* unsettles and convincingly challenges the *expectation* that authentic radicalism is tied to the loss of cultural embededness.

Perhaps the most comprehensive and influential recent revision of English popular history has been offered by Patrick Joyce. In *Visions of the People* Joyce questions the existing 'emphasis on the onward march of class, or class as the only or the main outcome of historical change'.[28] Indeed, for Joyce, the idea of 'class consciousness' has 'an antiquated ring to it' and may be placed alongside 'hopelessly idealised categories such as "revolutionary" or "labour

22 See also C. Calhoun, *The Roots of Radicalism: Tradition, The Public Sphere, and Early Nineteenth-Century Social Movements*, (Chicago: University of Chicago Press, 2012).

23 C. Calhoun, *The Question of Class Struggle: Social Foundations of Popular Radicalism During the Industrial Revolution*, (Chicago: University of Chicago Press, 1982), p. 55.

24 Ibid., p. 60.

25 Ibid., p. 55.

26 C. Calhoun, 'The radicalism of tradition: community strength or venerable disguise and borrowed language?', *American Journal of Sociology*, 88, 5, (1983), p. 911.

27 Calhoun, *The Question of Class Struggle*, p. 140.

28 P. Joyce, *Visions of the People: Industrial England and the Question of Class, 1848-1914*, (Cambridge: Cambridge University Press, 1991), p. 8.

consciousness"'.[29] Joyce's version of English radical history from 1848 up to 1914 emphasises the continuity of populism. Thus he is interested in the mobilising power of discourses about 'the people' and popular autonomy, as well as the interconnections between liberal, radical and socialist perspectives. Joyce's pluralistic approach has helped open the door for more sympathetic and nuanced approaches to radical nostalgia. This is evident from his appraisal — which focuses upon but is not restricted to the Independent Labour Party (ILP) — of the way the 'romantic, moral and aesthetic critique of "industrialism" was taken over intact by socialists'.

> The pantheon of Liberalism and radicalism was the pantheon of socialism — Dickens, Bunyan, Carlyle, Ruskin, and, later, Emerson, Thoreau and Tolstoy. Marx and Morris were not much bothered with. Strands of socialist thinking influential beyond as well as within the ILP preached a similar message: MacDonald's anti-urbanism was as evident as Blatchford's evocation of a 'merrie England' in which 'pre-industrial values' were exalted. Edward Carpenter attacked 'modern civilisation' rather than capitalism as a system.[30]

However, although Joyce's shared 'pantheon' usefully highlights continuities, it smoothes over the rupture in the radical attitude to nostalgia that occurred in the late nineteenth century. For one of the things that is striking about the politics of nostalgia found in Blatchford and Morris, is its self-conscious and defensive nature. By the end of the nineteenth century, the common sense, practical turn to the past found in earlier periods was no longer possible. In its place a kind of injured yearning came occasionally to the fore and, more commonly, into a awkward, broken, dialogue with anti-nostalgic and modernist aspirations.

Over recent years, the names of E. P. Thompson and Patrick Joyce have often been used to mark out opposing poles in the debate on the evolution of radical politics. The difference between them has been starkly framed as a argument between materialist and post-materialist/post-modern approaches to the nature and production of social meaning.[31] However, our interest in the dilemma of radical nostalgia points to political connections rather than theoretical distinctions. The dispute over the nature of social meaning between materialists and post-materialists should not blind us to the fact that Thompson and Joyce (and Calhoun) all seek to rescue forms of popular resistance from the 'condescension of prosperity'. Indeed, whilst Joyce and Calhoun have subverted the fetishisation of developmental narratives, it is Thompson who comes closest to, not simply recording, but offering a politics of nostalgia. Thompson's history has a vulnerable quality that finds space and accords value to sentiments of loss and yearning. 'I like these Muggletonians', he writes in his book about William Blake, *Witness Against the Beast*, 'but it is clear that they were not among

29 Ibid., p. 9.

30 Ibid., p. 77.

31 See for example, Marc Steinberg, 'Culturally speaking: finding a commons between post-structuralism and the Thompsonian perspective', *Social History*, 21, 2, (1996), pp. 193-214. Neville Kirk, 'History, language, ideas and post-modernism: a materialist view', *Social History*, 19, 2, (1994), pp. 221-240.

history's winners. Nor did they wish to be'.[32] The following wistful passage at the end of *The Making of the English Working Class* suggests a powerful sense of nostalgia for missed pathways within English political culture:

> both the Romantic and the Radical craftsmen opposed the annunciation of Acquisitive Man. In the failure of the two traditions to come to a point of junction, something was lost. How much we cannot be sure, for we are among the losers.[33]

Spence's Revolutionary Roots

Spence was already dead four years when Karl Marx was born, in 1818. But Spence's name lived on in English radical circles as a legend of incorruptible defiance. In *The German Ideology*, Marx included Spence in his short roll call of early English communists. In *Theories of Surplus Value* he speaks warmly of him as the author of a tract called *Private Property in Land* and as a 'deadly enemy' of this form of property.[34] It is worth staying with this lecture a moment. It is Spence's earliest statement and he stuck to its basic principles thereafter. It isn't hard to grasp: Spence's language is very plain and addressed to the 'free liberty' of the 'whole people'. Spence wants to see land ownership in the hands of democratic parishes: 'Thus are there no more nor other lands in the whole country than the parishes; and each of them is sovereign lord of its own territories'. In keeping with his consistent 'anti-giantism' Spence envisages that 'the land is let in very small farms'. Spence was not ideologically opposed to government but he was deeply suspicious of power that is not exercised at a local level. Thus he looks forward to the time when,

> the government ... having neither excisemen, customhouse men, collectors, army, pensioners, bribery, nor such like ruin-nation vermin to maintain, is soon satisfied, and moreover there are no more persons employed in offices, either about the government or parishes, than absolutely necessary.

What Spence wants is the *return* of the land to a free, self-governing, people. The idea that parishes could largely regulate their own affairs had considerable popular appeal in a society where locality and land still meant a great deal. But Spence had to repeatedly defend the possibility that ordinary people were capable or fit to be trusted. In the following dialogue from his *The End of Oppression* (1795), he uses a wondering 'Young Man' to elicit a Spencean defence of this principle:

> YOUNG MAN: Some seem to apprehend the mismanagement of the Parish Revenues, and so discourage People from thinking of that System.
> OLD MAN: That is the natural work of the Enemy, and must be

32 E. P. Thompson, *Witness Against the Beast: William Blake and the Moral Law*, (Cambridge: Cambridge University Press, 1993), p. 90. The Muggletonians were a millenarian free-thinking non-scriptural English sect of Dissenters. Thompson argues that they influenced by Blake.

33 E. P. Thompson, *The Making of the English Working Class*, p. 915.

34 K. Marx, *Theories Of Surplus Value*, Volume 1, (London: Lawrence & Wishart, 1969), p. 382.

> expected. But it does not become Democrats to doubt concerning it. For if Men cannot manage the Revenues and affairs of a Parish, what must they do with a State? It is almost as absurd to answer such quibbles as to make them. How strange that Men will turn the world upside down to get the management of a Nation, and yet pretend to despair concerning a Parish!!! It is too bad. The villainy is too barefaced. I am weary with combatting the vile sophistry of Scoundrels that are Oppressors, and of Scoundrels that would be Oppressors.

Spence's politics centred on his 'Plan', which he set out in this early work and stuck to throughout his life. Spence's Plan was a scheme to take the ownership of land away from individuals and place it under local (parish) ownership as common property. The model of self-government Spence foresaw was, as Mary Ashraf notes, based on the 'well-tested experience of the common people in organising their numerous benefit clubs and societies'.[35] For Spence, who saw himself as 'the poorman's advocate', autonomy was part of the political heritage of ordinary people.[36] Spence's implacability on the capacity of ordinary people to control their own affairs earned him a reputation as an extremist and an eccentric. Indeed, he worried that only the Government took him seriously. Imprisoned for a year for seditious libel in 1801, he complained,

> The people without treat me with the contempt due to a Lunatic … it is only the Government that wishes to make me appear of consequence, and the people within [the prison] treat me as bad or worse than the most notorious Felons among them.[37]

However, Spence disappointment with his countrymen must be judged in the context of his ambition. In fact, he had many followers. The term 'Spencean' was, in the first two decades of the nineteenth century, synonymous with ultra-radical opinion. Such was the Government's fear of the spread of his doctrines that three years after his death, an Act of Parliament was passed prohibiting 'all Societies or Clubs calling themselves *Spenceans* or *Spencean Philanthropists*'.[38] In the same year, 1817, Thomas Malthus observed that,

> it is generally known that an idea has lately prevailed among some of the lower classes of society, that the land is the people's farm, the rent of which ought to be divided equally among them; and that they have been deprived of the benefits which belong to them, from this their natural inheritance, by the injustice and oppression of their stewards, the landlords.[39]

---

35 Ibid., p. 128.

36 The full title of Spence's journal was *Pigs' Meat; or, Lessons for the Swinish Multitude: Collected by the Poor Man's Advocate (an Old Veteran in the Cause of Freedom) in the Course of his Reading for More than Twenty Years.*

37 Cited by Ashraf, *The Life and Times of Thomas Spence, p. 81.*

38 House of Commons, *An Act for the more effectually preventing Seditious Meetings and Assemblies*, 17th March, 1817. The *Act* further explains that certain Societies or Clubs calling themselves *Spenceans* or *Spencean Philanthropists*, hold and profess for their Object the Confiscation and Division of the Land, and the Extinction of the Funded Property of the Kingdom … it is expedient and necessary that all such Societies or Clubs as foresaid should be utterly suppressed and prohibited.

39 T. Malthus, *Additions To The Fourth And Former Editions Of An Essay On The Principle Of Population*, (London: John

Spence's intransigent hostility to aristocrats and landlords was based on two historical claims. First, that they had stolen the land from the people and second, that the power of this 'band of robbers' was a transgression of the people's 'native state' of natural, God-given, freedom.[40] The former argument was based on Spence's personal experience, the latter on a sweeping sense of rights being established and defended 'from the beginning'.[41]

For Spence, the enclosure of common land represented an attack on the traditional rights of the people. Today, he explained in his lecture of 1775, 'men may not live in any part of this world, nor even where they are born, but as strangers'.[42] Under his Plan this situation would be reversed, for 'All would be little farmers and little Mastermen'.[43] Despite being a city dweller himself, Spence's model for the future was almost entirely agrarian. As H. T. Dickinson notes, 'Mines, factories and cotton mills had no place in Spence's vision of Britain's green and pleasant land'.[44] Spence's idealised images of egalitarian and autonomous village communities, in which land was held in common, emerged from, and appealed to, a predominately rural society in which attachments to the land remained strong. It is important to note, in the light of later interpretations of his work, that Spence explicitly ruled out land nationalisation. His experience of political struggle and belief in popular democracy expressed itself as a distrust of national government,

> a Government that draws great Riches from sources which do not immediately affect the people, as from Loans, Mines, Foreign Tribute or Subsidies is sure to creep by Degrees into absolute power and overturn everything. It is for this reason I would not have the Land national, nor provincial, but parochial property.[45]

When Spence looked forward to the implementation of his Plan he was applying and developing his direct knowledge of co-operation and common ownership. This aspect of his nostalgia, like Cobbett's, offered a critique of the present that was based upon knowledge of the recent past. However, there is another, broader, aspect to Spence's nostalgia, an aspect which arose from the idea that there once existed a Golden Age of freedom and that the people had been brought low from this state by being deprived of their natural and God given rights. Tracing the developing of the myths of the Norman Yoke and Golden Age in radical thought, Christopher Hill writes that

> One of the great revolutions of radical thought, secularising Winstanley's

---

Murray, 1817), p. 40.

40 T. Spence, 'The Rights of Infants Written in the Latter End of the Year 1796', in T. Spence, *Pigs' Meat: Selected Writings of Thomas Spence*, (Nottingham: Spokesman, 1982), p. 116.

41 Ibid., p. 115.

42 T. Spence, 'The Rights of Man', pp. 61-62.

43 Cited by G. I. Gallop, 'Introductory essay: Thomas Spence and the Real Rights of Man', in T. Spence, *Pigs' Meat: Selected Writings of Thomas Spence*, (Nottingham: Spokesman, 1982), p. 33.

44 H. T. Dickinson, *Liberty and Property: Political Ideology in Eighteenth-Century Britain*, (London: Weidenfeld and Nicolson, 1977), p. 268.

45 T. Spence, 'The Restorer of Society to its Natural State', p. 146.

> demand for heaven on earth, was Thomas Spence's claim in 1783 that 'The Golden Age, so fam'd by Men of Yore/Shall soon be counted fabulous no more.'[46]

However, although Spence's religious convictions may not have been as dominant as those found amongst earlier radicals, it is misleading to ignore them entirely. Spence was brought up in an egalitarian dissident sect called the Glassites and often referred to the Biblical teaching that 'God hath given the earth to the children of men, given it to mankind in common'.[47] Seeking to explain Spence's frequent Biblical references T. M. Parssinen suggests that 'The cry of revolution entailed a new rhetoric' and that Spence 'found in his fundamentalist religious background a ready source of language to suit his purpose'.[48] However, in his detailed study of Spenceanism, Malcolm Chase corrects the suggestion that Spence was merely deploying Christian language for political ends. Spence's 'religious terminology', he notes 'meant more than a cynical means of self-promotion',

> A tendency to see Spence within the context of the development of socialist theory, as a far-sighted 'pioneer' and 'forerunner', has encouraged in historians an anachronistic disbelief that he actually *meant* what he wrote.[49]

When we do listen to Spence we hear an unselfconscious, 'common sense' assertion of the people's political heritage.

> the country of the people, in a native state, is properly their common, in which each of them has an equal property, with free liberty to sustain himself and family with the animals, fruits and other products thereof.[50]

Spence conflated his Plan with 'Nature's plan'.[51] Indeed, one notices again and again in his work a sense of nature that goes beyond Biblical teaching or political imperative and suggests a specific identification with animals as a repository of incorruptible freedom and defiance against novelty. The title of Spence's journal *Pig's Meat*, was a response to Burke's dismissal of the revolutionary masses as the 'swinish multitude'. But Spence's frequent use of the image of an angry hog, stamping upon the symbols of authority (a motif also found on many of the hundreds of political tokens he minted and distributed) and the abundance and diversity of references to other animals throughout his work, suggests that he found within the animal kingdom the kind of unchanging, primordial integrity that he wished to find in people. When Spence — who liked to describe himself

46 C. Hill, *Puritanism and Revolution: Studies in Interpretation of the English Revolution of the 17th Century*, (London: Pimlico, 2001), p. 49. The lines are from T. Spence, 'The Rights of Infants', p. 120.

47 T. Spence, 'The Rights of Infants', p. 111.

48 T. M. Parssinen, 'Thomas Spence and the origins of English land nationalisation', *Journal of the History of Ideas*, 34, (1973), pp. 139,135-41.

49 M. Chase, *The People's Farm: English Radical Agrarianism 1775–1840*, 2nd edition (London: Breviary Stuff, 2010 [first published by Oxford University Press, 1988]), p. 46.

50 T. Spence, 'The Rights of Man', p. 59.

51 T. Spence, 'The Rights of Infants', p. 121.

as 'free as a cat' — writes about dispossession it is towards a comparison with other creatures that he turns:

> A worm pays no rent: the Earth while he lives is his portion, and he riots in untaxed Luxuries. And, if perchance, a Crow, or other creature, should pick him up, why that is only Death, which may come in some shape or other to us all as well as he. But in this respect he had the advantage of us that while he lived he paid no Rent! And herein are all the Creatures to be envied.[52]

Spence's precise impact on later radicals is difficult to gauge. In *The People's Farm* Chase argues that Spence's agrarian radicalism, including elements of his Plan, fed into Chartism. Spence's fundamental conviction — that the land should be returned to the people as common property — retained a place in English socialism into the last century.[53] However, by the late nineteenth century, this idea had been largely absorbed by campaigns for the nationalisation of land. Moreover, the interpretation of Spence was increasingly shaped by socialist progressivism and socialist modernity.

Claiming Spence: Deracinating Radicalism

The emergence of land nationalisation campaigns in the 1880s provided fertile soil for Spence's rehabilitation.[54] When the leading British Marxist of the day, Henry Mayers Hyndman, came across Spence's work, in the Reading Room of the British Museum in the early 1880s he seized upon the chance to lay claim to an authentic English working-class thinker. Hyndman immediately set about shaping the way Spence should be 'correctly' interpreted. His *The Nationalisation of the Land in 1775 and 1882* reprinted one of the later editions of Spence's 1775 lecture. The title and introduction of Hyndman's pamphlet claim Spence as an early advocate of state control. It was a strange fate for an enemy of big government. Hyndman's discovery of Spence shaped his interpretation for the next one hundred years.[55] Spence was to become a key figure in Hyndman's rather desperate argument that 'In England … there was perhaps more practical Socialism than in any other nation'.[56]

---

52 T. Spence, 'The Restorer of Society to its Natural State', p. 144.

53 Chase, *The People's Farm*.

54 The idea of land nationalisation was popular in the 1880s, influenced by the work of, amongst other, Alfred Russel Wallace, Henry George, The Land Nationalisation Society and the English Land Restoration League. However, it is also pertinent to be reminded that the association, so important to Spence, between freedom, independence and land ownership also remained in the mind of some labour leaders. For Keir Hardie speaking in 1909, the peasant who has even three acres of land, a well filled pig sty, a cows grass on the common and a cottage which is his to use and hold so long as he pays the rent, is to all intents and purposes a free man. he cannot be starved into submission nor be coerced by eviction. It is an ideal worth fighting for. (cited by Michael Tichelar, 'Socialists, Labour and the land: the response of the Labour Party to the Land Campaign of Lloyd George before the First World War', *Twentieth Century British History*, 8, 2, 1997, p. 127).

55 H. Hyndman, *The Nationalization of the Land in 1775 and 1882: Being a Lecture Delivered at Newcastle-upon-Tyne by Thomas Spence, 1775* (London: E. W. Allen, 1882). Hyndman later noted the pamphlet 'has sold to the number of many thousands'. (Hyndman, *The Historical Basis of Socialism in England*, p. 448.)

56 Hyndman, *The Historical Basis of Socialism in England*, p. 409.

> From generation to generation the idea of nationalising the land has been kept alive among the people. A hundred years ago, Thomas Spence of Newcastle formulated a complete scheme to bring about this result through the action of parishes and municipalities. The time was not ripe.[57]

Frederick Engels enthused to Hyndman (in a letter of 13th March 1882) that he was 'very glad that glorious old Tom Spence has been brought out again'.[58] But what had happened to Tom Spence? He had developed what the Marxist historian Max Beer eulogised as a 'thoroughly honest, proletarian and consistent character'.[59] He was being transformed into a footnote in the evolution of scientific socialism. For William Stafford, Spence was one of those early English theorists who 'begin to grapple with the specifics of *capitalist* exploitation', a development which can 'justly be regarded as leading on to Marx'.[60]

To understand the growth of interest in Spence it is also useful to be reminded that Hyndman's main concern was to translate Marx into the common language of ordinary people. His worry was that Marxism was too theoretical to be readily comprehended. Indeed, in his *The Historical Basis of Socialism in England*, Hyndman notes that even the *Communist Manifesto* 'is by no means written in a popular form'.[61] With his no-nonsense rhetoric and irascible style Spence had the kind of common touch Hyndman saw was absent from Marx. Hence, within an increasingly intellectual and abstract radical discourse, Spence's plain speaking populism took on a class value. The argument can be taken further: in the context of revolutionary thought becoming established as a specialism of an educated, middle class, class faction with tenuous links to ordinary people, the hunt for authentic 'voices from below' whose message can be re-narrated as a primitive affirmation of the new, sophisticated, theories of liberation, took on a urgent and necessary quality. Thus the value of Spence was in his availability as a rudimentary forerunner and provider of cultural capital: a simple, honest man whose clumsy prose could be used to confirm the more educated and advanced status of later radical thinkers.

The most diligent attempt to pull Spence into a Marxist lineage was to come in the 1960s, with the research of Mary Ashraf, an English communist historian based in the German Democratic Republic.[62] A number of Marxist historians in the USSR were already familiar with Spence. He was a reference point in an existing debate on the origins of revolutionary communist consciousness. Ashraf was attempting to challenge the view, associated with V. P. Volgin, that Spence was an egalitarian but not a socialist, because he did not reject private property

57 Ibid., p. 448.

58 The letter is reproduced in Ashraf, *Thomas Spence*, plate XIX.

59 Beer continues: 'and to the end of his days took part in all revolutionary Labour movements at the cost of heavy sacrifices and sufferings'. M. Beer, *Social Struggles and Thought (1750-1860)*, (London: Leonard Parsons, 1925), p. 27.

60 W. Stafford, *Socialism, Radicalism, and Nostalgia: Social Criticism in Britain, 1775-1830*, (Cambridge: Cambridge University Press), p. 270.

61 Hyndman, *The Historical Basis of Socialism in England*, p. 409.

62 Ashraf was a researcher at the Institute for Marxism-Leninism in Moscow, where she undertook a study on the history of black radicals in Britain. She then moved to a university post in the GDR.

in anything other than land.[63] Ashraf's attempt to turn Spence into a modern socialist demanded that she counter this view and insert into his work her own conjecture:

> It seems clear that Spence intended large-scale industry to be public property or if not managed by the Parish as a whole, to be run by 'corporations' of workers collectively. From land confiscation which included these larger industries intimately associated with land tenure but already long established on capitalist lines, there is not a great step to the concept of the workers' ownership of the means of production.[64]

However, Spence will always disappoint this kind of appropriation. Indeed, there is an undertow of frustration in Ashraf's attempts to corral him. For Spence is not an amenable proto-Marxist; he is too wild in his determination to declaim about freedom, liberty and democracy, too localist, too contemptuous of authority. Kemp-Ashraf expresses a certain disappointment with her would-be hero:

> Spence himself is evidence that a consciously working-class point of view was taking shape and becoming articulate. Its actual demands naturally rejected the liberalism of the new democratic ideology of capitalism. But the conflict was often expressed as a condemnation of the old order which still prevailed, or in passionate denunciations that made no distinction between one method of accumulation and another.

Spence tries to 'articulate' but he can't; he's unfinished, ill formed, not really 'one of us'. But he is a taunting figure. It may be that Kemp-Ashraf didn't want him to entirely fit into the GDR's state sanctioned socialism. Between the lines was how criticism expressed itself in that society and, perhaps, Kemp-Ashraf was using Spence to voice criticism of the regime in the GDR. But, if so, it was a curious choice: for Spence's backward-looking evocations of better times and natural rights, along with his determined parochialism, always made him an unconvincing proto-Marxist. From a Marxist perspective, Spence, says a suddenly unenthused Ashraf, is indigestible; part of an 'inchoate tendency' of 'working class eccentrics'.[65]

Ashraf's attempt to claim Spence for orthodox Marxism must be judged a failure. Indeed, the flip-side of her notion that Spence was an embryonic, ill-formed proto-state socialist, is the, once common, dismissal of Spence as a crank. In *The Socialist Tradition* Alexander Gray writes that Spence was 'in himself a poor creature of little capacity and less gifts'. Gray adds that 'oddly, he became a symbol and played a certain part in history.[66] The idea that Spence was a mere oddity is repeated by E. P. Thompson and G. D. H. Cole. Thompson says that '[i]t is easy to see Spence … as little more than a crank',[67] whilst for Cole he

63 See Ashraf, *Thomas Spence*, p. 141, note 2 (1), p. 143, note 18.

64 Ashraf, *Thomas Spence*, p. 121.

65 Ibid., pp. 139-140.

66 A. Gray, *The Socialist Tradition: Moses to Lenin*, (London: Longmans, 1963), p. 257.

67 Thompson, *The Making of the English Working Class*, p. 177.

had 'little practical bearing on the contemporary development of British radical or working-class thought'.[68] A final blow comes from Knox, who argues, on the basis of Spence's localism, that he was 'less a harbinger of modern revolutionism than a mutation of the past'.[69]

My argument has been that Spence was, indeed, a mutation of the past. But I have also claimed that that is what *made* him an authentic radical thinker whose ideas reflected the common culture of the ordinary people of England. The rupture between the street-level organic politics of Spence and the socialist modernity offered by his later critics and admirers renders him incomplete, incoherent and available to be co-opted. It is only with the disintegration of Marxism's certainties, over the past few decades, that Spence's voice can re-emerge and be allowed to speak in terms which he might have recognised. The attention he is receiving today is notable for its openness to the localist and anti-authoritarian aspects of his Plan.[70] The commemorative Blue Plaque put up at the Quayside in Newcastle in 2010 to celebrate his birth symbolises a new interest in this once forgotten 'poorman's advocate'. It may also mark a willingness to listen to Spence and his deeply rooted plans for the future.

68 G. D. H. Cole, *Socialist Thought: The Forerunners 1789-1850*, (London: Macmillan, 1959), p. 25.

69 T. Knox, 'Thomas Spence: The Trumpet of Jubilee', *Past and Present* 76, (1977), p. 98.

70 See for example, Brian Morris, 'The agrarian socialism of Thomas Spence', in Brian Morris, *Ecology and Anarchism* (London: Images Publishing, 1996).

8
Thomas Spence's Spelling Reform

•

Robert W. Rix

Thomas Spence is known as one of the most important radicals to emerge out of the politically turbulent 1790s. As an editor of his work writes: 'Spence was *the* socialist theorist of his generation and deserves his place in the history of British political thought for this reason alone'.[1] But, he also deserves notice as an innovative linguist.[2] In most critical accounts, however, Spence's plan for redistributing the ownership of land (examined elsewhere in this volume) eclipses his attempt to redistribute the power of language. Nonetheless, for Spence, the one very much depended on the other. Spence published a spelling reform in the name of social reform. This was in form of a 'dictionary' of English, entitled *The Grand Repository of the English Language* (1775). Spence knew that the lower orders had to be able to use the language of the authorities, if they were to gain entry into the public sphere of politics. Spence's new system of spelling was meant to facilitate reading and writing while teaching the most 'accurate' pronunciation. Subsequently, he printed several of his political and educational pamphlets in the new spelling, which he sometimes named the 'Crusonian alphabet'. This article will describe Spence's spelling reform and discuss it in the context of the social and political conceptions that determined the study of language in the eighteenth century.

Spence's Spelling Reform

The political significance of Spence's spelling reform is often passed over in criticism. In his anthology of Spence's *Political Works*, H. T. Dickinson downplayed its political significance, explaining in the preface that the 'edition is restricted to Spence's political writings and hence ignores his work on English language and on coins'.[3] The spelling reform has also been described as a folly that is best left out when assessing Spence's political achievements. For instance, H. M. Hyndman wrote that young Spence 'wasted much time and energy in his endeavours to establish a phonetic system of spelling', but can assure us that 'the

1 *Pigs' Meat: The Selected Writing of Thomas Spence, Radical and Pioneer Land Reformer*, ed., G. I. Gallop (Nottingham: Russell Press, 1982), p. 51. Emphasis in the original.

2 In *English Pronunciation in the Eighteenth Century: Thomas Spence's Grand Repository of the English Language* (Oxford: Clarendon Press, 1999), Joan C. Beal gives close attention to the *Grand Repository*. The book is a study of eighteenth-century pronunciation, and as the nature of such a specialist linguistic study dictates, only cursory attention is paid to Spence's politics. See also her more recent 'Evidence from Sources after 1500', in *The Oxford Handbook of the History of English*, ed. Terttu Nevalainen and Elizabeth Closs Traugott (Oxford: Oxford University Press, 2012), pp. 63-78.

3 Thomas Spence, *The Political Works of Thomas Spence*, ed., H. T. Dickinson (Newcastle upon Tyne: Avero, 1982), p. v.

young man … soon turned his thoughts to more important matters'.[4] Such evaluations should be weighed against Spence's own words and actions. In *The Important Trial of Thomas Spence for a Political Pamphlet* entitled 'The Restorer of Society to its Natural State', on Monday 27th, 1801, at Westminster Hall …' (1807), Spence explicitly links linguistic renewal with political regeneration: 'When I first began to study, I found every art and science a perfect whole. Nothing was in anarchy but language and politics. But both of these I reduced to order, the one by a new alphabet, the other by a new Constitution'.[5]

It is significant that this pamphlet is a 'second edition' (as stated on the frontispiece), since it was first printed in the new alphabet four years earlier, after Spence's acquittal for a charge of sedition. The first edition gives an account of Spence's trial in the new spelling under the title of *D'he Imp'ort'ant Tr'al ov T'om'is Sp'ens F'or a P'ol'it'ik'al P'amf'lit 'entitld "Dhe Restorr ov Sosiete tw its natural Stat"* (1803). This version was produced for general sale, but primarily intended for the benefit of those of his friends who had contributed to his defence or payment of the fine. To aid the uninitiated, the pamphlet contains a table of unfamiliar symbols. This goes to show that Spence did not give up a belief in the efficacy of his spelling reform even in later years.

Before we look at the political implications of the proposed spelling reform, it is useful first to examine the formal features of the new system, which Spence published in the form of a 'dictionary' in 1775. On the frontispiece for the volume, the full title is:

> The Grand Repository of the English Language containing besides the excellencies of all other dictionaries and grammars of the English tongue, the peculiarity of having the most proper and agreeable pronunciation of the alphabetical words denoted in the most intelligible manner by a new alphabet, with a copperplate exhibiting the new alphabet both in writing and printing characters, intended for the use of everyone whether native or foreigner that would acquire a complete knowledge of the English language with the least waste of time and expense but especially for those who are but indifferent readers from not having been taught to pronounce properly.
>
> By Thomas Spence, Teacher of English in Newcastle, Newcastle-upon-Tyne. Printed by T. Saint for the Author and sold by him at his school on the Keyside, and by all the Booksellers in Town and Country. 1775.[6]

The main body of this work is the 'Accurate New Spelling and Pronouncing Dictionary' with 14,536 entries on 342 pages.[7] This was a substantial number for a one-man project, but, in comparison, the first edition of Samuel Johnson's

4 Thomas Spence, *The Nationalization of the Land in 1775 and 1882. Being a lecture delivered … 1775*, edited with introduction by H. M. Hyndman (London: E.W. Allen, 1882), p. 23.

5 Thomas Spence, *The Important Trial of Thomas Spence*…. (London: A. Seale, 1803), p. 59.

6 Only two copies of the book survive today. One is held in Boston Public Library, Massachusetts, and one in Newcastle Central Library. Spence's *Preface*, from which I will be quoting, is not paginated. Henceforth, page references to this will be given in brackets and will refer to the copy in Boston Public Library, which has been reprinted in facsimile by Scolar Press (Menston, 1969).

7 Joan Beal, *English Pronunciation*, p. 4.

Dictionary of the English Language (1755) contains around 40,000 entries. The purpose of the *Grand Repository* is two-fold: to facilitate writing and to teach proper pronunciation. The form of the entries is so that a word is first given in conventional spelling, with main stress marked; then Spence's 'new alphabet' follows in brackets.

The purpose of Spence's 'new alphabet' is to transcribe the phonetic quality of words, so that all misleading spellings were done away with. It is an easy-to-use system in which one symbol will only ever represent one sound. The new alphabet consists of forty characters and is based on the traditional alphabet. The symbols for the vowels are primarily the upper-case forms of conventional printing. But due to his self-imposed 'one sound, one sign' rule, new symbols are added. For example, to distinguish the vowel sound found in 'mane' from that found in 'man', Spence uses the conventional upper-case 'A' for the former, while the latter is represented by cutting the 'A' in half to create a new symbol. The new alphabet follows the order of the conventional list of letters, so after distinguishing four different A-sounds, he lists B' and so on. After 'Z' follows a series of ten symbols that are not represented by a single familiar letter. These symbols are created by ligaturing two traditional symbols from the conventional alphabet. For instance, the diphthong in 'oil' is represented by splicing together the upper-case symbols for 'O' and 'I', while the /ŋ/ sound in 'loving' is a splicing together of 'N' and 'G'.

Over three introductory pages, the new orthography is explained and tabulated. There are also guides to how the letters should be printed, and how they should be rendered in longhand. The phonetic type was created with the help of the famous illustrator Thomas Bewick (1753-1828), who is otherwise known for founding the English school of wood engraving. Bewick had first met Spence in the Newcastle workshop of the bookbinder Gilbert Gray, which in the evenings doubled as a lending library and a debating society. Bewick also designed the images Spence would later impress on his radical tokens.[8]

The problem with phonetic spelling is that pronunciation will undergo changes over time. Samuel Johnson considered this problem in the 'Preface' to his *Dictionary*: 'To accommodate orthography better to the pronunciation … is to measure by a shadow, to take that for a model or standard which is changing while they apply it'.[9] Apparently, Spence's determination to advance the lower orders through reforming English spelling, making it more like the spoken language, made him disregard such warnings.

Nonetheless, proper language in contemporary speech as a means of social mobility was one of Spence's major concerns. In the 'Preface' to the *Grand Repository*, Spence quotes several pages from *Dissertation on the Causes of the Difficulties Which Occur in Learning the English Tongue* (1761) by the Irish actor

8 Thomas Bewick, *Memoir of Thomas Bewick Written by Himself, 1822-28*, ed., Selwyn Image (London: John Lane, 1924), pp. 54-55. Spence's interest in the pressing of radical tokens resulted in the publication *The Coin Collectors Companion* (London: T. Spence, 1795).

9 Samuel Johnson, *A Dictionary of the English Language in which the Words are deduced from their originals and illustrated in their different significations by examples from the best writers to which are prefixed a history of the language and an English Grammar*, 2 vols. (London: W. Strathan, 1755). I quote from the unpaginated 'Preface' in vol. 1.

Thomas Sheridan (1719-1788), who set himself up as a professional elocutionist. Spence explains that Sheridan is quoted so extensively because he 'was so much in my mind with regard to the difficulties in learning English, and the methods, which ought to be taken to remove them'.[10] In the passage Spence quotes, Sheridan discusses the fact that several vowels and several consonants could denote one and the same sounds in English, and that the same sound could be represented, orthographically, in different ways. Therefore Sheridan wondered whether a new alphabet might be in order but had decided against it: 'to this it will be immediately objected, that however right the design might appear in theory, it would be impossible to carry into execution' since 'the whole graphic art must be changed; that new characters must be 'reprinted according to the new alpabet [*sic*]; and that people must be taught their alphabet anew to enable them to read such reprinted texts'. Consequently, Sheridan concludes that such a plan must be abandoned because people are creatures of habit and thus reluctant to accept something that will render all their existing knowledge superfluous.[11] In response to the long quote from Sheridan, Spence rejects that custom can 'be made an objection'.[12] Against Sheridan, he argues that all sensible people will get on with the new system while those who take a pleasure in history may still read the old spelling.

With the use of a new phonetic alphabet, the *Grand Repository* combines the *genres* of dictionary, spelling book and pronunciation guide, which were often found together in eighteenth-century works of lexicography. I will now discuss these *genres* in their cultural and social context in order to bring into view Spence's attempt at democratising lexicography.

Dictionaries of the Eighteenth Century

As a dictionary, the *Grand Repository* follows the standard eighteenth-century mode of giving brief entries that explain a word or define a concept. The entries are most often in the form of synonyms, a short explanatory phrase, or, occasionally, a sentence. Spence was evidently not attempting to compete with current dictionaries, such as Dr Johnson's famous two-volume work, which provided supplementary learning, long quotations illustrating usage and traced etymology. For Spence, it was the new spelling system which carried most weight. An effect of the emphasis on spelling rather than semantics is an occasional vagueness in the definitions, as when hemlock is defined as 'a kind of plant'.

It was common among eighteenth-century compilers of dictionaries to borrow the stock of words and their definitions from previous lexicographic

10 'Preface', *Grand Repository*, [1].

11 A similar attitude was expressed by Thomas Dyche in *A Dictionary of All the Words Commonly Us'd in the English Tongue; and the most usual Proper Names; with Accents-directing to their true Pronunciation* (1723). Dyche also considered making very moderate changes to the spelling, but, like Sheridan, abandoned his plan because 'to propose my single Opinion against the public vogue, I must confess, is a Hazardous Enterprise; for Custom will bear a Man down, unless he find a good Number of Candid Friends to support him', quoted in Manfred Görlach, *Eighteenth-Century English* (Darmstadt: C. Winter Heidelberg, 2001), p. 82.

12 'Preface', *Grand Repository*, [11].

works. For Spence, the most important source is evidently Johnson's *Dictionary*. The synonyms he uses as definitions in his entries are frequently simply the heads of Johnson's lists of meanings without the wealth of background material and quotations. But Spence's definitions of words also follow Johnson closely, at times even taking over his explanations wholesale. When the latter is the case, Spence occasionally makes the fallacy of transferring Johnson's tendency to complicate the understanding of a word rather than explaining it. An example of this is the definition of horse, which Spence copies verbatim from Johnson: 'a neighing quadrupede used in war, draught or carriage'. However, most of the time, Spence edits Johnson's learned definitions, so the simplest and clearest meaning is provided. For example, cough is explained as 'a convulsion of the lungs'. This is taken from Johnson, but Spence sensibly leaves out the subsequent qualification '... vellicated by some sharp serosity'. After all, Spence aimed at a less educated audience than those attracted to Johnson's book.

In connection with this, the different classes of vocabulary that Spence included deserve attention here. Spence lists a number of words that Johnson marked out for criticism as 'low', 'barbarous' or 'cant'.[13] These include *banter*, *mob*, and *bamboozle*. But, unlike Johnson, Spence does not express disapproval. Cant was defined by Johnson as 'a corrupt dialect used by beggars and vagabonds', and he talks about it as that used by the 'vulgar'. In Spence's *Grand Repository*, the definition of 'cant' is not to the same extent loaded with class-bias: 'a form of speaking peculiar to some particular class or body of men'. If Spence's intention, according to the frontispiece, was to teach the 'most proper and agreeable pronunciation', there is no trace of prescriptivism in terms of usage, nor is there any attempt at differentiating semantic categories according to their perceived propriety. To some extent, Spence can be seen to cater to the 'vulgar' classes by listing a great number of common words they would be expected to use (some of them dialect forms), such as: *bilk* ('to cheat, to defraud'), *buss* ('a kiss' or 'a kind of fishing boat'), *chuf* ('a blunt clown'), *cully* ('one deceived or imposed on'), *mope* ('a stupid lifeless person'), and so on.

The farmhands, to whom Spence appealed in his political pamphlets on land reform, were among the intended audience of the *Grand Repository*. Thus, it provides coverage of terms such as *coulter* ('the sharp iron fixed in the beam of a plough'), *dung* ('the excrement of animals used in manure'), *loam* ('a sort of fat earth') etc. Interestingly, this vocabulary connected with practical farming is complemented by a related set of terms concerned with the power relations among those labourers tilling the land and the landlords owning it. We find, for example, *copy-hold* ('a tenure, for which the tenant hath nothing to shew but the copy of the rolls made by the steward of his Lord's court'). In the light of Spence's emphasis on democratic land reform, such a definition seems politically motivated. But, generally, the word definitions display no bias. Instead, the politics of the *Grand Repository* must be understood in a wider context.

---

13 Johnson uses this derogatory nomenclature respectively 248, 48, and 154 times, according to a count based on *A Dictionary of the English Language on CD-ROM*, ed., Anne McDermott (Cambridge: Cambridge University Press, 1996).

Despite the many examples of words in popular use, Spence understood – like dictionary compilers before him – that mastery of 'proper' English was a passport to social mobility and success. So most of the time, the *Grand Repository* falls into the genre of 'hard words' dictionaries, which had dominated English lexicography since the publication of Robert Cawdrey's *A Table Alphabeticall* (1604). The title-page of Cawdrey's pioneering work specified that the purpose was to aid 'the true writing, and understanding of hard usuall English wordes'.[14] The 'hard words' dictionary dealt with terminology that was believed to be troublesome or cause problems for those of the urban elite who had no classical schooling, but wanted to require refinement in speech and manners.[15]

Many of the words Spence chose to include were specialised terms, often of Latin, Greek, or French origin. For instance, in just a single column on a page under 'E', we find *ebriety* ('drunkenness'), *ebriosity* ('a habitual drunkenness'), *ebullition* ('the act of boiling up'), *eccoprotics* ('a gentle purgatives'), *echinate* ('bristled like a hedgehog'), *eclaircissement* ('explanation'), and *éclat* ('splendour'). This vocabulary was undoubtedly meant to aid comprehension of terms that were above the level of the worker or artisan labourer who had only limited school learning.

Being a work intended for the instruction in language, it is not surprising that linguistic terminology is widely covered. Much of this would have been helpful for those unfamiliar with grammars or textbooks of language learning. Spence includes separate entries on the irregular verbs, since they often caused confusion among uneducated speakers. He lists *was*, *had*, *rid* ('preter of ride'), and *ridden* ('the participle of ride'). He also lists both *got* and *gotten*, which Johnson had given as possible variations.

The *Grand Repository* provides terminology related to geography, geology, astronomy, philosophy, physics, science, etc., but some branches of learning were given particular attention. For instance, it contains a large body of words related to anatomy and medicine. If we pick a random page under 'D', Spence lists *dysentery* ('the bloody flux'), *dyspnoea* ('a difficulty of breathing'), *dysury* ('a difficulty in making urine'). In this respect, the dictionary can be said also to have a practical function related to the instruction books on health and medicinal remedies that were popular among the lower classes.

Spence's definitions and the selection of words were motivated by a desire to enable the lower orders to understand and participate in the world beyond the workshop. Thus, one well-represented category is terminology related to the courts of law. In immediate sequence we get definitions of *jurat* ('a magistrate in the nature of an alderman'), *juridical*, *jurisdiction*, *jurisprudence*, *jurist*, *juror*, and *jury*. The political agenda that compelled Spence to undertake work on the *Grand Repository* is sometimes discernible, as when he defines bench only as 'the

14 Robert Cawdrey, *A Table Alphabeticall, conteyning and teaching the True Writing, and Vnderstanding of Hard Vsuall English Wordes, borrowed from the Hebrew, Greeke, Latine, or French, &c. With the interpretation thereof by plaine English words, etc.* (Printed by J. R. [James Roberts] for Edmund Weauer: London, 1604).

15 For a full list on early lexicographic works and the audience to which they were addressed, see Tetsuro Hayashi, *The Theory of English Lexicography, 1530-1791* (Amsterdam: John Benjamins B.V., 1978) p. 33.

seat whereon judges sit' rather than the primary sense of 'seat, distinguished from a stool by its greater length', as Johnson has it.

In terms of politics, there is more to be said about the selection of entries. Although nearly all of Spence's words can be found in Johnson's *Dictionary*, Spence features a notable selection of words with political contexts. The *Grand Repository* includes a large proportion of words connected with current titles of heraldry and the military. These can be seen to have a direct relevance to the political situation in Britain at the time. Hence, Spence gives *landgrave* ('a German title'), which was the tide of the ruler of Hesse Cassel, from whom George III hired mercenaries to fight for the British army on several occasions.

The political agenda behind Spence's project also becomes visible at several junctures. For example, following *birth*, the only compound word Spence lists is *birthright*, which he defines, in outright political terms, as 'the rights and privileges to which a man is born'. In contrast, Johnson has six compounds, including *birthday*. To give another example, Spence has no entry on *less*, yet he lists *lessee* ('one who takes a lease') and *lessor* ('the granter of a lease'), which were both important terms in connection with his radical discussion of land distribution.

Finally, a category which receives extensive coverage is religion. As we will see, Spence believed that the lower orders would be interested in reading the Bible, as this was often the only book they owned. We find entries for biblical terms such as *Levite* and *levitical*. This may seem innocent enough, but the words should be seen as useful in the context of Spence's radical ideas of returning land to its rightful owners, which he based on the millennial notion of the Jubilee from Leviticus 25:10.

Writing for Children in the Crusonian Alphabet

As it should now be clear, Spence's focus was on educating the poor, which had a strong political inflexion. The educational dimension is advertised on the frontispiece of the *Grand Repository*, when Spence signs himself 'Teacher of English'. In the conclusion of the 'Preface', Spence claims that his new system is particularly suited for 'the laborious part of the people, who generally cannot afford much time or expence [*sic*] in the educating of their children, and yet they would like to have them taught the necessary and useful arts of reading and writing'.[16]

One must view Spence's dictionary project on the background of the history of poor education in the eighteenth century. Access to politics and opinion hinged on a person's literacy; education was the great divide. This was why the foremost radical of the day, Thomas Paine, would argue for a complete reversal of state education, as part of his plan for a new social order in his *Rights of Man* (1791-1792). Spence had, years before, seen the unpredictable and quirky nature of English spelling as a barrier to the poor. The complexity of spelling prevented the lower orders from becoming articulate and asserting their rights against the

16 'Preface', *Grand Repository*, [12].

rulers. Realising that the poor would stay poor from their deficiency in education, Spence undertook work on the *Grand Repository* as an 'Accurate New Spelling and Pronouncing Dictionary'. The spelling reform was intended as the foundation for an extensive program of self-education for those who could not otherwise afford school. It was Spence's belief that removing the barrier that conventional spelling was for the poor, it would enable them to challenge the political status quo.

Throughout the eighteenth century, children's education was the centre of a prolonged debate over class and social divisions in Britain. Thus, it is not wholly unexpected when Spence began publishing texts for the instruction of the young in his new alphabet. These differed not only in form, but also in political content from other books of education used at the time. In 1782 he published *A S'upl'im'int too thi Histire ov Robinsin Kruzo being TH'I HISTIRE 'ov KRUZONEA or R'OB'INS'IN KRUZO'z IL'IND Doun too thi prezint Tim*. In the short 'Preface', Spence explains (in standard spelling) that the purpose of the new spelling reform is 'to free the poor and the stranger, the industrious and the innocent from vecsatious [*sic*], tedious and ridiculous absurdities: and also to make Charity schools and in great measure, all schools for teaching English unnecessary'. He further admonishes: 'Courteous reader of whatever size or Degree, you need not blush at being found with this diminutive performance in your hand; for though small, it sufficiently conveys to the world a great design'.[17] The book was also printed in conventional spelling the same year (1782). The version in standard spelling is marked on the frontispiece as *A New Edition*, indicating that it was printed second of the two.

A S'upl'im'int too thi Histire ov Robinsin Kruzo was advertised in the liberal *Newcastle Courant* (which was also printed by Thomas Saint) on 12 January 1782, selling at sixpence bound. In the short notice, the motives behind the publication were made clear:

> This book is printed and planned as to be the best adapted for a Reading Made Easy or First Book for teaching English upon at any time ever offered to the world, the transition from this book to others being also easy, as a proof of which Mr. Spence, Teacher of English in St. Ann's School Newcastle, instructs it with the greatest ease and pleasure to himself and scholars ... This he does at his school in the daytime, and at his house Head of the Side from 6 o'clock in the evening, and by experiments he has made, he is so far certain of answering the highest expectations of success that he leaves his reward to be regulated according to the progress of his pupils.[18]

The *S'upl'im'int* contains two stories: 'The History of Crusonia' and 'An History of the Rise and Progress of Learning in Lilliput'.[19] The first story is a

17 Thomas Spence, *A S'upl'im'int too thi Histire ov Robinsin Kruzo being TH'I H'IST'IRE 'ov KRUZONEA or R'OB'INS'IN KRUZO'z IL'IND Doun too thi prezint Tim ... (Nuk'a"il. Printed and sold bi T. SANT)*, ii.

18 Quoted in *Bless'd Millennium: The Life & Work of Thomas Spence*, ed., Keith Armstrong, with introduction by Malcolm Chase (Tyne and Wear: Northern Voices, 2000), p. 11.

19 The standard spelling edition, *A Supplement to the History of Robinson Crusoe Being the History of Crusonia or Robinson Crusoe's Island down to the present time ..., a new edition* (Newcastle: T. Saint, 1782), added two new stories: 'The

vision of the European having intermarried with the natives of Crusoe's island, and (as an extension of Spence's plans for land reform) having abolished all landlords and private property holdings. To quote from the standard spelling edition, this is a Utopia, in which one finds 'great encouragement for parents to bring up their children properly'. There no one needs be inferior in education, because 'every parish has a free-school, with the best of teachers, as also a public library, containing copies and translations of all the best books in the world, so that every one may read and inform himself as far as he pleases'.[20] 'Crusonia' and the 'Crusonian Alphabet' became terms that Spence would use to refer to his new spelling system, since the figure of Robinson Crusoe was the very symbol of self-invention in the reconstruction of civilisation. Spence evidently saw his spelling reform as instrumental in alleviating the social imbalances of society.

Whereas the 'The History of Crusonia' was an original piece, the 'Lilliput' story was an adaptation from a story that had appeared in the *Lilliputian Magazine*, published by the eighteenth-century entrepreneur of children's books, John Newbery. Newcastle was second only to London in publishing for children, and, since the *Lilliputian Magazine* has no publication date, it is possible that Spence, who came from Newcastle, may be the author of the original. It is certain, however, that, in transferring the story, it was changed from a simple way of explaining the alphabet to serve as a plug for the Crusonian alphabet.

In this story, the young Billy Hiron observes that 'the Language of the Lilliputians was irregular and difficult to be understood', and that their 'Spelling too was all confused being without Rule or Order, and the only sure Maxim they had laid down was, that all Words which could be sounded different Ways were to be written according to the hardest, harshest, longest, and most unusual Sound; so that a Life time was little enough to learn their Spelling in'. Therefore the young master Hiron sets out to establish 'the Crusonian Alphabet and Manner of Spelling'. The effect of the spelling revolution brings about an 'important Revolution occasioned in the Customs, as well as Manners, of Lilliput ... as they could now learn as much in a Month, as formerly in a Year'. This means that 'the very poorest soon acquired such Notions of Justice, and Equity, and of the Rights of Mankind'. As the poor familiarised themselves with the 'Customs of Crusonia', 'Landlords appeared despicable and burthensome, in Proportion as the Happiness of being without them was perceived; and the least Ill-treatment from them was now borne with the greatest Uneasiness and Impatience'. The final result is a revolution where the people in 'flagrant Incitement' will throw their 'Riders' in the 'Dirt'.[21]

The spelling reform was intended to hasten the spread of truth among those who were kept in darkness by illiteracy. Spence expressed an Enlightenment confidence in the dissemination of knowledge. In the verses of the radical song 'The Progress of Liberty', Spence states that when 'man begins to know his

---

History of the Mercolians' and 'An Account of what passed on a Journey with old Zigzag'.

20 The first story is reprinted in *Political Works*, pp. 5-15, quote on p. 13.

21 Thomas Spence, *Supplement to the History of Robinson Crusoe*, pp. 39-42.

Rights / The iron yoke we crumbling see'.[22] Like many radicals at the time, Spence put faith in the distribution of cheap prints as the most important channel for dissemination of knowledge. In no uncertain terms he argued that the 'Progress of Reason' was 'aided by the Art of Printing'.[23]

Spence had imagined that his new easier spelling system was to be promoted through books for the young. Following the 'Preface' in the *Grand Repository*, he placed an advertisement for a 'just published' work sold by him at his 'School on the Keyside, and the Booksellers and News-carriers'.[24] This was the first issue of a series of cheap penny-pamphlets titled *The Repository of Common Sense and Innocent Amusements*, which were to be continued as weekly installments, as soon as 'a competent number of subscribers is obtained'. Only the first issue seems to have been published, but no copy is known to have survived. The pamphlet series was 'Designed chiefly for those who cannot spare time, expence [*sic*], and patience sufficient for learning to read and spell the usual way' and was to consist of 'Extracts from the best Authors', in which 'every word is spelled according to the best pronunciation by the new alphabet'. If Spence claimed the amusements the series was 'innocent', the 'common sense' it disseminated was undoubtedly (like the excerpts of various kinds that appeared in *Pigs' Meat*) politically motivated.

The two versions of the 'Supplement' to Robinson Crusoe were not the only books Spence printed in 1782. There was also *The Real Reading-Made-Easy; or a Foreigner's and Grown Person's Pleasing Introduction To Reading English, Whereby all Persons, of whatever Age or Nation, may soon be taught, with Ease and Pleasure, to read the English Language*. This publication begins with an introduction to Spence's alphabet, followed by short biblical sentences and sayings written in the new spelling. These are arranged in a line that teaches key words by repetition.

The use of the Bible in teaching young children language was a mainstay of eighteenth-century education and an integral part of the Sunday School movement that grew up in the 1780s. Spence's use of religion in his children's education warrants attention. In the *S'upl'im'int*, Spence explains that his new spelling 'is calculated to render both the teaching and learning of it a pleasure, and die well-inclined will think it only an agreeable pastime, to instruct their own children, servants, and neighbours'. Thus it will be, as it is 'according to the prophet', that 'the earth be filled with the knowledge of die Lord, as the waters cover the sea' (*my translation*).[25] Spence often consolidated the discussion of his social program with millennial rhetoric. Time and again, we find a close connection between the apocalyptic image of a new earth and the implementation of his agrarian plan for land reform.

Nonetheless, there has been a tendency among political historians to present

---

22 Printed in *Pigs' Meat* I (1793): pp. 280-281.

23 Thomas Spence, *The Important Trial of Thomas Spence, for a political pamphlet, intitled 'The Restorer of Society to its Natural State'*, 2nd edn. (London: A. Seale, 1803), p. 9. This pamphlet was published after Spence was acquitted of charges for publishing seditious material.

24 'Preface', *Grand Repository*, [13].

25 Spence, *A S'upl'im'int too thi Histire ov Robinsin Kruzo*, p. iii.

Spence as a son of rationalism and therefore also a reluctance to accept that Spence — in phrasing his language in biblical metaphors, references, diction, and cadences — used religion for anything but opportunistic reasons.[26] However, the connection between the Christian utopianism and the inherent rights of man runs deep in his writing. Spence's famous and often reprinted 'Jubilee Hymn' refers to Leviticus 25, which contains the promise of a Jubilee where lost land and property is returned to each family. The idea that the land was owned by God and thus subject to a higher authority than the landed gentry underpins Spence's philosophy of land reform. Significantly, the 'Jubilee Hymn' first appeared as verses sung on Robinson's island in the *S'upl'im'int*.

Education for poor children can be traced back to the establishment of the Society for Promoting Christian Knowledge in 1699. The Society educated poor children in charity schools all over the country. In this connection, one should mention an interesting precursor to Spence's spelling reform, which aimed to facilitate Bible reading for charity school children. This was the anonymous *The Needful Attempt, to Make Language and Divinity Plain and Easie* (1711). The author complains in the 'Introduction' that 'our present wai auf speling iz so veri unrezonabul and irregular' that it was rendered impossible 'to teeatsh a Lairner dhe present wai auf pronounsing aul Words so speld'.[27] Despite the good intentions behind this and other such schemes, commentators often pointed out that the charity school system worked to bolster existing social patterns, since the schools emphasised the teaching of humility and that the poor should fulfill their station in life, while becoming grateful to their superiors. Spence's religious programme runs counter to this in focusing on passages of eschatological prophecy. In the preface to the *S'upl'im'int*, Spence directly criticises the Bible societies for propagating religious knowledge 'in vain', since he believed 'books distributed among those who cannot read' were of no use.[28]

The Bible was often the only book poor families owned, and it was therefore an ideal text to use for the introduction of Spence's new spelling system. In the 'Preface' to the *Grand Repository*, Spence referred to a project of re-transcribing the whole Bible in the new spelling. Seven years later, in the *S'upl'im'int*, Spence advertised for subscriptions for the Bible in the 'Crusonian alphabet' to be had in instalments at a mere penny a week. The testaments were to be transcribed into 'what may be called pure English in contradistinction to the hotch potch so long, (to the dishonour of the country) now be the name of English' (*my translation*).[29] Evidently, Spence's intention was to provide labour-class readers with evidence that the promises of redistribution of land, which he propounded in his many pamphlets, were authenticated in the biblical text.

After relocating from Newcastle to London, Spence had a few pages printed (by the booksellers Cook and Debrett) of *The Pronouncing and Foreigners'*

26 For a critique of this position, see Michael Scrivener, *Seditious Allegories: John Thelwall and Jacobin Writing* (Pennsylvania: Pennsylvania State University Press, 2001), pp. 135-137.

27 Anon. *Needful Attempt, to Make Language and Divinity Plain and Easie* (London: J. Matthew, 1711 [repr. in facsimile by Scolar Press in 1969]), p. 3.

28 Spence, *S'upl'im'int*, p. ii.

29 Ibid. p. 12.

Bible, containing the old and New Testament being, not only the properest book for establishing a uniform and permanent manner of speaking, the sonorous, harmonious and agreeable English and also infinitely preferable to any introductory book hitherto contrived for teaching children or grown persons upon whose mother-tongue it is ... recommended as the most proper book for Sunday Schools. A transcription of the beginning of Genesis survives on an undated proof sheet found among the papers in the British Library of the avid commentator on radical culture, Francis Place.[30] However, Spence's Bible project did not go ahead, presumably because it lacked subscribers.

Spence and Proper English

Evidently, Spence wanted to give power to the people through advancing standards of literacy in England. For the last decades of the eighteenth century, the literacy of the labouring classes and artisans rose. Forced to work long hours and with little money for instruction, the only option for the lower orders were the charity schools, in which 'the sense of obedience and responsibility' and that everyone should be 'God-fearing and do their part in society' was inculcated.[31] To aid self-instruction — in the spirit of Crusonian independence — Spence's *Grand Repository* contains more than dictionary entries. Following the preface is a short grammar (10 pages). Placing sections on grammar in books of lexicography was not unusual, and Spence copied much of this grammatical instruction from Ann Fisher's *A New Grammar* (1750).[32] Ann Fisher (1719-1778) was a Newcastle schoolmistress, whose grammar achieved much success for its simplicity (going through thirty-three editions). Spence is likely to have used it in his own Newcastle classrooms.

In the eighteenth century, the study of language was generally subsumed under larger socio-cultural and national concerns. In the latter half of the eighteenth century, proper grammar was seen as a necessary tool for achieving social refinement. R. C. Alston lists only about 106 publications on grammar from 1700 to 1750, but almost 400 between 1751 and 1800.[33] A new order of prescriptivism that differentiated 'the language of the upper classes from the language of the illiterate mob' became the order of the day.[34] Thus, the common denominator of the many new grammars in the second half of the century is their long lists of concrete injunctions against improper use. The most significant radical who, like Spence, took up grammar and language instruction was William Cobbett. In order to allow the lower orders to articulate their

30 Add. MS. 27808 (249). Francis Place, known as a campaigner for trade unions and a commentator on radical culture, also left an unfinished biography on Spence.

31 Devon Lemire, 'A Historiographical Survey of Literacy in Britain between 1780 and 1830', *Constellations* 4.1 (2012): pp. 248-261, quote on p. 258.

32 A. F. Shields, 'Thomas Spence and the English Language', *Transactions of the Philological Society* 73.1 (1974): pp. 33-64. Fisher's grammar was first published in 1748 under the title *The Pleasing Instructor*.

33 For a full list, see R. C. Alston, *A Bibliography of the English Language from the Invention of Printing to the Year 1800*, vols. i-xvii (Leeds: Arnold, 1965-1973).

34 Carey McIntosh, *Common and Courtly Language: The Stylistics of Social Class in Eighteenth-Century English Literature* (Philadelphia: University of Pennsylvania Press, 1986), pp. 46-47.

dissatisfaction with the political system in a language that was 'correct', and therefore would be taken seriously, he published *A Grammar of the English Language in a Series of Letters intended for the use of Schools and of young Persons in General: but more especially for the use of Soldiers, Sailors, Apprentices, and Plough-Boys, To which are added six Lessons, intended to prevent Statesmen from Using False Grammar, and from writing in an Awkward Manner* (1819). As Cobbett writes in the introduction, 'tyranny has no enemy as formidable as the pen'.[35]

Cobbett had already clarified the issues at stake in a series of discussions on language in his *Weekly Political Register* of 1817. Cobbett's intentions were summarised in the publisher's 'Preface': 'The present project, ostensibly, is, to communicate to all uneducated Reformers, a knowledge of Grammar. The people, you know, were accused of presenting petitions not grammatically correct. And those petitions were rejected, the petitioners being "ignorant" though some of them were afterwards put into prison for being better-informed'.[36] This refers to the fact that between 1797 and 1818, several petitions to Parliament proposing extended suffrage were thrown out on the grounds of the crudeness of their language. As Olivia Smith has shown, this was a concrete culmination of the hierarchical ideas about 'refined' and 'vulgar' language, which had developed during the eighteenth century.[37]

The late eighteenth and early nineteenth century was still very much an oral culture. Thus, the phonetic system of spelling outlined in the *Grand Repository* was not only useful for reading and writing but equally for teaching how to 'pronounce properly'. In the appendix titled 'Christian Names of Men and Women both as spelled and pronounced', a list of male names from Aron to Zedekiah and female names from Abigail to Winifred are included with a guide to pronunciation. In an article titled 'An infallible way to correct Provincialisms and other Vulgarisms in Speech', which Spence wrote for *The Giant Killer, or Anti-Landlord*, it is asked: 'Why should People be laughed at all their lives for betraying their vulgar education, when the Evil is so easily remedied. How ridiculous it is to hear People that can read saying *Any Think – A Horange – Idear – Noar*'.[38]

In the wake of *Johnson's Dictionary*, a new emphasis on fixing pronunciation became apparent. Five times as many works on elocution appeared between 1760 and 1800 than had done so in the years before 1760.[39] Thomas Sheridan, who Spence quotes extensively in the preface to the *Grand Repository*, developed a detailed system to indicate pronunciation in *Complete Dictionary of the English Language* (1780). This included not only accent marks, but it also made use of a system of diacritics for representing vowel qualities and consonant forms. For

35 William Cobbett, *A Grammar of the English Language...* (London: T. Dolby, 1819), p. 4.

36 *Weekly Political Register* (1817): 1059-60.

37 Olivia Smith, *The Politics of Language, 1791-1819* (Oxford: Oxford University Press, 1984), pp. 30-31.

38 *The Giant Killer, or Anti-Landlord* 1 (1814): 2.

39 Lynda Mugglestone, *Talking Proper: The Rise of Accent as a Social Symbol* (Oxford: Clarendon Press, 1995), p. 4. See further Arthur J. Bronstein, 'The History of Pronunciation in English-Language Dictionaries', in *The History of Lexicography*, ed. R. R. K. Hartmann (Amsterdam: Philadelphia: John Benjamins, 1986), pp. 23-33.

Sheridan, this was meant only to help pronunciation, never to replace conventional spelling. Although Sheridan was not as rigidly prescriptive as John Walker in *Critical Pronouncing Dictionary and Expositor of the English Language* (1791), he believed that English should be standardised.

As early as 1761, Sheridan had envisaged that if a standardising dictionary was published, 'a uniformity of pronunciation' among all classes could be attained. At a time when Britain was expanding its empire overseas, it made sense that 'the rising generation, born and bred in different Countries, and Counties' would be 'as subjects of one King, like sons of one father' and have 'one common tongue'. Hence, all 'natives of these realms' would be 'restored to their birthright in commonage of language, which has been too long fenced in, and made the property of a few'.[40] This may sound like Spence, but those Sheridan believed would benefit from his instructions in 'proper' English were not the lower orders, but the urban elite of the middle class, who had grown politically powerful in the course of the eighteenth century.

Spence wrote in a period when ideas of language and improvement were intrinsically connected, for which reason linguistics was seen as a progressive and (emphatically) *social* science. Spence knew that literacy and correctness in language provided the means for social change. The 'Crusonian' alphabet was the crucible to reform the existing order and establish a hope for new world in which the divisions between men were thrown out with the old system of spelling.

40 Thomas Sheridan, *A Dissertation on the Causes of the Difficulties which occur, in teaming the English Tongue, with a scheme for publishing an English Grammar and Dictionary upon a plan entirety new the object of which shall be, to facilitate the Attainment of the English Tongue, and establish a Perpetual Standard of Pronunciation* (London: R. and J. Dodsley, 1761), p. 36.

9
A Radical Plan for the English Language

•

Joan C. Beal

Two hundred years after the death of Thomas Spence, the teaching of English and especially literacy in English, is a highly contested area. Since the introduction of the National Curriculum in England, Wales and Northern Ireland following the 1988 Education Reform Act, a regime of testing children at various Key Stages, the first of which is at age 7, has led to league tables of performance and an annual moral panic about levels of attainment, especially in mathematics and English. The latest steps taken by the current Conservative-led coalition government have been to introduce what is known as the SPAG (spelling, punctuation and grammar) test for children at the age of 11, and to require the use of synthetic phonics as the method for teaching reading in primary schools. Literacy, both in the strict sense of ability to read and write, and in the looser sense of being able to write what is perceived as correct (i.e. Standard English) is presented as the key to advancement and social mobility. Whilst this 'back to basics' approach to the teaching of English is particularly associated with right-wing politicians, concern about literacy and social mobility is also expressed by those on the left. Thomas Spence could not have been further from the current government on the political spectrum, but he was acutely aware of the importance of literacy and had an innovative and radical plan to teach it.

Spence is best known for his political writings and activities, with most early biographers paying little or no attention to the aspect of his work for which he is best known amongst linguists: his invention of a phonetic system of spelling as an aid to literacy. The general view has been that this was a distraction from his more important political writings, and that he gave it up once he moved away from Newcastle. For example, Rudkin writes that 'except for an occasional broadside, Spence made little use of his phonetics in London'.[1] However, the new *Dictionary of National Biography* entry by H. T. Dickinson sets the record straight.

> Spence continued to propagate his phonetic alphabet for the rest of his life. Several of his later radical works were printed in this alphabet as well as in standard English, and modern philologists now treat his efforts seriously.[2]

1 Olive D. Rudkin, *Thomas Spence and His Connections.* (London: G. Allen & Unwin,1927), p. 229.

2 Harold T. Dickinson, 'Spence, Thomas (1750–1814)', *Oxford Dictionary of National Biography*, Oxford University Press, 2004. [http://www.oxforddnb.com/view/article/26112, accessed 4 March 2014]

Spence saw his plan for spelling reform as inextricably linked to, and just as important as, his better-known plan for political change. In *The Important Trial of Thomas Spence* (which was printed first in Spence's alphabet), he explicitly links these two plans:

> When I first began to study, I found every art and science a perfect whole. Nothing was in anarchy but language and politics. But both of these I reduced to order, the one by a new alphabet, the other by a new Constitution.[3]

In other words, in 1775, at the age of 25, Spence had solved all the problems of society, if only society would listen.

As a teacher, Spence would have had first-hand experience of the difficulties of teaching children to read and write, given the inconsistency of conventional spelling in English. Such concerns had been voiced since English first began to rival Latin in the school curriculum in the sixteenth century, and the current educational debates concerning the advantages and disadvantages of phonics show that these problems have not gone away. Spence believed that education was the key to liberating what he called 'the laborious part of the people',[4] and that the notoriously unphonetic spelling of English was a barrier to this. In one of his utopian works, *A Supplement to the History of Robinson Crusoe*, Spence describes how the people of Lilliput, having been given the benefit of a phonetic alphabet (the Crusonean being one of Spence's names for his orthography), found it very easy to learn to read, with revolutionary consequences:

> As they could now learn as much in a Month, as formerly in a Year, the very poorest soon acquired such Notions of Justice, and Equity, and of the Rights of Mankind, as rendered unsupportable, every species of Oppression.[5]

Spence first introduced his alphabet in a dictionary published in 1775, the same year as his address to the Newcastle Philosophical Society. The *Grand Repository of the English Language* is a small, pocket-sized dictionary (14, 536 entries on 342 pages) with short definitions, some of which show Spence's political leanings (e.g. 'Whig: a friend to civil and religious liberty'). What marks it out from other dictionaries of the time, even those, like Thomas Sheridan's *General Dictionary of the English Language* and John Walker's *Critical Pronouncing Dictionary*, which set out to provide clear and explicit guidance on pronunciation, is that Spence respells every word in his 'New Alphabet'. The key to this alphabet is provided here in Figure 1 and the first page of the *Grand Repository* in Figure 2. Spence writes of his 'New Alphabet' that 'to read what is printed in this alphabet, nothing is required but to apply the same sound immutably to each character (in whatever position) that the alphabet directs.'[6] In other words, this is a completely phonetic system in which one letter always

3 Thomas Spence, *The Important Trial of Thomas Spence*, (London: A. Scale, 1807).

4 Thomas Spence, *The Grand Repository of the English Language* , (Newcastle: T. Saint, 1775).

5 Thomas Spence, *A Supplement to the History of Robinson Crusoe* (Newcastle: T. Saint, 1782).

6 Thomas Spence, *The Grand Repository of the English Language*, (Newcastle: T. Saint, 1775), Sig C1, Verso.

represents the same sound and any sound is always represented by one letter. This contrasts with conventional English spelling in which 'gh' can represent all the different sounds in *enough*, *ghost*, and *plough*, or be completely silent as in *caught*, and the short 'i' sound in, e.g. *hit* can also be spelt with an 'e' as in *sorted*, or even an 'o' as in *women*. The part played by the New Alphabet in Spence's new society is first hinted at in the preface to the *Grand Repository* itself. Spence envisages his new spelling taking over from the traditional orthography and being used in books: as a start, he proposes a 'weekly miscellany', which he thinks should succeed 'especially among the laborious part of the people, who generally cannot afford much time or expence [*sic*] in the educating of their children, and yet they would like to have them taught the necessary and useful arts of reading and writing.'[7]

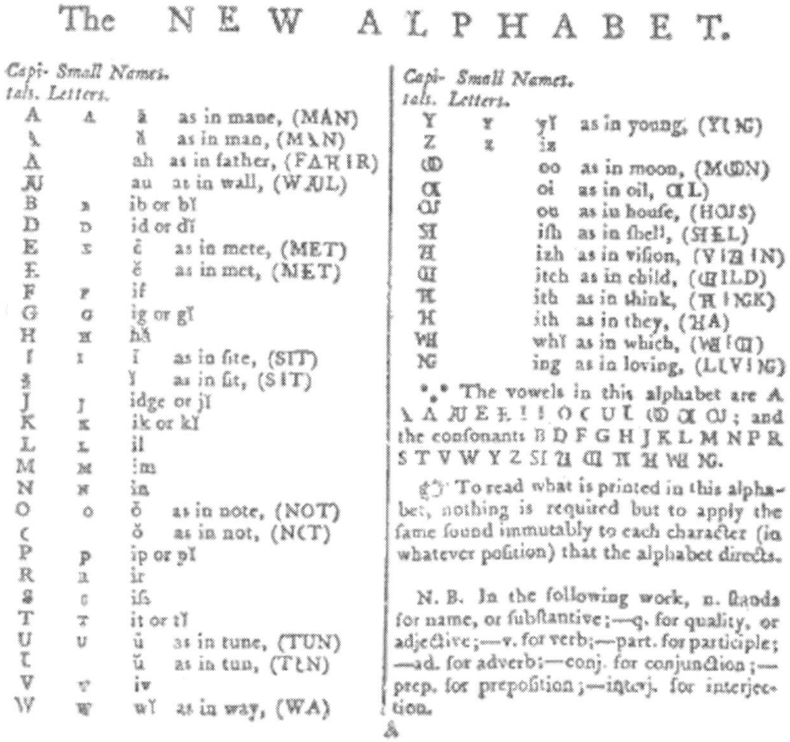

The NEW ALPHABET.

Capitals.	*Small Letters.*	*Names.*	
A	A	ā	as in mane, (MAN)
\		ă	as in man, (M\N)
Δ		ah	as in father, (FΔTHIR)
AU		au	as in wall, (WAUL)
B	B	ib or bY	
D	D	id or dY	
E	E	ē	as in mete, (MET)
Ē		ĕ	as in met, (MĒT)
F	F	if	
G	G	ig or gY	
H	H	hĀ	
I	I	ī	as in fite, (SIT)
ɩ		Y	as in fit, (SɩT)
J	J	idge or jY	
K	K	ik or kY	
L	L	il	
M	M	im	
N	N	in	
O	O	ō	as in note, (NOT)
(		ŏ	as in not, (N(T)
P	P	ip or pY	
R	R	ir	
S	S	iſs	
T	T	it or tY	
U	U	ū	as in tune, (TUN)
Ɩ		ŭ	as in tun, (TƖN)
V	V	iv	
W	W	wY	as in way, (WA)
Y	Y	yY	as in young, (Y(NG)
Z	Z	iz	
Ꝏ		oo	as in moon, (MꝎN)
Œ		oi	as in oil, (ŒL)
Ȣ		ou	as in houſe, (HȢS)
SH		iſh	as in ſhell, (SHĒL)
ZH		izh	as in viſion, (VɩZHɩN)
CH		itch	as in child, (CHILD)
TH		ith	as in think, (THɩNGK)
DH		ith	as in they, (DHA)
WH		whY	as in which, (WHɩCH)
NG		ing	as in loving, (LƖVɩNG)

*** The vowels in this alphabet are A \ Δ AU E Ē I ɩ O (U Ɩ Ꝏ Œ Ȣ; and the conſonants B D F G H J K L M N P R S T V W Y Z SH ZH CH TH DH WH NG.

☞ To read what is printed in this alphabet, nothing is required but to apply the ſame ſound immutably to each character (in whatever poſition) that the alphabet directs.

N. B. In the following work, n. ſtands for name, or ſubſtantive;—q. for quality, or adjective;—v. for verb;—part. for participle;—ad. for adverb;—conj. for conjunction;—prep. for prepoſition;—interj. for interjection.

A

Figure 1

David Abercrombie was the first linguist to notice Spence's contribution to phonetics, including a section about him in a paper entitled *Forgotten Phoneticians*. Here, Abercrombie writes that 'in 1775 there appeared a dictionary in which the pronunciation was "parenthesized" … in a genuine, scientific, phonetic alphabet with seventeen new letters.'[8]

7 Thomas Spence, *The Grand Repository of the English Language*, (Newcastle: T. Saint, 1775), Sig B2 Recto.

8 David Abercrombie, "Forgotten Phoneticians," *Transactions of the Philological Society*, *p.* 47 (1948), reprinted in *Studies in Phonetics and Linguistics* (London: Oxford University Press, 1965), p. 68.

As can be seen in Figure 1, the 'new letters' were based on the English alphabet, but adapted, so, for instance, the short 'a' in MAN is represented by a capital A cut in half, the long 'a' in FATHER by an A without the cross-bar, and so on. This would make the script very 'user friendly' to teachers and to students who had started to read using the conventional alphabet. Spence intended his alphabet to be used in writing and printing: as well as the capitals used in his dictionary, he provided a lower-case version and even a copper-plate one for handwriting. The punches for printing these scripts had been made by none other than Spence's friend and sparring partner, the famous engraver Thomas Bewick.

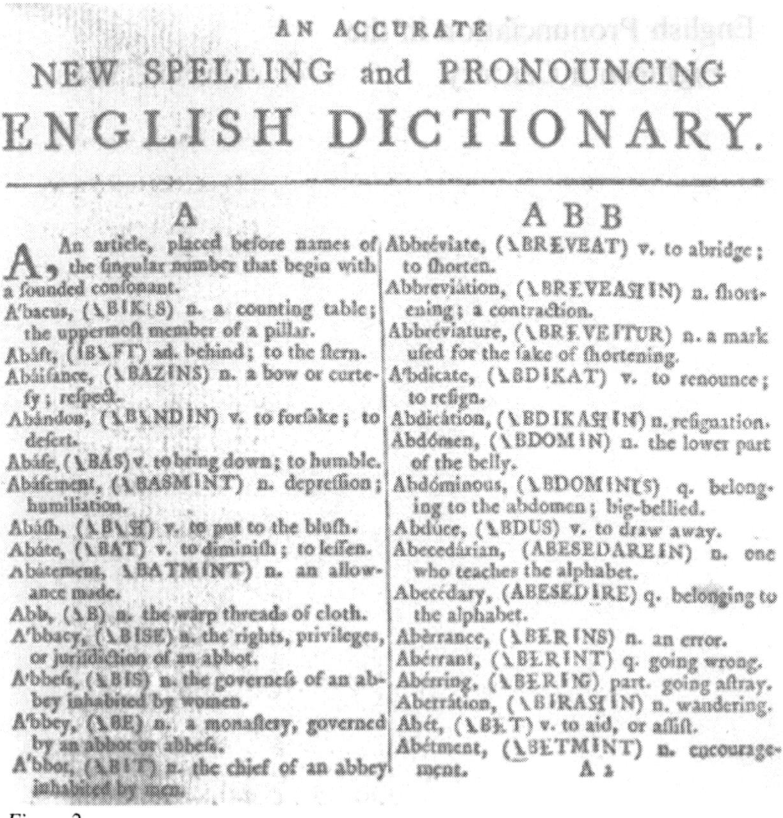

AN ACCURATE

NEW SPELLING and PRONOUNCING

ENGLISH DICTIONARY.

A

A, An article, placed before names of the ſingular number that begin with a ſounded conſonant.
A'bacus, (ABIKIS) n. a counting table; the uppermoſt member of a pillar.
Abáft, (IBAFT) ad. behind; to the ſtern.
Abáiſance, (ABAZINS) n. a bow or curteſy; reſpect.
Abándon, (ABANDIN) v. to forſake; to deſert.
Abáſe, (ABAS) v. to bring down; to humble.
Abáſement, (ABASMINT) n. depreſſion; humiliation.
Abáſh, (ABASH) v. to put to the bluſh.
Abáte, (ABAT) v. to diminiſh; to leſſen.
Abátement, ABATMINT) n. an allowance made.
Abb, (AB) n. the warp threads of cloth.
A'bbacy, (ABISE) n. the rights, privileges, or juriſdiction of an abbot.
A'bbeſs, (ABIS) n. the governeſs of an abbey inhabited by women.
A'bbey, (ABE) n. a monaſtery, governed by an abbot or abbeſs.
A'bbot, (ABIT) n. the chief of an abbey inhabited by men.

A B B

Abbréviate, (ABREVEAT) v. to abridge; to ſhorten.
Abbreviátion, (ABREVEASHIN) n. ſhortening; a contraction.
Abbréviature, (ABREVEITUR) n. a mark uſed for the ſake of ſhortening.
A'bdicate, (ABDIKAT) v. to renounce; to reſign.
Abdicátion, (ABDIKASHIN) n. reſignation.
Abdómen, (ABDOMIN) n. the lower part of the belly.
Abdóminous, (ABDOMINIS) q. belonging to the abdomen; big-bellied.
Abdúce, (ABDUS) v. to draw away.
Abecedárian, (ABESEDAREIN) n. one who teaches the alphabet.
Abecédary, (ABESEDIRE) q. belonging to the alphabet.
Abèrrance, (ABERINS) n. an error.
Abérrant, (ABERINT) q. going wrong.
Abérring, (ABERING) part. going aſtray.
Aberrátion, (ABIRASHIN) n. wandering.
Abét, (ABET) v. to aid, or aſſiſt.
Abétment, (ABETMINT) n. encouragement.

A 2

Figure 2

Although Spence used versions of his New Alphabet throughout his life, there is no evidence that anybody else did. In Britain, spelling reform was not a fashionable cause in the eighteenth century, when the 'correct' spelling had been determined by authorities such as Samuel Johnson, who, in the preface to his dictionary, formulated the principle that 'for pronunciation, the best general rule is to consider those as the most elegant speakers who deviate least from the written word'.[9] In other words, 'correct' spelling was sacrosanct, and, if anything, pronunciation should be altered to conform to spelling, not *vice versa*. Across the Atlantic, in the wake of the American Revolution, radical ideas about spelling were more favourably received and discussed by the likes of Benjamin Franklin and Noah Webster. The only three copies of Spence's *Grand Repository* in existence today can be found in Newcastle Central Library, Boston, Massachusetts and the Houghton Library at Harvard University. The last of these was only recently discovered, and had been owned by a British soldier stationed at Fort George, Maine during the Revolutionary War.[10]

Because it is a phonetic system, Spence's New Alphabet gives us clues about what he thought was 'the most proper and agreeable pronunciation'. Since, by all accounts, Spence had quite a broad Northumbrian accent, his contemporaries were sceptical about his credentials for providing a guide to pronunciation. Welford relates the following story:

> When soliciting subscriptions to this curious work (The Grand Repository) he called upon the Rev. H. Moises, master of the Grammar-School, morning lecturer of All Saints' Church, for the purpose of requesting him to become a subscriber to the work. As Mr. Spence had a strong Northern accent, Mr. Moises enquired what opportunities he had had of acquiring a just knowledge of the pronunciation of the English Language. "Pardon me," said Spence, "I attend All Saints' Church every Sunday Morning!"[11]

This is a typical Spencean reposte, but makes the serious point that the clergy would have been the models of "good" speech to the citizens of places like Newcastle, far from the fashionable standards of London. The speech represented in the *Grand Repository* is a sort of modified, northern version of standard speech, different from both broad Northumbrian and the educated standard then developing in London. A quick glance at Figure 2 tells us that this is definitely a northern phonetic alphabet, for there is only one letter representing a short 'u'. Then, as now, one of the most obvious differences between northern and southern accents of English was that pairs of words such as *could* vs. *cud*; *puss* vs. *pus*; and *put* vs. *putt* are pronounced differently in the south, but exactly the same as each other in the north: in other words, *could* and *cud* etc. are homophones. This linguistic marker of the North-South divide was noticed by the London-based elocutionist, John Walker, who wrote:

> If the short sound of the letter **u** in *trunk*, *sunk* etc., differ from the sound of that letter in the northern parts of England, where they sound it like the **u** in bull, and nearly as if the words were written *troonk*, *soonk*, etc., it necessarily follows that every word where that letter occurs must by these provincials be mispronounced.[12]

9 Samuel Johnson, *A Dictionary of the English Language*, (London: C. Dodsley, 1755), Sig A2 Verso.

10 John Overholt, "A Grand if Worse for Wear Repository", accessed 4th March 2014, http://blogs.law.harvard.edu/hydeblog/2012/03/10/a-grand-if-worse-for-wear-repository.

11 Richard Welford, *Men of Mark 'Twixt Tyne and Tweed*, volume 3, (Newcastle: Walter Scott, 1895), pp. 432-433.

12 John Walker, *A Critical Pronouncing Dictionary*, (London: G. G. J. and J. Robinson, and T. Cadell, 1791), p. xiii.

Spence was probably not aware of the southern pronunciation when he wrote the *Grand Repository*, but, in any case, he seems not to have been concerned about regional accents *per se* so much as helping the lower classes avoid the stigma of sounding uneducated. In his very last publication, he wrote:

> Why should People be laughed at all their lives for betraying their vulgar education, when the Evil is so easily remedied. How ridiculous it is to hear People that can read saying *Any Think — A Horange — Idear — Noar.*[13]

Here, Spence picks up on stigmatised pronunciations that he had probably heard in London, and that still sound familiar today: 'ink' for *–ing*, use (or not) of 'h', and linking 'r' as in '*lawr* and order' (*Noar* represents the Biblical name Noah with linking 'r'). His motivation, in his last publication as in his first, was to use his knowledge of the English Language and his unfashionably radical New Alphabet to advance 'the laborious part of the people'.

Of course, Spence did not succeed in implementing either of his plans: ownership of the land is still in private hands, and the spelling of English is still unphonetic. There are many reasons why a radical spelling reform has never been accepted in the UK, and even the reforms implemented in American English are much less radical than in Noah Webster's original vision. Opponents of phonics today point out that a teacher presenting a word like *bath* to children in the North of England would cause confusion if she taught the long 'a' vowel of Received Pronunciation, and the same argument can be used against phonetic spelling. Other reasons why Spence's reform was not accepted at the time include Spence's own notoriety after his move to London and the generally conservative attitude to linguistic change in the eighteenth and early nineteenth centuries. Another possible reason, which Spence would have acknowledged, may have been a fear that Spence's vision of an educated and therefore rebellious proletariat, as expressed in his depiction of Crusonea, might actually come about. This might seem fanciful, but at the time, even such a strong advocate of education as Hannah More held just such a view. S. J. Skedd points out that 'More was adamant that the poor should not be taught writing, as it would encourage them to be dissatisfied with their lowly situation.'[14] However, the *Grand Repository of the English Language* stands as a testament to Spence's genius: 111 years before the invention of the International Phonetic Alphabet, Spence had invented a workable and practicable phonetic alphabet. For a historical linguist like the present author, this has proved immensely valuable as an aid to reconstructing what passed for correct pronunciation in the Newcastle of the late eighteenth century.

13 Thomas Spence, *The Giant Killer, or Anti-Landlord* 1, (London: August 6. 1814).

14 S. J. Skedd, 'More, Hannah (1745–1833)', *Oxford Dictionary of National Biography*, Oxford University Press, 2004; online edn, May 2009, accessed 8th March 2014, http://www.oxforddnb.com/view/article/19179.

10

'Meet and Sing, and Your Chains Will Drop Off Like Burnt Thread' The Political Songs of Thomas Spence

•

Michael T. Davis

By the mid-1790s, Britain was waging a bitter war against a determined and evil force. But this was not a war against France or a distant enemy. This was a war being fought on home soil against a perceived enemy from within. The battleground was in the bookshops, streets, taverns and public spaces in practically every corner of Britain, and at stake were the hearts and minds of the British people. With the political future of the nation potentially at risk, the importance of this struggle could not be underestimated and required the mobilization of extensive resources. The opponent was a group of radical pamphleteers and activists, who used a network of booksellers, pedlars and hawkers to launch a barrage of what was seen as vulgar and seditious productions. One of their weapons of choice was songs, placing Britain under auditory assault. The only way forward was for conservative forces to fight fire with fire, confronting radicals head-on with their own weapons. One person who undertook this challenge was the Evangelical writer and social reformer, Hannah More, devising a plan of counter-attack in 1794 that included the regular publication of ballads designed to inculcate loyalism in the community.[1] When she communicated her plan to Beilby Porteus, the Bishop of London, he expressed how he was 'perfectly well aware, not only of the real existence, but of the magnitude and extent of the evil you mean to combat'.[2] Porteus reflected upon 'a central set of booksellers' and 'the lowest rabble [that] flock to their shops', envisaging the day when they could claim victory over their opponents: 'It would be a most edifying spectacle to see this ragged regiment all drawn up there together, and chanting forth our admirable compositions to the astonished villagers, with their ballads'.[3] The historical significance of this battle was not lost on the Bishop of London, and he thought the radical songs and tracts that

1 On the counter-revolutionary campaign of Hannah More, see Kevin Gilmartin, *Writing Against Revolution: Literary Conservatism in Britain, 1790-1832* (Cambridge: Cambridge University Press, 2007), pp. 55-95; Anne Stott, *Hannah More: The First Victorian* (Oxford: Oxford University Press, 2003), pp. 169-190; and Susan Pedersen, 'Hannah More Meets Simple Simon: Tracts, Chapbooks and Popular Culture in Late Eighteenth-Century England,' *Journal of British Studies* 25 (1986): pp. 84-113.

2 William Roberts, *Memoirs of the Life and Correspondence of Mrs. Hannah More* (New York: Harper & Brothers, 1836), p. 456.

3 Roberts, *Memoirs*, pp. 456-457.

More had collected would in the future be displayed as artefacts of this war: 'they would form the best *sans culotte* library in Europe, and will, I dare say, someday or other be visited by travellers, as we now do the Vatican or the Museum.'[4]

Among the leading combatants on the radical side, whose works would undoubtedly be driven from the streets and displayed on the shelves of this chimerical "sans culotte library", was Thomas Spence. Many contemporaries would have awarded Spence this dubious distinction on the perception he was an unrespectable radical, a worthy contributor to the *sans-culottes* collection but someone unworthy of inclusion elsewhere in civil society. As the sociologist Jeffrey Alexander has shown, societies use a symbolic code of civility to construct identities, to determine who should be trusted and who should be treated with suspicion.[5] Like other British reformers of the late eighteenth century, Spence was identified within the structure of this code as someone dangerous, and the object of disgust and alarm. He was looked upon 'as irrational and inclined towards hysteria, excitable, disorderly and passionate, and given to fantasy' — someone who deserved to be relegated to the margins of society.[6] Stigmatized by his contemporary critics as a rabble-rouser, there seemed to be some evidence of Spence's commitment to a Jacobin-style conspiratorial revolution. During the 1790s, he published works that espoused the idea of a French-assisted insurrection in England and he called for action to 'get rid of oppression' in 1795: 'In a country so prepared, let us suppose a few thousands of hearty determined fellows, well armed and appointed with officers, and having a committee of honest, firm, and intelligent men to act as a provisionary government and to direct their actions to the proper object .... if the aristocracy arose to contend the matter, let the people be firm and desperate, destroying them root and branch and strengthening their hands by the rich confiscations. Thus the war would be carried on at the expense of the wealthy enemy and the soldiers of liberty beside the hope of sharing in the future felicity of the country, being well paid, would be steady and bold.'[7] In the previous year, government spies were convinced they had uncovered Spence's active involvement in a shadowy and deceptive group known as the Lambeth Loyal Association.[8] Founded in November 1793 and disguised by its loyalist title, the

4 Roberts, *Memoirs*, p. 457.

5 See Jeffrey C. Alexander, 'Citizen and Enemy as Symbolic Classification: On the Polarizing Discourse of Civil Society,' in *Cultivating Differences: Symbolic Boundaries and the Making of Inequality*, ed. Michèle Lamont and Marcel Fournier (Chicago and London: University of Chicago Press, 1992), pp. 289-308; and Jeffrey C. Alexander, *The Meanings of Social Life: A Cultural Sociology* (Oxford: Oxford University Press, 2003), pp. 120-154. For a discussion of radicals and radicalism of the 1790s within this framework, see Michael T. Davis, 'The Mob Club? The London Corresponding Society and the Politics of Civility in the 1790s,' in *Unrespectable Radicals? Popular Politics in the Age of Reform*, ed. Michael T. Davis and Paul A. Pickering (Aldershot: Ashgate, 2008), pp. 21-40.

6 Davis, 'The Mob Club,' p. 25.

7 Thomas Spence, *The End of Oppression* (1795) , in *The Political Works of Thomas Spence*, ed. H. T. Dickinson (Newcastle upon Tyne: Avero, 1982), pp. 36-37.

8 On the Lambeth Loyal Association, see Malcolm Chase, *The People's Farm: English Radical Agrarianism 1775-1840*, 2nd edition (London: Breviary Stuff, 2010 [first published by Oxford University Press, 1988]), pp. 55-56; Albert Goodwin, *The Friends of Liberty: The English Democratic Movement in the Age of the French Revolution* (Cambridge, MA: Harvard University Press, 1979), pp. 350-352; Alan Wharam, *The Treason Trials, 1794* (Leicester: Leicester

Association sometimes drilled at Spence's bookshop in Holborn where the spy, Frederick Polydore Nodder, once discovered behind closed curtains, three men being exercised with 'an old rusty Musket and a Brook Stick or two'[9] — hardly the weapons of a menacing cadre. Nevertheless, Spence was interrogated in 1794 on suspicion of high treason for his connection with the Association but this was not his only entanglement with the law. In the twelve months following his first arrest in December 1792, nervous authorities had Spence hauled before the courts three more times but he was never found guilty. When the government turned its attention to the revolutionary United Englishmen in 1798, there was deep suspicion that Spence was involved in this clandestine movement but again he was set free. Only in 1801 did the government succeed against Spence, arresting him for publishing a seditious libel in *The Restorer of Society to its Natural State* and having him sentenced to a year in Shrewsbury prison. The prosecutorial campaign against Spence was symptomatic of what some historians have dubbed a "reign of terror" against radicals during the late eighteenth and early nineteenth centuries, but as Harry Dickinson notes: 'Spence was evidently not intimidated by the repressive policy of the government or the campaign of harassment aimed at him personally.'[10]

But perhaps worse than being viewed as a resilient and dangerous political fanatic — and perhaps because of this view — many contemporaries also considered Spence to be an outright lunatic. When the *Annual Register* reported on Spence's trial in 1801, it referred to him as 'a poor insane, though mischievous bookseller',[11] and a Member of Parliament questioned whether it was more appropriate for Spence to be admitted to a hospital for the mentally ill than it was to prosecute him: 'Whether any individual of the numerous audience upon that occasion did not feel a sort of indignation at a man's being put upon his trial who was a fitter object of confinement in Bedlam?'[12] Spence himself was astutely aware of such aspersions, once commenting that he was 'looked on as a lunatic' by the majority of people.[13] Even some of his acquaintances could see his activities and behaviour at times seemed to justify this perception. The engraver, Thomas Bewick, who knew Spence from his Newcastle days, recalled a moment that highlights Spence's sometimes violent commitment to his politics: 'to reason with him was useless — he began by calling me (from my silence) a

---

University Press, 1992), pp. 78-79; and David Worrall, *Radical Culture: Discourse, Resistance and Surveillance 1790-1820* (Hemel Hempstead: Harvester Wheatsheaf, 1992), pp. 20-21.

9 The National Archives [TNA], TS 11/963/3509, examination of Frederick Polydore Nodder, 22 May 1794.

10 Dickinson, *Political Works*, xvi. On the political trials of this period, see Clive Emsley, 'An Aspect of Pitt's Terror: Prosecutions for Sedition during the 1790s,' *Social History* 6 (1981), pp. 155-184; Clive Emsley, 'Repression, 'Terror' and the Rule of Law in England during the Decade of the French Revolution,' *English Historical Review* 100 (1985), pp. 801-825; Michael Lobban, 'From Seditious Libel to Unlawful Assembly: Peterloo and the Changing Face of Political Crime, c. 1770-1820,' *Oxford Journal of Legal Studies* 10 (1990), pp. 307-352; Philip Harling, 'The Law of Libel and the Limits of Repression, 1790-1832,' *The Historical Journal* 44 (2001), pp. 107-134; and Michael T. Davis, 'The British Jacobins: Folk Devils in the Age of Counter Revolution?,' in *Moral Panics, the Media and the Law in Early Modern England*, ed. David Lemmings and Claire Walker (Basingstoke: Palgrave Macmillan, 2009), pp. 221-244.

11 *Annual Register*, 13 June 1801, p. 20.

12 *The Parliamentary History of England, From the Earliest Period to the Year 1803*, ed. William Cobbett (London: T.C. Hansard, 1819), 34:1512.

13 Thomas Spence, *The Important Trial of Thomas Spence* (1803), in Dickinson, *Political Works*, p. 93.

sir Walter Blackett, and adding "If I had been as stout as you are I would have thrashed you" ... he then produced a pair of cudgels — and to work we fell, after I had black'ned the insides of his thighs and Arms, he became quite outrageous, and behaved very unfairly, which obliged me to give him a severe beating.'[14] Francis Place, Spence's fellow reformer of the 1790s, saw in him 'a very simple, very honest single-minded man, querulous in his disposition, odd in his manner, he was remarkably irritable.'[15] The characterization of Spence as someone who was mad and lacking self-control has proven difficult to erase, filtering down into some modern-day interpretations. E. P. Thompson, for instance, thought it was 'easy to see Spence ... as little more than a crank',[16] while Alastair Bonnett finds 'the most irritating remark ever made about Spence'[17] coming from Thomas Knox who interprets Spence's career as 'stunted' by his zealous commitment to land reform and characterizes him as nothing more than 'a radical crank'.[18]

However, not all historians have interpreted Spence in such negative light. His importance within the reform movement once hinged upon his status as the "first modern socialist" in Britain. As G. I. Gallop states: 'Spence was *the* socialist theorist of his generation and deserves his place in the history of British political thought for this reason alone.'[19] Similarly, Malcolm Chase acknowledges 'Spence's contribution to radical thought was one of substance, vitality, and longevity,'[20] while other historians have come to appreciate the enduring influence of Spence on mobilizing radicals in the late eighteenth and early nineteenth centuries.[21] Although Iain McCalman describes Spence as 'an eccentric pamphlet-seller and land-reformer', he also positions him as the inspiration for a rich and potent underworld of ultra-radical Spencean disciples that emerged in the 1790s and extended well beyond Spence's death in 1814.[22] As Kenneth Johnston notes, McCalman and other recent scholars have encouraged us to think of radicals like Spence not so much as part of the lunatic fringes 'but serious-in-their-way voices and figures of political prophecy who envisioned a much broader and more modern vision of reform than the standard program the reformers usually put forward.'[23] Much of this re-assessment has

---

14 Thomas Bewick, *A Memoir of Thomas Bewick Written by Himself*, ed. Iain Bain (Oxford: Oxford University Press, 1975), p. 53.

15 British Library, Francis Place Papers, Add. MS 27808, fo. 152.

16 E. P. Thompson, *The Making of the English Working Class* (London: Pelican Books, 1968), p. 177.

17 Alastair Bonnett, 'Spence Died Nearly Two Hundred Years Ago. Why Should We Care About Him Today?,' http://thomas-spence-society.co.uk/8.html.

18 Thomas R. Knox, 'Thomas Spence: The Trumpet of Jubilee,' *English Historical Review* 76 (1977), p. 75.

19 G. I. Gallop, *Pigs' Meat: The Selected Writings of Thomas Spence, Radical and Pioneer Land Reformer* (Nottingham: Spokesman, 1982), p. 51. Cf. G. D. H. Cole's remark: 'the writings of Thomas Spence ... had little practical bearing on the contemporary development of British radical or working-class thought.' G. D. H. Cole, *A History of Socialist Thought* (London: Macmillan, 1959), 1: p. 25.

20 Chase, *The People's Farm*, p. 17.

21 For instance, see Noel Thompson, *The Real Rights of Man: Political Economies for the Working Class 1775-1850* (London: Pluto Press, 1998), pp. 1-15.

22 Iain McCalman, *Radical Underworld: Prophets, Revolutionaries and Pornographers in London, 1795-1840* (Cambridge: Cambridge University Press, 1988), p. 7.

23 Kenneth R. Johnston, *Unusual Suspects: Pitt's Reign of Alarm and the Lost Generation of the 1790s* (Oxford: Oxford University Press, 2013), p. 11.

focused on Spence's contribution to radical culture, and the techniques he used to manipulate and manoeuvre within the boundaries of a repressive environment. As Marcus Wood notes, 'Spence's influence on and relevance for early nineteenth-century radicalism lay not so much in what he thought but in how he attempted to disseminate that thought.'[24] In an age when communications were being closely monitored, Spence employed an impressively diverse range of methods to spread his message: 'he was a token dealer and manufacturer, a philologist and phonetician, a graffiti artist, a journal editor, a leader of debating societies in London and Newcastle, a printmaker, and a publisher of extraordinary courage and ambition.'[25] Spence was a resourceful and dexterous political agitator, making him one of the leading 'multi-media propagandists in the republican cause' of his times.[26]

An important part of Spence's multi-media repertoire was songs and political hymns.[27] They can be found scattered throughout his journal *Pigs' Meat* (1793-95), collected in songbooks published around 1811, and printed as broadsides that were distributed on the streets.[28] As the written word intersected with oral culture and as alcohol lubricated the voices of participants, renditions of Spence's verses could often be heard performed as drinking songs in the taverns of London. Spence attracted to his group a number of followers who were accomplished at political serenading, ensuring his lyrical messages were heard on every possible occasion. Among the dedicated Spenceans fond of singing was the lame publican and balladeer, William Tilly, and the rugged stone-cutter and alleged pickpocket, Thomas Porter, who was conspicuous for performing in the white apron of his trade and renowned for his powerful voice.[29] With such diverse and wide circulation, songs were a central and compelling part of Spence's propaganda campaign. As Michael Scrivener notes, 'Spence used songs as a principal means of spreading his political ideas' and 'exploited the form with considerable sophistication.'[30]

While the dense lyrics of some of Spence's songs, such as "Burke's Address

24 Marcus Wood, *Radical Satire and Print Culture 1790-1832* (Oxford: Clarendon Press, 1994), p. 67.

25 Wood, *Radical Satire*, p. 66.

26 James Epstein, *In Practice: Studies in the Language and Culture of Popular Politics in Modern Britain* (Stanford: Stanford University Press, 2003), p. 89.

27 On Spence's songs, see P. M. Ashraf, *The Life and Times of Thomas Spence* (Newcastle upon Tyne: Frank Graham, 1983), pp. 187-91; Michael Scrivener, *Seditious Allegories: John Thelwall and Jacobin Writing* (Pennsylvania: Pennsylvania State University Press, 2001), pp. 102-11; and Joan C. Beal, 'Why Should the Landlords Have the Best Songs? Thomas Spence and the Subversion of Popular Song,' in *United Islands? The Languages of Resistance*, ed. John Kirk, Andrew Noble and Michael Brown (London: Pickering & Chatto, 2012), pp. 51-62.

28 The songbook, *Spence's Songs*, is usually dated as 1807. For instance, see Ashraf, *Life and Times*, 189; and Dickinson, *Political Works*, pp. 130-134. However, Malcolm Chase has made a more plausible dating of *Spence's Songs*: 'the conventional dating of the publication, 1807, is unacceptable, given that every surviving copy is printed on paper watermarked 1811 ... its small jobbing printer was unlikely to carry large stocks of paper, making publication within a year or so after 1811 likely.' Chase, *The People's Farm*, p. 26.

29 TNA, HO 42/172, MS note on *A Humorous Catalogue of Spence's Songs*. On Spencean tavern culture, see Iain McCalman, 'Ultra-Radicalism and Convivial Debating-Clubs in London, 1795-1838,' *English Historical Review* 102 (1987), pp. 309-333.

30 Scrivener, *Seditious Allegories*, p. 102.

to the Swinish Multitude",[31] must have made them nearly impossible to sing and were probably more often read as text, all of his lyrical compositions were inherently didactic. This politically instructive character of Spence's songs was consistent with his long-standing commitment to educate and enlighten the lower classes. Dating back to at least the publication in 1775 of his phonetic dictionary, *The Grand Repository of the English Language*, the one-time schoolmaster sought to level class distinctions by educating what he called 'the labouring part of the people".[32] To instruct the common people in the English language was Spence's way of reconstructing their identities, ensuring they were not 'laughed at all their Lives for betraying their vulgar Education'.[33] In a similar way, his songs were aimed at acquainting the lower classes with their political rights and the Spensonian future. They would be informative but 'political song is a speech act with illocutionary and perlocutionary force.'[34] Spence recognized the potential for songs to turn instruction into action, to be rousing, cause upheaval and, as Michael Scrivener points out, to 'be more symbolically defiant than ordinary political prose.'[35] In the lyrics of "Spence and the Barber" which was to be sung to the tune of "Tally heigh ho, the Grinder", the power of song was explicitly identified: 'When all feel alike in a cause / Small trouble's requir'd in teaching / A song that attracts their applause / Is better than speeches or preaching / Let's hear then no more of despair / But sing your dear rights to each other'.[36] In Spence's mind, songs appeared to be unassailable and liberating when combined with the conviviality of free-and-easy meetings: 'Even under the modern tyrannies of China, France, Turkey, etc., what can hinder small companies from meeting in a free and easy convivial manner, and singing their rights and instructing each other in songs? Can tyrants hinder people from singing in their work, or in their families? If not, despair no longer but begin immediately, too much time has already been lost. Sing and meet and meet and sing, and your chains will drop off like burnt thread'.[37]

This notion of liberation and free will is one of the recurrent themes in the political songs of Spence. In the typical style of late-eighteenth and early-nineteenth century radicals, the monarchy, church and aristocracy are often caricatured as oppressors of the people but Spence's songs give them hope of political freedom. In "The Downfall of Feudal Tyranny", which was published in *Pigs' Meat* in 1795, Spence draws his audience into the political myth of the Norman yoke but envisages the coming of emancipation:

31 Michael Scrivener, *Poetry and Reform: Periodical Verse from the English Democratic Press 1792-1824* (Detroit: Wayne State University Press, 1992), pp. 65-67.

32 Ashraf, *Life and Times*, p. 150. On *The Grand Repository*, see A. F. Shields, 'Thomas Spence and the English Language,' *Transactions of the Philological* Society 61 (1974), pp. 33-64; and Joan C. Beal, *English Pronunciation in the Eighteenth Century: Thomas Spence's Grand Repository of the English Language* (Oxford: Oxford University Press, 1999).

33 Thomas Spence, *The Giant-Killer; or Anti-Landlord* 1 (1814): 2.

34 Michael Scrivener, 'Reading the English Political Songs of the 1790s,' in Kirk, Noble and Brown, *United Islands*, p. 50.

35 Scrivener, *Seditious Allegories*, p. 97.

36 Dickinson, *Political Works*, p. 133.

37 Thomas Spence, *An Address to All Mankind*, in *Spence's Songs, Part the Second* (London: Seale & Bates, 1811?).

That conquering blade, who did us invade,
Ev'n William the Norman by name,
Among his proud band he divided our land,
Nought leaving but slav'ry and shame,
My poor boys.
Nought leaving but slav'ry's shame.

These plundering bands, thus strengthen'd by lands,
For ages have rul'd us with awe,
Whilst we once so free, now without property,
From conqu'rors received the law,
My poor boys.

The priests them to aid, they lib'rally paid,
And gave them good share of the spoil,
The poor to persuade, that if nothing they said,
In heav'n they should end all their toil,
My poor boys.

Thus lords and priests leagu'd together intrigu'd,
Completely poor man to enthrall,
And when thus befool'd, their vassals they rul'd,
And kept them in chains one and all,
My poor boys.

But now reason's ray, begins to display,
To man his dear rights once again,
While all wond'ring how they've been duped till now,
Make haste to declare they are men,
My brave boys.

The sons and the heirs of those old murderers,
Observe how they fly now to arms,
For mankind they see, are resolv'd to be free,
Which ev'ry proud tyrant alarms,
My brave boys.

Sad ruin's their fate, though they associate,
No rents now the poor will soon pay,
For when in a mass, like a flood o'er they pass,
They'll sweep all their greatness away;
My brave boys.

For whom do we toil and feed with our spoil?
Is now through the nations the cry,
Infuriate men sing, till heav'ns concave ring,
O, give me death or liberty!
My brave boys,
O give me death or liberty![38]

38 Scrivener, *Poetry and Reform*, pp. 73-75. On the place of the Norman yoke myth in radicalism in the eighteenth and nineteenth centuries, see Thompson, *The Making of the English Working Class*, pp. 94-96; and F. K. Donnelly, 'Levellerism in Eighteenth and Early-Nineteenth Century Britain,' *Albion* 20 (1988), pp. 261-269.

Similarly, in "The Progress of Liberty" to the tune of "Britannia Rule the Waves", Spence witnesses the breaking of the common people's metaphorical chains as 'No more the grinding hand of Power / The op'ning bud of Reason blights / On eagle's wings fair Truth shall tower / For man begins to know his Rights / The iron yoke we crumbling see / Beneath the Cap of Liberty'.[39] In Spence's eyes the future for the oppressed lower classes was bright:

> No longer lost in shades of night,
> Where late in chains we lay!
> The sun arises, and his light
> Dispels our gloom away.
>
> No longer blind, and prone to lye
> In slavery profound,
> But for redress aloud we cry!
> And tyrants hear the sound.
>
> The pomp of courts no more engage,
> The magic spell is broke,
> We hail the bright reforming age!
> And cast away the yoke.[40]

For those experiencing hardship, lyrics such as these must have been inspiring, filling them with optimism and energy. Songs like "The Rights of Man For Me", which was published in *Pigs' Meat* in 1795 and set to the cheerful tune of "Maid of the Mill", were deliberately enlivening and heartening while at the same time calling the people to action: 'Then cheer up all you who have been oppress'd / Aspire unto sweet liberty / No Fetters were form'd for a Nation to bind / Who have the brave Wish to be free / To reason attend and blush at your Chains / And throw off vile Slavery / And let each Man sing till loud Echoes ring / The Rights of Man Boys for me'.[41]

By the time this song was published, the "Rights of Man" was a phrase indelibly and enduringly associated with the democrat and polemicist, Thomas Paine, who published in *The Rights of Man* (1791-92) what has been called 'a Bible to the radicals'.[42] As Amanda Goodrich has noted, Paine's work 'heralded a new radicalism in English politics'[43] and it inspired a whole generation of political reformers in the democratic cause. While Spence would have appreciated Paine's republicanism and attack on the aristocracy, and even faced legal persecution for selling his publications, he did not see himself as a mere follower of Paine. Spence actually laid claim to being the first writer to use the "Rights of Man" phrase in a ballad of the same name published in 1783, which outlined his plan to abolish private property and establish equal common rights

39 Dickinson, *Political Works*, p. 122.

40 Ibid., pp. 123-24.

41 Ibid., p. 129.

42 Lucyle Werkmeister, *A Newspaper History of England 1792-1793* (Lincoln: University of Nebraska Press, 1967), p. 40.

43 Amanda Goodrich, *Debating England's Aristocracy in the 1790s: Pamphlets, Polemics and Political Ideas* (Woodbridge and New York: The Boydell Press, 2005), p. 6.

to the land.[44] Spence's vision of reform was distinctive to that of Paine, engendering a more radical and revolutionary utopia. Inflicted with 'self-dramatization' — the so-called characteristic vice of the English Jacobins identified by E. P. Thompson[45] — and without a sense of false modesty, Spence exclaimed: 'I hear there is another RIGHTS OF MAN by *Spence*, that goes farther than *Paine's* ...It is amazing that Paine and other democrats should level all their artillery at kings, without striking like Spence at this root of every abuse and of every grievance.'[46]

The 'root of every abuse and grievance' was landlordism. Spence believed economic freedom was more important to the common people than political liberty, and he saw the right to vote as little use to those who were oppressed by the system of private land ownership. His songs expressed a sensitive awareness of the distress of the people and the need to invert the *status quo* in order to improve the condition of the lower classes. As Britain entered a protracted war against Revolutionary France in 1793 and the 'wretched faces' of the common people came to embody their distress, Spence published a song in *Pigs' Meat* called "The Year Ninety Three" that captures the perilous situation of the population: 'Each day and each hour a merchant then stops / Only shutters are seen, they all shut up their shops / Whole families ruined! 'twas piteous to see / Oh what a fine year was the year Ninety-Three!! / Trade's now at an end, there's no work to be found / Brave Britons are dying with hunger around / Or at a famine's approach to the Continent flee / And York lets their blood — that's the year Ninety-Three'.[47] Added to the stress of hunger and financial hardship, Spence underscores the oppressiveness of the English government and judicial system: 'Now pillory, whipping post, British bastille / The loss of old times makes each Englishman feel / No spirit, no thought, now dare circulate free / For Pitt, Kenyon, Dundas, in curst Ninety-Three'.[48] Spence carries further the linking of economic distress to tyranny in his satirical song, "Edmund Burke's Address to the Swinish Multitude" published in 1794. Burke's "swinish multitude" metaphor in *Reflections on the Revolution in France* was meant to define and dehumanize the common people of England and, in the witty words of the radical satirist, Charles Pigott, it was 'an epithet applied ... to the English people, because they tamely suffer their rights to be wrested from them, and their wrongs to remain unredressed'.[49] Spence parodies Burke at the same time he uses irony to attack the wealthy as corrupt and responsible for the plight of the enslaved working classes: 'Ye apron men to labour bred / How dare ye this to quarrel / We'll take your children's beer and bread / And you shan't smell the barrel / 'Tis ours to take your needful scot / When e'er we lack assistance /

44 Ashraf, *Life and Times*, pp. 160-161.

45 Thompson, *The Making of the English Working Class*, p. 173.

46 Dickinson, *Political Works*, pp. 34-35.

47 Ibid., p. 120.

48 Ibid., p. 121.

49 Charles Pigott, *A Political Dictionary Explaining the True Meaning of Words*, ed. Robert Rix (1795; rpt. Aldershot: Ashgate, 2004), p. 140. For the 'swinish multitude' reference, see Edmund Burke, *Reflections on the Revolution in France*, ed. L.G. Mitchell (1790; rpt. Oxford: Oxford University Press, 1999), p. 79.

Passive obedience is your lot / And humble non-resistance'.[50] Without change, Spence warned the government and aristocracy would 'take two thirds of all you get / To keep you poor and humble',[51] and the people would remain fettered by their social superiors: 'Then hence ye Swine, nor make a rout / Forbearance but relaxes / We'll clap the muzzle on your snout / Go work and pay your taxes'.[52]

The solution to this situation, according to Spence, was to be found in his visionary and distinctive mantra known as "Spensonianism" or what has been called his "Land Plan".[53] The control of and income derived from the land was by far Spence's greatest preoccupation, first articulated in 1775 in a lecture to the Newcastle Philosophical Society and repeatedly elaborated over the next forty years of his life. As Max Beer suggested, Spence saw the land 'as necessary to human existence as light, air, and water; to deprive a man of the land was to deprive him of his life.'[54] Songs became a vehicle for Spence to remind people of the critical importance of the land and to further acquaint them with his ideas of land reform. In an "Address to Posterity, Warning Them Against the Landlord Judas", Spence emphasized the need to redress the system of land ownership because 'No Freedom with Landlords, enjoy e'er you can / For land, I say land, is the whole *Rights of Man*'.[55] All landlords were 'Judases', according to Spence, and the 'Touch-stone of Worthiness' was whether they would be 'willing to grant all a Right to the Ground'.[56] Spence rallied this point in "The Touch-Stone of Honesty" set to the tune of "Lillibullara":

> The Lands ought of Right to be held by us all,
> No Privates should lord it o'er their Fellow Men,
> The whole Human Race Old, Young, Great and Small
> Share and Share alike of the Rents would have then.
> All those who say no, it shall not be so,
> We Murderers cruel and Traitors them call,
> Be they rich or poor we may be full sure,
> At Heart they are nothing but Judases all.[57]

In the autobiographical ballad, "The Propagation of Spensonianism. Written in Shrewsbury Jail in the Year 1801", Spence announces the imminent 'end of Oppression and Lordship being come / We'll then all rejoice in the bless'd millennium'.[58] What he visualized was 'a kind of social revolution',[59] a complete upending of the system in which 'All ancient Oppressions were then swept away / And Virtue and Freedom for every did sway'.[60] He believed it was

50 Dickinson, *Political Works*, p. 125.

51 Ibid., p. 125.

52 Ibid., p. 126.

53 See Ashraf, *Life and Times*, pp. 120-45; and Chase, *The People's Farm*, pp. 26-33.

54 M. Beer, *A History of British Socialism* (London: George Allen & Unwin, 1919), 1: p. 107.

55 Dickinson, *Political Works*, p. 131.

56 Ibid., p. 131.

57 Ibid., p. 131.

58 Ibid., p. 134.

59 J. R. Dinwiddy, *Radicalism and Reform in Britain, 1780-1850* (London and Rio Grande: The Hambledon Press, 1992), p. 190.

60 Dickinson, *Political Works*, p. 135.

possible for the people to "turn the world upside down" and even called on this powerful radical motif in a ballad published in 1805.[61] His songs summoned them to unite against the government and aristocracy, an enlistment that promised a better future and would be impossible to resist:

> Said Spence, if a few hearty men,
> Said come let us have Spence's system,
> What would your behaviour be then,
> Would you hinder or would you assist 'm?
> Said Strap them I could not oppose,
> My interest would not allow me,
> I never can count those my foes,
> Who wish with such bliss to endow me.[62]

Spence furthered this message with an arousing tone in the self-applauding song, "The Progress of Spensonianism", set to the evocative tune of "The Battle of the Nile":

> Arise! Arise! Let all Mankind arise
> And join in the Shouts of this patriotic Throng,
> Arise! Arise! Come all Mankind arise,
> And let the Heavens echo with our Song;
> While the Genius of Freedom,
> Spence's Plan proclaiming,
> Flies through the World,
> Our natural Rights maintaining,
> And Partnership in Land
> To Eternity shall stand,
> And through all future Ages applauded shall be.
> Then Huzza! Huzza! Huzza! Huzza Boys,
> Spence shews the World what Nature did for Man ordain,
> Huzza! Huzza! Huzza! Huzza! Huzza Boys
> For ever and forever 'twill remain.[63]

In these calls for defiance and change, Spence appeared as a brother-in-arms to the lower classes, and implored them to 'hearken to Reason and Friend Thomas Spence'.[64] But he was much more than a companion in the cause. Spence saw himself as the saviour of the people and something of a prophet. His revelation was said to have come during his time in prison in 1801: 'One night as a slumb'ring I lay on my bed / A notable Vision came into my Head / Methought I saw Numbers forth going to teach / And Justice and Peace among mankind to

61 Christopher Hill, *The World Turned Upside Down: Radical Ideas during the English Revolution* (Harmondsworth: Penguin, 1984), p. 380. As Penelope Corfield notes: 'The satirical tradition of *The World Turned Upside Down* or *The World Turned Topsy-Turvy* had long been represented in European popular song and prints, associated with ideas of inversion and misrule ... The concept also had a sharper application in periods of political upheaval.' P. J. Corfield, 'Class By Name and Number in Eighteenth-Century Britain,' *History*, 72 (1987): p. 41, n. 19.

62 Dickinson, *Political Works*, p. 132.

63 Ibid., p. 135.

64 Ibid., p. 134.

preach'.[65] In true prophet style, Spence's song "The Progress of Spensonianism" proclaimed: 'Lo! See but how Eden Spence has set in View / And who keeps us from it, he has shewn us too' and, like an apostle, he is presented as the 'Guide who has spied out the land / So plain he instructs you, you must understand'.[66] Some of Spence's songs are infused with millenarian and Christian imagery, which was powerfully invoked in his most well-known ballad, the "Jubilee Hymn":

> Hark! how the trumpet's sound
> Proclaims the land around
> The Jubilee!
> Tells all the poor oppress'd,
> No more they shall be cess'd,
> Nor landlords more molest
> Their property.
>
> .... Since this Jubilee
> Sets all at Liberty
> Let us be glad.
> Behold each man return
> To his possession
> No more like doves to mourn
> By landlords sad![67]

This song borrows from Leviticus 25 the vision of an approaching "Jubilee", in which the land is owned by God and the people recover their lost property every fifty years. This positioned Spence within a tradition of using the concept of "Jubilee" to justify radical resistance of the established order, and conjured up images of emancipated slaves and the restitution of monopolized lands.[68] Although this was an extremely provocative anticipation in the late eighteenth and early nineteenth centuries, Spence saw the 'grand rising Dawn of the social Jubilee' as divine providence.[69] 'God was a very notorious Leveller',[70] in Spence's mind, and the use of biblical references in his songs and other works was a way of giving his land revolution a level of legitimacy as well as appeal to his largely sectarian audience.

All of this can be seen as an extension of Spence's religious upbringing which, as Malcolm Chase suggests, was 'unusually pious, perhaps, even by the standards of the time.'[71] From his net-maker father, Spence gained a critical understanding of the Bible and he recalled how his 'father used to make my

---

65 Ibid.

66 Ibid.

67 Scrivener, *Poetry and Reform*, 63-65.

68 On the use of the biblical Jubilee as a radical concept, see Malcolm Chase, 'From Millennium to Anniversary: The Concept of Jubilee in Late Eighteenth- and Nineteenth-Century England,' *Past and Present* 129 (1990), pp. 132-147; and Peter Linebaugh, 'Jubilating; Or, How the Atlantic Working Class Used the Biblical Jubilee against Capitalism, with Some Success,' *Radical History Review* 50 (1991), pp. 143-180.

69 Dickinson, *Political Works*, p. 136.

70 Cited in McCalman, *Radical Underworld*, p. 63.

71 Chase, *The People's Farm*, p. 35.

brothers and me read the Bible to him while working in his Business, and at the end of every chapter encouraged us to give our opinions on what we had just read'.[72] We can also see in Spence's blending of millenarian themes with singing the influence of the radical dissenting sect, the Glassites. It has been pointed out that the 'Glassites were the pioneers of congregational hymn singing' and, through one of his brothers who was a member, Spence would have found inspiration in the way they used 'the more lively metres of secular songs and set them to traditional tunes rather than ecclesiastical music.'[73] But, by the time Spence had moved to London, he probably found a more immediate inspiration for the use of songs from across the English Channel. Evidence of the politically alluring power of music and song can be seen in the way lyrics articulated popular feelings and raised enthusiasm during the French Revolution.[74] Songs like "Ḉa Ira" and "La Marseillaise" were performed in the streets and cafés of Paris, 'reflecting and affecting the changing political currents of the Revolution'.[75] At the same time the French revolutionaries exploited the subversive capacity of songs, Spence provocatively aligned himself at times with their cause. He endorsed the French call for liberty when he published the first English translation of "La Marseillaise" in *Pigs' Meat*,[76] and in one ballad Spence goes so far as to foreshadow the time when British and French radicals fraternised and crusaded together:

> Come cheer up my lads, lo! the day draweth near,
> When Britain's brave sons Freedom's standard will rear;
> And joining with Frenchmen, all tyrants o'erthrow,
> Th' oppress'd world releasing wherever they go.
>
> Then mankind rejoice,
> France and Britain agree;
> Their faiths they have plighted,
> Fleets and armies united,
> To drive tyrants from you,
> And set the world free.[77]

By arousing the Francophobic fears of British conservatives through these lyrics, Spence was entering the centre of the contested space of political songs in the late eighteenth century and appealing to a long tradition of balladry as an expression of counter-hegemonic dissent as well as a means of soliciting subversion.[78] Scholars have shown how music and songs can be as much tools of

72 Dickinson, *Political Works*, p. 94.

73 Ashraf, *Life and Times*, p. 189.

74 Laura Mason, *Singing the French Revolution: Popular Culture and Politics, 1787-1799* (Ithaca: Cornell University Press, 1996); Lenora Cuccia, 'Songs That Speak: Popular Vocal Music as Propaganda during the Revolution, 1789-1793,' *Consortium on Revolutionary Europe 1750-1850. Selected Papers* (1999), pp. 177-185.

75 Laura Mason, 'Popular Songs and Political Singing in the French Revolution,' *Princeton University Library Chronicle* 52 (1991), p. 172.

76 Ashraf, *Life and Times*, p. 189.

77 Dickinson, *Political Works*, p. 121.

78 On the politics of songs in the late eighteenth and early nineteenth centuries, see Mark Philp *et. al.*, 'Music and Politics, 1793-1815,' in *Resisting Napoleon: The British Response to the Threat of Invasion, 1797-1815*, ed. Mark Philp

hegemonic control as sources of anti-power that express the discontent of the common people and a means of animating popular political action. John Street, for instance, notes the 'potential of music to promote approved causes is linked to its potential to fuel rebellion'.[79] By the late eighteenth century, songs had become an 'expression in the idiom of the people'[80] and 'reflected but seldom manipulated working-class opinion'.[81] It is little wonder that political singing was an enduring concern of the government and their conservative supporters during the course of the eighteenth century and into the next. In the early 1730s, George II legislated against Jacobite balladry as a way of controlling insurgent popular opposition but in the heated atmosphere of the 1790s radical song culture seemed to be more potent and less controllable than ever before. The magistrate and police reformer, Patrick Colquhoun, observed that 'it has never been possible, under the existing Laws, to suppress the herd of Ballad-Singers which are to be found in such multitudes in every part of the Metropolis, and indeed, in all the large Towns in the Kingdom: and which at present are under the controul [*sic*] of a very feeble Police, which does not, and indeed cannot, restrain effectually the immoral and often seditious tendency of the Songs sung to the listening multitude'.[82]

Spence was shrewdly aware of this chink in the chain of repression. Although brave and tenacious, Spence was understandably risk averse and this partially explains why he used songs as a means of political expression. As a widespread and palpable panic about political stability spread throughout Britain during the 1790s, the government responded by spinning a repressive web of legislation, spies and trials to catch radical activists. Progressively, conventional sites of popular discourse came under increasing surveillance and radicals were forced to develop an innovative repertoire of tactics designed to avoid prosecution. Spence deliberately moulded his propaganda in a way that was legally evasive. As Marcus Wood points out, he 'generally steered clear of openly blasphemous or obscene expressions … while he looked to the infiltration of rapidly developing communications networks such as token coin production, the political print, the advertising industry, and children's book publishing.'[83] To this list can be added Spence's political ballads. While Home Office dossiers filled with reports of seditious singing, songs managed to give radicals like Spence some important and distinct advantages. Songs were effective ways to communicate his political and agrarian reforms, being 'subversive yet entertaining and difficult to

(Aldershot: Ashgate, 2006), pp. 173-204; and Kate Horgan, *The Politics of Songs in Eighteenth-Century Britain, 1723-1795* (London: Pickering & Chatto, 2014). On radical song culture in the 1790s, see Michael T. Davis, '"An Evening of Pleasure Rather than Business": Songs, Subversion and Radical Sub-Culture in the 1790s,' *Journal for the Study of British Cultures* 12 (2005), pp. 115-126.

79 John Street, '"Fight the Power": The Politics of Music and the Music of Politics,' *Government and Opposition* 38 (2003), p. 117.

80 Roy Palmer, ed., *A Touch on Times: Songs of Social Change 1770-1914* (Harmondsworth: Penguin, 1974), p. 8.

81 Martha Vicinus, *The Industrial Muse: A Study of Nineteenth-Century British Working-Class Literature* (London: Croom Helm, 1974), p. 13. This is also a point made in Robin Ganev, *Songs of Protest, Songs of Love: Popular Ballads in Eighteenth-Century Britain* (Manchester and New York: Manchester University Press, 2009).

82 Patrick Colquhoun, *Treatise on the Police of the Metropolis* (London: H. Fry, 1797), p. 625.

83 Wood, *Radical Satire*, p. 64.

prosecute': 'Songs were an important response to the government's campaign against radical communication: like reading aloud, songs and singing made political ideas available to a wide audience, a means of discourse that could be responded to and received by almost all.'[84]

As singing and songs generally were not solitary means of expression, they helped Spence spread his word. In some ways, songs were an early form of mass communication and social media, connecting more people than conversation or other forms of oral transmission. With the setting of his songs to popular tunes, Spence was able to propagate his radical visions even to semi-literate and illiterate audiences. This was both a logistical and logical tactic for Spence to employ, as Joan Beal points out: 'Spence's choice of tunes was certainly subversive, but it was also practical: there was no need for his followers to learn new tunes, newcomers could join in without embarrassment'.[85] Singing would also have an appeal for those involved beyond its inclusiveness. As Iain McCalman suggests, it was a ritual — like toasting and linking hands — that could be cathartic and expressive, lifting morale and allowing participants to escape momentarily the hardships of life.[86]

But, like all rituals, singing was about much more than mere escapism for British radicals. At a time when government legislation was designed to suppress the spatial collection of people and thereby inhibit their sense of union, Spence could use his songs as a means of community building and to encourage a collective sense of identity. Social scientists have highlighted the importance of social cohesiveness to marginalized publics: 'community building is critical. Groups on the political or social fringes of society often, either consciously or unconsciously, build collectivities that bind together their members'.[87] These groups construct an oppositional consciousness that challenges the dominant hegemony 'through symbolic action and the creation of rituals'.[88] For Spence, his songs were an integral part of this "symbolic action" and "ritual" that fostered a sense of bonding. Communal singing was a way for Spence to attract recruits and produce solidarity among his followers: 'One of the great things that happens in choral groups is that people of all kinds and stations and abilities can get a very real sense of togetherness, and common concern, and accomplishment ... It gives people a chance to work together for a common goal'.[89] Songs and singing also have an egalitarian functionality, which Spence sought to exploit: 'There is no question but that, particularly in choral groups, people who are diverse in backgrounds, diverse in age, diverse in cultural environment, can relate very beautifully and get to understand each other through music participation'.[90]

---

84 Davis, 'An Evening of Pleasure Rather than Business,' p. 122.

85 Beal, 'Why Should the Landlords Have the Best Songs,' p. 58.

86 McCalman, 'Ultra-Radicalism and Convivial Debating-Clubs in London,' pp. 316-317.

87 Susan Herbst, *Politics at the Margins: Historical Studies of Public Expression Outside the Mainstream* (Cambridge: Cambridge University Press, 1994), p. 2.

88 Herbst, *Politics at the Margins*, p. 24.

89 Cited in Colin Durrant and Evangelos Himonides, 'What Makes People Sing Together? Socio-Psychological and Cross-Cultural Perspectives on the Choral Phenomenon,' *International Journal of Music Education* 32 (1998), p. 64.

90 Cited in Durrant and Himonides, 'What Makes People Sing Together,' p. 64.

In a way, this democratic characteristic of singing reflects the overall nature and objective of the reform movement in the late eighteenth and early nineteenth centuries. But it also captures the culture of conviviality and sociability that was distinctive about Spencean radicalism.[91] In the network of taverns that made up Spence's "free-and-easies", his songs were nurtured and his followers nourished with a rich blend of anti-establishment sentiments as well as promises of a utopian future. But this was far from the ideal discursive space outlined by Jürgen Habermas, in which citizens 'confer in an unrestricted fashion'.[92] Radical meetings were infiltrated by government spies and informers, and even private conversations in public spaces could be eavesdropped upon and lead to prosecution.[93] In this highly sensitive surveillance culture, the act of singing Spence's songs might have helped unnerve its participants, providing some level of safety in numbers. It was also a disguise for what was actually going on; 'given that Spence was constantly watched by spies, the tunes could well have acted as a cloak for his activities: anybody passing by the pub would just hear patriotic songs being sung.'[94] But, of course, this was far from the reality. We can understand Spence's songs as a 'struggle with the dominant culture at many levels'[95] and they formed part of the counter-rituals staged by radicals, playing out the interaction E. P. Thompson identified 'in which rulers and crowd needed each other, performed theatre and counter-theatre'.[96] When Spence adapted his songs to tunes that were a key part of polite British musical culture, he surely relished the chance to play the upper classes at their own game and to invert the tunes original message. The best example of this is his "Jubilee Hymn", which was to be sung to the tune of "God Save the King" but proclaims 'The sceptre now is broke'.[97] In a brilliantly ironic twist, those who sung this song were imagining the downfall of the monarchy while singing it to the beat of the song that had assumed the status of a national anthem and was intended to give voice to Protestant patriotism as well as the divine right to rule.[98]

With such slick skill as a radical songster, it was fitting that one of his devoted followers, Thomas Evans, should declare in a song: 'Here's Tommy so clever / We hail thee forever'.[99] Spence was able to create a powerful and evocative political space through his songs at a time when government crackdowns on freedom of expression made it increasingly difficult and perilous to do so. He captured his own resilient and unshakeable character in the song,

91 See McCalman, 'Ultra-Radicalism and Convivial Debating-Clubs in London,' pp. 309-333.

92 Jürgen Habermas, 'The Public Sphere: An Encyclopaedia Article,' *New German Critique*, 1 (1974), p. 49.

93 See James Epstein, "Equality and No King': Sociability and Sedition. The Case of John Frost,' in *Romantic Sociability: Social Networks and Literary Culture in Britain, 1770-1840*, ed. Gillian Russell and Clara Tuite (Cambridge: Cambridge University Press, 2002), pp. 43-61; and John Barrell, 'Coffee-House Politicians,' *Journal of British Studies* 43 (2004), pp. 206-232

94 Beal, 'Why Should the Landlords Have the Best Songs,' p. 58.

95 Scrivener, *Seditious Allegories*, p. 111.

96 E. P. Thompson, 'Patrician Society, Plebeian Culture,' *Journal of Social History* 7 (1974), p. 396.

97 Scrivener, *Poetry and Reform*, p. 64.

98 On the song 'God Save the King', see Percy Alfred Scholes, *God Save the Queen! The History and Romance of the World's First National Anthem* (London: Oxford University Press, 1954).

99 London School of Economics, 'Spence and the Spenceans', *Spence's Songs*, fo. 17.

"The Rights of Man For Me", when he recalled 'in black Newgate I did pen this Song / My theme I've not altered you see / In jail or abroad whatever betide / My Struggles for Freedom shall be / Whatever Fate bring I will think, speak and sing'.[100] And, indeed, "think, speak and sing" is exactly what he did throughout his life. When Spence wrote a motto at the head of his pamphlet, *The Restorer of Society to its Natural State*, it ended with some self-implied and poetic words of wisdom about the 'bold political innovator': 'He leads us beyond the bounds of habit and custom, a necessary step to future advances; and though he may sometimes lead us wrong it is better perhaps to go wrong sometimes than stand still too long.'[101] What he failed to add was that this 'bold political innovator' would have them singing every step of the way.

100 Dickinson, *Political Works*, p. 129.

101 Ibid., p. 69.

THE CIVIL CITIZEN
1796
Publish'd by T Spence Turn-stile Holborn

Spence caricature, 'The Civil Citizen', 1796.
The crawling figure says: 'If The Law requires it we will Walk Thus'

11
The End of Oppression

•

Thomas Spence

(London 1795; 2nd edition of 1795)

YOUNG MAN: I hear there is another RIGHTS OF MAN by Spence, that goes farther than Paine's.

OLD MAN: Yet it goes no farther than it ought.

YOUNG MAN: I understand it suffers no private property in land, but gives it all to the parishes.

OLD MAN: In so doing it does right, the earth was not made for individuals.

YOUNG MAN: But people of all conditions have been so accustomed to think that the completion of all earthly felicity consists in the possession of landed property, that it is not likely they will generally be brought to give up the darling hopes of one time or other possessing a snug estate.

OLD MAN: It is true, if there were no injustice attending the state of a landlord, it is the most desirable and enviable state in the world, even infinitely more so than that of a king, or any placeman or pensioner whatsoever.

YOUNG MAN: It is indeed. Every body knows that well. For the landlord is entirely supreme, independent, and arbitrary, in his own domains, hence the title lord, and nothing binds him but his own leases, which he for his own interest grants. He is in no danger of losing his revenues, for he pays himself in a most haughty and lordly manner, without process, and without hardly condescending to ask. And when his rents are brought to him on the very hour they are due, his dignity will not permit him to be thankful.

OLD MAN: Why, I find you are at least half a Spensonian: You understand something of the nature of the enemy; and I dare say we shall not differ much in opinion.

YOUNG MAN: I have heard, read, and seen enough of their oppressions to make me wish them at an end, if possible.

OLD MAN: Whether it be possible we shall see by and by. But for the reasons before-mentioned, unless it be necessary that there should be in a state freemen and slaves, lordly men, and mean men, landlords cannot be suffered.

YOUNG MAN: But most people believe it would be unjust to deprive landed men of their property, as many of them have purchased their estates.

OLD MAN: Landed property always was originally acquired, either by conquest or encroachment on the common property of mankind. And as those public robbers did never show any degree of conscience or moderation and enslaved for ages, should in the day of reclamation, through an effeminate and foolish tenderness, neglect the precious opportunity of recovering at once the whole of their rights.

YOUNG MAN: But I am speaking of the seeming hardships of depriving modern purchasers of their property.

OLD MAN: Those modern purchasers are not ignorant of the manner in which landed property was originally obtained, neither are they sorry for it, nor for any other imposition by which they can get revenue. And every one knows that buying stolen goods is as bad as stealing.

YOUNG MAN: You are entirely right. The conduct of our rich men is not such as to create much respect for their property. The whole of their study is to create monopolies and to raise rents and revenues; and, like the grave, their endless cry is, Give! Give!

OLD MAN: And what was originally obtained by the sword, they determine to detain by the sword. Are not they and their minions now in arms under the name of yeomanry, volunteers etc? And what means the inveterate war commenced by the aristocracy of the world against France? They know that mankind once enlightened will not brook their lordliness, nor be content with their rights by piece-meal; therefore they exert every nerve to prevent light from spreading, and the union of the people.

YOUNG MAN: Indeed there cannot be any thing said for them. They exhibit to us too plainly all the properties and practices of robbers. Plunder, spoil and contributions they will at all events have though their ill-gotten lands should swim with blood; fully declaring themselves the true heirs and successors of the ancient Nimrods from whom they hold.

OLD MAN: Then let all men say, Spence has done right in rooting up such a combination of spoilers, and setting the world free from all exactions, imposts, and abuses, at once and for ever.

YOUNG MAN: It is amazing that Paine and the other democrats should level all their artillery at kings, without striking like Spence at this root of every abuse and of every grievance.

OLD MAN: The reason is evident: they have no chance of being kings; but many of them are already, and the rest foolishly and wickedly hope to be sometime or other landlords, lesser or greater.

YOUNG MAN: But do you think mankind will ever enjoy any tolerable degree of liberty and felicity, by having a reform in parliament, if landlords be still suffered to remain?

OLD MAN: You should first ask if the landed interest will let you have a reform, which they will take care to prevent. For a convention or parliament of the people would be at eternal war with the aristocracy. But granting they should so far forget their interest, they would soon recollect their mistake, and set about their true interest again, which is to counteract every species of public good. And full well are they furnished with every requisite for the diabolical work. The perpetual influx of wealth by their rents without toil or study, leaves them at full liberty and leisure to plot, and supplies them also with the means of fighting successfully against the interests of the working part of the community, and turn their labours to their own advantage.

YOUNG MAN: Yes, it is natural to expect that whether in the legislature or out of it, their whole study will be under every kind of government, to encrease the prices of what their estates produce, that their rents may rise. What shall we then account such a body of people, whose interests are only their own, and so opposite to all others, but a public enemy, a banditti that must always be watched and sometimes resisted.

OLD MAN: There you are wrong with your watching and resisting. Who is to watch and resist? Must not all the rest of the world do something for their bread? And are they not disarmed by the game laws, awed by the military, and by monopolies, state tricks, rents and taxes reduced to continual drudgery and starvation? How many days do you think such a brood of beggars could maintain themselves in a state of insurrection against their oppressors? They must away to their work again. The cries of the famished families break up their campaigns before they are well begun, and they must again return to the yoke, like other starved animals, for mere subsistence.

YOUNG MAN: O hopeless state of mankind!

OLD MAN: No, it is not yet hopeless, though the enemy like a numerous army, be garrisoned and quartered every where among us, and have all the strong holds, all the arms, and every advantage that triumphant and cruel invaders could wish for, yet will a true and universal knowledge of Spence's plain and simple system overturn them, and sweep all their greatness and lordliness away in one day, and leave the world in perpetual and perfect peace.

YOUNG MAN: Some seem to apprehend the mismanagement of the parish revenues, and so discourage people from thinking of that system.

OLD MAN: That is the natural work of the enemy, and must be expected. But it does not become democrats to doubt concerning it. For if men cannot manage the revenues and affairs of a parish, what must they do with a state? It is almost as absurd to answer such quibbles as to make them. How strange that men will turn the world upside down to get the management of a nation, and yet pretend to despair concerning a parish!!! It is too bad. The villainy is too barefaced. I am weary with combatting the vile sophistry of scoundrels that are oppressors, and of scoundrels that would be oppressors. But in Spence's *Pigs' Meat*, you will find the parish system represented in such a variety of ways, and so plainly evidencing to every reader, the easy and practicable transition from this scene of oppression and woe, to perfect freedom and felicity, that I must refer you to that incomparable work for complete satisfaction on the subject.

YOUNG MAN: I thank you. I will take the first opportunity of perusing that excellent book. But in the mean time, for the sake of conversation, let us suppose that a whole nation no matter whether America, France, Holland, or any other, but as to England, it is entirely out of the question, were fully convinced of the excellence of this system, and universally wishing its establishment, I should be glad to know the most easy method of doing so, and with least bloodshed.

OLD MAN: In a country so prepared, let us suppose a few thousands of hearty determined fellows well armed and appointed with officers, and having a committee of honest, firm, and intelligent men to act as a provisionary government, and to direct their actions to the proper object. If this committee published a manifesto or proclamation, directing the people in every parish to take, on receipt thereof, immediate possession of the whole landed property within their district, appointing a committee to take charge of the same, in the name and for the use of the inhabitants; and that every landholder should immediately, on pain of confiscation and imprisonment, deliver to the said parochial committee, all writings and documents relating to their estates, that they might immediately be burnt; and that they should likewise disgorge at the same time into the hands of the said committee, the last payments received from their tenants, in order to create a parochial fund for immediate use, without calling upon the exhausted people. If this proclamation was generally attended to, the business was settled at once; but if the aristocracy arose to contend the matter, let the people be firm and desperate, destroying them root and branch, and strengthening their hands by the rich confiscations. Thus the war would be carried on at the expence of the wealthy enemy, and the soldiers of liberty beside the hope of sharing in the future felicity of the country, being well paid, would be steady and bold. And wherever the lands were taken possession of by the people, (which by all means should be as early accomplished as possible) the grand resource of the aristocracy, the rents, would be cut off, which would soon reduce them to reason, and they would become as harmless as other men.

YOUNG MAN: If people could but thus become honest and wise enough to cut off at once the resources of the enemy, they might soon get rid of oppression. But it is a pity they do not perceive the immediate and inexpressible blessings that would infallably result from such a revolution.

OLD MAN: The good effects of such a charge, would be more exhilirating and reviving to the hunger-bitten and despairing children of oppression, than a benign and sudden spring to the frost-bitten earth, after a long and severe winter. Only think of the many millions of rents that are now paid to those self-created nephews of God Almighty, the landed interest, which is literally paid for nothing but to create masters. — I say only think of all this money, circulating among the people, and there promoting industry and happiness, and all the arts and callings useful in society; would not the change be unspeakable? This would neither be a barren revolution of mere unproductive rights, such as many contend for, nor yet a glut of sudden and temporary wealth as if acquired by conquest; but a continual flow of permanent wealth established by a system of truth and justice, and guaranteed by the interest of every man, woman, and child in the nation. The government also of such a people could no longer be oppressive. The democratic parishes would take care how they suffered their money to be lavished away upon state speculations. And their senators, who could not be men of landed property, would be found to be much more honest and true to the services of their constituents than our now-a-days so much boasted gentlemen of independent fortunes.

When a people create landlords, they create a numerous host of hereditary tyrants and oppressors, who not content with their lordly revenues of rents, seize also upon the government, and parcel it out among themselves, and take as enormous salaries for the places they occupy therein, as if they were poor men; so that the rents which the foolish people foolishly pay for nothing, and the poor dull ass the public, become thus loaded, as it were, with two pair of panyers. So then, whoever will be so silly good-natured and over-generous as to pay rents to a set of individuals, must not be surprized, if their masters by all ways and means and pretences should keep them to it, and give scope sufficient to their liberal propensities.

FINIS.

12

A Supplement to the History of Robinson Crusoe Being the History of Crusonia, or Robinson Crusoe's Island

•

Thomas Spence

(Newcastle Upon Tyne, 2nd ed., 1782)

After giving a stale description of courses and storms, manner of landing. etc. I now proceed to tell you something of the government, religion, and customs of this famous island, as they are at present, and to give you some idea of their rise and progress.

Soon after Robinson's last visit to this island, the people he left, established a good understanding with the savages on the continent, and got wives from thence; by which means, and on account of many of their new relations by these marriages, coming over, and settling with them, it quickly became so populous, that every foot of land was occupied, and claimed by some or other; and by leaving it to their eldest sons as in England, (for the Europeans taught them their customs) the better half of the rising generation could get no vacant spot to live on, which occasioned great uneasiness in the minds of those unfortunate youngsters. The disturbances from this cause, became at length so serious, as to make it necessary to settle some authority and government to keep the peace, and to determine what people might call their own. Accordingly for that purpose, the whole of the people assembled; when some of the old Europeans, being yet alive, spoke to this effect.

"The customs hitherto followed, with regard to holding possessions, are not of our invention, but are copied from our native country, Europe; and as far as we know, are used in all the world beside. But as the business we are upon, is the settling of a form of government for our common good, security, and satisfaction, it is fit that every man offer that scheme, which to him appears most eligible; that from the many proposed, the best, or that which shall appear the best, drawn from them all, be chosen. And as we have not experienced, nor indeed know of any other than what we have already introduced from Europe, we beg leave, once more, to lay before you the outlines as there practised, viz.

1. The land, in Europe, was at first possessed, and handed down to posterity, as hath been done among us; which method you are

nevertheless dissatisfied with.

2. The possessors, there, may let out, or not let sell, or make over their landed property, to whom, and upon what conditions, they will.

3. None but land-owners are admitted into senates or parliaments, and other offices of state or trust, or allowed to vote for a representative; and their estates must always be in proportion to their trust; as they believe men of great estates to be farthest above temptations to dishonesty.

This plan, is the foundation, upon which some of the freest, and most renowned governments of the world are built; which, if we reject, we likely will adopt a worse; but if any can propose better, he, is welcome."

"That may soon be done," cried the malcontents, "for sure it is not possible worse can be proposed for our interest. For we would thereby not only be reduced to tenants, but tenants at will; and we could not be certain but some time or other we might be denied a habitation on the island, even for rent, and so be obliged to seek abode among the savages on the continent whenever the interests or fancies of the landlords should prompt them thereto. Besides, as the legislature and all other authority would be wholly in the landed interest, we, and others hereafter in our condition, would be rendered mute, insignificant slaves, living on the earth only by permission: having our lives, liberty, and subsistence, lying wholly at their mercy. No, you must first get us to believe we are of some other species, for at present we think we are men as well as our fathers, or elder brothers, or any land-owners whatever, and shall act accordingly. We have the same right to liberty, subsistence (and consequently to land) and to be of the legislature, and other offices, as they; and our posterity, through all generations, will be born with the same privileges. So to do justice to ourselves and posterity we intend to have no landlords but the parishes, and to make every parish a corporation, and every man a parishioner, or member of that parish, and that only, he last dwelt a full year in, notwithstanding from what other parish, country, or nation, he might come prior to such settlement. A small rent or rate, shall, according to the determination of the parishioners, be paid by every person, suitable to the valuation of the housen and land he possesses, to the parish treasury to be put to such uses as the majority please; and each parish shall have all the uncontrollable power that can possibly be made good use of by a corporation, and be connected only by a parliament for the common strength and welfare of the whole."

This scheme so favourable to the malcontents, was immediately adopted by them, nor could all the precedents, their opponents, deduced from other nations, avail any thing; for as in all disputes the right commonly goes with the might, so here, the landlords being the weaker party, were obliged to submit, and the parish system took place.

The above relation, which I had on my first enquiries soon after landing, though confirmed by all I spoke with, could not gain my entire credit, on account of the numberless objections my mind raised against this scheme, and impossibilities I thought attended it, till my own senses found the truth of the story in every one of their customs; nay, my prepossessions were so strong, that I was clear a society could not subsist upon a plan so repugnant to any thing I had either heard or thought of: so to ease my disturbed mind I set to work to examine every thing I saw, with the greatest strictness; and the first subject, that fell under my consideration, was the town I reside in, which is the capital of the island, and all its colonies.

This town is built on each side of a commodious harbour, a considerable river falls into it, and at the upper end of the harbour there is a most elegant bridge. The town extends about a mile on each side along the shore, and about half a mile outward towards the country, and contains about fifty thousand inhabitants. Four parishes meet and have their churches in it, two on each side, whose steeples are very magnificent, and a great ornament to the town. It is full of superb and well furnished shops, and has every appearance of grandeur, opulence, and convenience, one can conceive to be in a large place, flourishing with trade and manufactures.

This view quite astonished me, for instead of anarchy, idleness, poverty, and meanness, the natural consequences, as I narrowly thought of a ridiculous levelling scheme, nothing but order, industry, wealth, and the most pleasing magnificence! So being anxious to know the utmost of this new fashioned commonwealth, I took occasion to fall into the following dialogue, with one of my informers, whose name is Mann.

Captain: And so none, notwithstanding the splendid appearance they make, and the extensive manner they carry on trade, have estates nor can purchase any?

Mr. Mann: No, nor is it likely ever will, nor does the happiness of human life, or business require it to be.

Capt: Would it not tend to make people more industrious if they could lay out their riches in possessions?

Mann: I am surprised to hear you ask that question. Look either to us or to the Jews, and see if there be any want of industry in acquiring wealth as far as law allows, though we can buy no land; but on the contrary you will find a general industry, not one idle; for riches unsupported by an estate, would soon take wings and fly away, without some other supply, which consideration sets every one on doing something, though they may have plenty. But in your country, what great incitement, pray, can it be to industry, to be obliged to give the cream of one's endeavours, unthanked, to the landlord? For what landlord was ever yet thankful for his rents? They think the tenants rather owe thanks to them for permission to live on their earth forsooth! I can never think of them but with detestation. I can compare them and their castles to nothing but the giants, and their castles in romances, who were said to be a terror and destruction to all the people around; and must certainly have been invented for a satire upon landlords. For what is there that the giants did, which the landlords do not? Did the giants eat the people and their children? The landlords eat their meat, and wear their cloaths. Did the giants confine them in horrid dungeons? How many have the merciless landlords destroyed in goals? How many executed; and how many more, of their poor vassals, have they led to the wars like bull-dogs by virtue of their feudal tenures? And in countries where those gigantic powers, are curtailed a little, do they not still make the laws? Harass and imprison the miserable tenants for their exorbitant rents? Impress them to defend and conquer countries wherein, as a reward for their labour, they would be severely punished for pulling a nut or eating grass if they could? And which of them dare meddle with a hare, or a partridge? Wherefore I must be allowed to pronounce landlords proper and real giants, the heirs and successors of the greatest and vilest monsters ever walked the face of the earth. Giant-killer must then be, as it hath ever been esteemed, a highly honoured name; and here you have the satisfaction of beholding a whole nation of giant-killers, and a land where no such monsters as landlords can breed.

Capt: But I am afraid landlords are as much the produce of all lands, as other kinds of monsters are of the Nile, and it will be difficult to part or keep them long asunder.

Mann: I agree with you. that where there are men, there will be landlords, so heaven hath ordained; but then, we have so provided, that we are *all* landlords, and yet no giants; so that the least change in our excellent system, would effect the interest of every one, which makes every one a guardian to the commonweal.

Capt: Very true: but I have heard of bribery doing mischievous things to societies, and even overturning some; for it will make men vote, fight, or do any thing against the interests both of the present generation, and all that are to come, which makes me tremble for your state.

Mann: And why not tremble for others if they be worth purchasing? Or would you have us throw away what is good that we may not lose it? You shall see we have done all we can to secure our rights, but, if they will go. after all, then, let them go; when all is over, and at the worst, we can but have landlords. But in all human probability neither voting nor fighting can hurt us. For you must understand we never vote but by ballot, or in a secret manner, either in parochial or parliamentary business. Now suppose you would bribe the whole of the voters in any affair, and I were one of them, I would reason thus with myself: If I vote as I am bribed, I wrong the interest of the publick. Posterity, and myself, and if there be but one vote, against my briber, he may say it is mine, and if I deny it, so may he that really voted, and has as good a chance to be believed, there being no witness; whereby I will have the mortification to think I have wronged my country and conscience without being able to clear myself of your suspicions. So in consequence of this reasoning I would vote against you and so would all the others from the same consideration. Let us see how the case will stand then? Why you would chide me privately (for you durst not do it publicly) for not voting for you though hired. I would say, how do you prove that? Because say you I have not one vote, and therefore not yours; (for if you had but one vote I would lay claim to it.) Well then I would answer, I have the comfort to think I am no worse than others. Besides if I had voted for you, others would have had as good a claim to the merit of the action in your sight, while I would have had the whole of the guilt, and an equal share of the blame. You will be ready to say. I did not act like a man of honor to you, after taking the wages, not to do the work. True. I broke faith, with a bad man, that wanted to bring some evil on my country, and posterity; but. at the same time, I pleased God and my conscience and did a signal service to my country, For, we will suppose you so powerful, that it would be dangerous to refuse you to your face, and so could have no other way of saving ourselves, which I hope will do so effectually, even from such temptations; so there is an end to your hurting us by voting.

Capt: I must own so long as you vote by ballot or secretly there is no hurting you in that quarter. But is it not beneath freemen to vote in such a clandestine manner as if you had not the courage to act honestly in the face of the world? Moreover, you lose all the praise of your good deeds, which is a general incitement to worthy actions.

Mann: In your country they vote in the open manner you commend. What is the consequence? Why, the minister tells you, it is necessary to have a majority at any rate for the dispatch of business, which is the same thing as to plead for no parliament at all. So a majority he gets, who vote for him. through thick and thin, in spite of the sun, and all the eyes of their country. The minority, indeed, harangue and fume, as if something were the matter, to get the majority to understand what they know as well as themselves; but they are too fast asleep, in the lap of corruption, to regard either them, or the praises of their country. So you see the weak influence of fame, even among senators; what effect can it then have among the poor freeholders, and burgesses after such an example! This general corruption, and jarring, sets all your newswriters, and pamphleteerers, on work to shew their cobbling genius in their schemes for mending the constitution, and redressing grievances, by their place and triennial bills, &c. whereas the shoes were so ill made at first, are so worn, rotten, and patched already, that they are not worth further trouble or expence, but ought to be thrown to the dunghill, and a new pair made, neat and handsome, yet, easy, as for the foot of one that loves freedom and ease. Then would your controversies about this and the other method of cobbling be done away, and you walk along the rugged and dirty path of life, easy and dry-shod.

And now you shall witness with your own eyes that force is as unlikely to succeed against us as your secret corruption. Therefore you must go with me to-morrow to a neighbouring parish about two miles off, it being their general review day, when all the men thereof are to go through their military exercise. Every parish has a general field day once in a quarter of a year appointed by act of parliament, when they are reviewed by an able general chosen by the same authority, who goes constantly about from parish to parish through his district, which consists of thirty-nine contiguous parishes, so that he has three to review in a week, or one every other working day throughout the year, except when the appointed day happens to be improper on account of weather, when it is deferred to the next; but if that also will not suit, then that parish will not be reviewed that quarter, and he goes to the next parish in rotation. These field-days are kept very punctually and are noted in the almanacs as the fairs, and serve the young people instead of wkes.

Accordingly when next morning came, which was exceedingly fine, we went to the military ground of the aforesaid parish, which was very neat and convenient, and tolerably large, surrounded with several rows of trees, with seats underneath for the spectators, and kept entirely for that and such like public uses. The parish bells rung merrily, numbers of spectators from the neighbouring parishes, with all the old men, women, and children that could get from the same parish were solacing themselves in the morning sun around the place. Presently the men of the parish appeared, those who had good horses on horseback, those of a colour together, others trailing field-pieces of brass, and others with muskets. The boys too were classed according to their sizes, with small muskets and cannon, suitable to their strength, and the whole with proper officers, colours. music, and an uniform dress, which last was peculiar to the parish, as every parish has its uniform, which they generally chuse to wear at all times. They made a gallant appearance, and all in their most happy countenances, as if going to some agreeable sport. Each emulated another in obedience to command, and dexterity of action. What contributes greatly to this. is. that nothing but conspicuous merit can advance any to be officers and they must go gradually through every station to the highest, if their merit can carry them so far. They went through their several manoeuvres like veterans, but the boys in particular were a pleasing sight. No play whatever gives them such delight as this military exercise, which they apply to with such eagerness, that before they leave school, or are fit for any other employment, they have it as compleatly as the oldest among them. For this purpose all due encouragement is given them, a particular Instance of which appeared at this time. They made a mock fight with the men and drove them off the field, which closed the scene.

We spent the remainder of the day in the same parish, where there was nothing but festivity and joy; and among other sports, were shooting-matches, and cudgel-playing, which are favourite diversions, and frequently encouraged by medals and premiums from the parish treasuries.

I can never enough admire the beauty of the country; it has more the air of a garden, or rather a paradise, than a general country scene; and indeed it is properly a continuation of gardens and orchards. For besides the infinite number of real gardens, all the fields, even for meadow and pasture, are strewed very thick with fruit-trees, and appear like as many orchards; and the corn is cultivated in rows, and as carefully as garden-herbs. The houses and every thing about them, are surprisingly neat, and resemble in every respect the habitations of gentry, even so much that I could not imagine for some time, where the labouring people resided. The parish provides good, substantial, and elegant houses, but obliges the inhabitants to keep them clean. There is no such thing through all the country as a dirty or patched window, a smoky house, or a broken pavement. And as the people never dread their leases being ended or the being turned out. So like other freeholders they spare no pains in making such conveniencies as suit their different callings and inclinations, nor in ornamenting their walls and gardens with all the pride of the vegetable world. These delightful dwellings are scattered, very rank over the whole country; and, in a word, it seems to have been intended both by God and man, for a nursery and habitation, suitable to the chief of the creation, and convinces one sufficiently, what the deity, and rational creatures can effect.

We growing pretty hearty, and partaking of the universal joy around us, referred our political observations till another time, and so concluding the day, marched homeward well satisfied with our entertainment. But meeting again a day or two after, we fell naturally into the following dialogue.

Mann: Now our whole country is trained and peopled as you have seen, I suppose you have now no hopes of fighting us out of our liberties; and if there were a possibility of voting them away, we would not nevertheless part with them. Nay. we will not suffer any act in the least impolitic, to give us uneasiness long; for we are too knowing and powerful to be gulled or browbeat, which makes our parliament very careful how they pass acts.

Capt: I agree with you that you have good reason to think yourselves secure; yet, I have many doubts, which you must be kind enough to resolve, and this is one: I am surprised how an uninhabited island should, in scarce a century, become so populous.

Mann. You know what number of men Robinson left on the island; you have seen how they got wives, with a fresh addition of people, the relations of their wives coming along with them; and how the parish system took place. This last no sooner happened, than they made a law to admit all strangers to visit them, and to encourage them to settle among them; and to that end, to naturalize every one that should rest a twelvemonth in any parish; and at the expiration of that term, they were to become free parishioners, or members of that parish; with the same privileges of voting, holding offices, etc. as any mn. This law was made to encrease the number of men in the state, and you shall see how well it answered the purpose. But you must understand, though they had just before fallen out about the insufficiency of land for them all, yet it was not because there was too little to maintain them; far from it, for it is impossible to determine how many, by good culture, a country is capable of maintaining; but those that were first, carved too largely; for instead of taking as much as just to serve themselves and families, without wasting it, and leaving the rest for others to do the like, as is done with the fish of the sea and the water of the well, every one took as much as he could with any face mark off; by which means many had more than would maintain a thousand; and yet their younger sons, by their fine European customs, could not get an inch, which was the reason, as you have already seen, of the parish system taking place. So, to return, as they wanted men for strength, and had plenty of country and traffic for their support, they took all opportunities of informing the savages of their resolutions, and of inviting them over to make trial of living among them. Many therefore came, and proud of acquiring equal property and privileges, in a parish, or rather little common-wealth, with every one else, on so short a settlement, each presently pitched upon a residence, got a piece of ground, and a house built on it by the parish, and so fell to work; and which was no small encouragement, what every one earned was his own, without deduction of toll or tax, except the parish rate to the treasury; which they could not murmur at paying, as it was no more to them than to the oldest inhabitants, and as they would soon have a vote in the laying it on, and its management too. So, one few led the way for another, and the more that came, the more were ready to come, till no parish had an uninhahited spot left.

In the mean time the country was filling with husbandmen who required room; so were the villages with merchants, and Robinson Crusoe's, Jack-of-all-trades' disciples, the mechanics; with ingenious persons accidentally, or on purpose, from all the nearest civilized countries, who only required houses, shops, etc. suitable to their respective businesses. Some villages, on account of accidents and conveniencies for trade, encreased above others, and became towns; and this town, on account of the excellent harbour, encreased above them all. and became the capital. And thus has this island become what you see it.

But this is not all. Our excellent government, by refusing to take none of the human race under its protection, and allowing every man to be equal in his own neighbourhood, or parish, with every other privilege of his birthright, and, at the same time, all the blessings of society, has not only peopled this island with multitudes of happy beings, but a large extent of the continent opposite to us, on the same plan; for by the continual confluence of people, and the surprising increase from matrimony, (which every body entered readily into, and does yet, and will do, while the parish system lasts, from the easiness of living, and the few pernicious distinctions, etc. we have to lie in the way to break off love affairs, so that it is as rare here to be deprived of one's first love as it is in your barbarous countries to enjoy them) it was at last feared, enough of food could not be raised for the support of them all, notwithstanding the prudent methods taken by the parishes, to let no individual possess more land than he was likely to manage in the best manner; and the giving of medals and premiums out of their treasuries, for the greatest improvements in husbandry and gardening; and for raising the best crops according to the extent of ground, etc. so it was resolved in parliament, to take a considerable piece of the continent, on the side next us, into possession, and constitute a few new parishes on the shore; to settle their bounderies, and build a guildhall in the most convenient place for each; to make a present to the treasury of each new parish, of a sum of money, from the national treasury, as a stock for them to begin upon; and also a gratuity to each person that should first go and settle in them. Whereupon numbers of all trades, especially husbandmen, went over, and soon put them upon a respectable footing, and in a short time they were able to send us as much provisions as we chused. But these too in a small time, becoming sufficiently stocked, other parishes were marked out at the back of them, and begun in the same manner; and so we encrease continually, laying parish to parish as occasion requires. But nobody is allowed to go beyond the parishes to carve for himself, for nothing less than a whole parish is taken off the waste at once, and that is by parliamentary authority, as before described; which is taken care not to be done so quickly, as to occasion a thinness of inhabitants, or an uncultivated aspect in the old parishes. People may hunt, or feed flocks, and herds, beyond the bounds of the parishes, and pitch tents; but not appropriate or build.

Capt: Will you please now to let me know the nature, number, etc. of your parliament.

Mann. The number of members was settled at three hundred at the first, when there were but few parishes and has never been encreased since; for it is thought to be a sufficient number, to determine on any affair; and they propose new subjects, debate, and make their laws much in the manner of British parliaments, excepting that they vote by ballot, or secretly. At first when the number of parishes were few, four or five would have fallen to the share of each parish to elect; and when it happened there were odd members, besides giving each an equal number, they cast lots to know which parishes should elect them. But there are now, by the vast encrease of parishes on the continent, which have the same privileges as these on the island, more parishes than senators; wherefore every so many neighbouring ones, are classed together to elect one among them, that is, the whole number of parishes including new and old, wherever situated, are divided into three hundred lots or classes, as equal as possible, and each class is to elect one representative.

But these elections being by ballot, and every man voting in his own parish, occasion neither animosity nor confusion; and bribery as already shewn, being of no use, is without existence. So, as all the parishes in a class vote always in the same day, it is presently and quickly decided, by adding the votes in each parish for each candidate together.

It makes no odds to them whether the person they chuse for the senate, or any other office, be poor or rich, if he be but properly qualified; for all parish officers have suitable cloaths and salaries, out of their parish treasury, and those whose offices extend beyond the bounds of a parish, or to the service of the nation in general, as senators, officers of state, ambassadors, generals, admirals, etc. have suitable cloaths and salaries out of the national treasury: and so is every thing whatever for the public service in general supported by this general treasury.

Capt: Pray how is this national treasury supplied?

Mann: In a manner, perhaps, very different from your conceptions. The landlords the parishes, pay all the taxes here. The expences of the state, which the parliament regulates, are divided among them according to their abilities, and they send their shares at the time appointed, and so it is done; and thus our nation has no occasion to run in debt. The parish treasuries are supplied as said before, by the rate they lay on the houses, lands, mines. etc. according to their valuation, as well as by the sale of wood. etc. and there is neither toll nor tax beside. The parishes build and repair the houses, make proper roads and hedges, plant trees, and in a word, do all the business of a landlord. And you have seen what sort of landlords they are. I suppose you do not meet with much amiss, or out of repair. And it is no wonder, for a parish has many heads to contrive what is proper to be done, and the contriver has also the happiness of being qualified both to propose and vote for the performance of it. Instead of debating on this and the other method of cobbling the state, as with you, for ours needs no cobbling, it is common to see all degrees of people debating how any thing in their own neighbourhood might either be embellished or improved to the public good. As whether such an unprofitable spot might be drained, this planted with trees, or that made into a close or garden, etc. for every man that wishes to rise to preferment, must be shewing his neighbours, who have power to do it, some specimens of his public spirit; which keeps up a constant emulation among them. And you may frequently hear the fond mother caressing her darling boy, and crying he will be an admiral, general, senator, or any great officer she pleases to mention, and yet none can contradict it; as he may, for ought any body knows, be one or all that she prophesies, one after another, if his merit be sufficient. This is great encouragement for parents to bring up their children properly, and indeed makes our youth, as was observed of Jephthah's children, each one resemble the children of a king. And truly in education they need not be inferior, for every parish has a free-school, with the best of teachers, as also a public library, containing copies and translations of all the best books in the world, so that every one may read and inform himself as far as he pleases. There is also a national university, which every parish is allowed to keep one at, where all human learning is taught to perfection; and this one, is chosen by ballot out of the most promising youths. But this spirit of emulation would make continual strife, and dissension, if the manner of deciding every affair were not by ballot, or in a secret manner, so that none can know who is for or against him, which makes every one sit down contented with his fate. The being indecently eager for preferment would be the surest way to prevent it. — I must not omit that even our amusements are elegantly provided for out of this parish treasury, for every parish has its theatre and assembly rooms, to which all have access gratis. Thus each parish is a little polished Athens, as well as warlike Sparta.

Capt: This delights me much, but I must beg leave, to make another objection: Does nobody repine that the place they occupy is not their own; that they have to pay to the parish rent for it; that they cannot sell or give it away; and, that they cannot put their posterity in possession thereof, and all the improvements they may have made, at their decease?

Mann: You could not in any country possess a place more properly, or have more encouragement to make improvements than here. For there is no fear of enemies to dispossess you, none would be so mad as to attempt it. As to what you are pleased to call rent, have possessions where you will, you must still pay towards public affairs, and that to some purpose. Where are all your land-taxes, your cesses, customs tolls, and tithes which every freeholder pays. What is paid here is only for the same purposes that landlords pay these taxes, viz. for public affairs; so in that point you are as properly a landlord here as any where, and with regard to the permanency of possessions: Indeed a man with us would not be allowed to let his land run wild, or destroy his houses, for this would be to the hurt of the society of which he is a member, and a misusing of their talent; they would in consequence of such behaviour have a right to resent it, and put their talent into other hands. For the land is not made for this man or that man, but for all mankind in general. Even among savages a man cannot have an uncontrollable liberty; he would not be allowed to make wanton havock of the animals and fruits of the country, so as to cause others feel the effects of it. In such a case they would declare war upon him, and extirpate him as a nuisance and pest to the earth. But if a person here behave any thing tolerably, he may remain in his possession for a thousand years, if he could live as long, and leave it to any of his posterity that had not a possession; but if he have no posterity, or they be all settled, and unwilling to give up what they have to go to it, (for none can enjoy two inheritances) then it falls to the disposal of the parish, who gives it to the first that applies for it that has not a possession; but if more candidates than one appear, then the competition is determined by ballot: thus is every indulgence granted that the nature of real society can permit, and he that would have more may go live by himself.

Capt: Aye, and very fit he should.

Here, after proper acknowledgements on my part, for his civility, we ended our political dialogue, when I had been about a month here, and now I have been over great part of the country, both on the island and continent, and find every thing not only agreeable to what I was told, but far exceeding all description. So that I am determined never more to visit poor wrangling Britannia, once so dear to me, till I be certain this paradisical system has taken place in it; and then I would do my utmost to be with you to sing "Britons never will be Slaves." but as it is, Crusons never will be slaves, seems much the properest.

This puts me in mind to tell you of the names given to this famous island, and these are Cruson or Crusonia,from Robinson Crusoe, the founder of the empire; and the inhabitants Crusons or Crusonians. They likewise have him, poor fellow, upon all their standards, ensigns, flags, etc. just as represented on the frontispiece of his history, which I was mightily pleased to see, as I always respected him from my first acquaintance. They name the continent, which they have colonized, Fridinea, from his Man Friday, because it was his country, but this is only a provincial name, to distinguish the continent, from the island, for the general name, of the whole nation, both on the island and continent, is the United Parishes of Crusonia; intimating, that each parish is as independent of each other, as distinct and separate states can be of so small a size, that like other petty states must be united under one guardian head, to hinder them from altering their own constitutions, and for mutual defence both against the injustices of one another, and of greater societies: and as an emblem of their united strength, they have a bundle of rods on the colours, lying on the ground before Robinson Crusoe, with this motto, "Who can hurt us while thus combined."

The Independence of these little communities prevents going out of the parish for justice, and renders all lawyers and attornies unnecessary. For the laws are few, explicit, and the same in every parish, being made by their common legislature; and there being no estates to contend for, litigations are seldom: and the mayor, with the other magistrates, together with a jury, decide in cases of debt, fraud, assault, or any thing else, in a final manner. In these courts every one pleads his own cause, and is certain of having justice speedily administrated, without a fee!

As to religion, which I had almost omited, toleration is allowed to all opinions, so long as they do not appear prejudicial to society; and whatever religion the majority of a parish is of, is supported by the parish treasury, which pays the clergymen's salaries without any tithes; no perquisites, fees, or collections whatever, being allowed but the aforesaid parish-rate for publick matters of any kind. This religion has also the use of the parish church, but the minority if they set up any other religion must bear the expence of it themselves. So you will find Lutherianism, Calvinism, Anabaptism, Quakerism, and almost all opinions, have their parishes, yet all live in love and unity; for they are all too knowing, as remarked before, to differ about the way of getting to heaven; they are glad to see people going by any road.

It would be endless expatiating on the executive power, magistrates. judicial proceedings. Trial by jury, liberty of the press, and of speech, etc. which I assure you equal any thing of the kind in your country; for not only your government, but all governments, are as well known to Crusonians as to you; and they are more likely to adopt such things as suit them, from their uncommon facility of knowing, and the impossibility of opposing reason and truth among them.

And now be not uneasy though your curiosity with regard to every item should not be fully satisfied, but comfort yourself with this reflection, that things may be done properly though you should not be completely informed of the manner; and indeed I have hopes you will excuse a more circumstantial detail, as I have given you, in so particular a manner, the construction and movement of the great wheels of the machine, that you cannot mistake the motion of the smaller. — I shall now conclude with the *Crusonian Creed* on matters of property, viz.

All men, to land, may lay an equal claim;
But goods, and gold, unequal portions frame:
The first, because, all men on land, must live;
The second's the reward industry ought to give.
I am, etc.

13
The Constitution of Spensonia

•

Thomas Spence

(London, 1803)

Declaration

The Spensonian People convinced that forgetfulness and contempt for the natural Rights of Man, are the only cause of the Crimes and Misfortunes of the World, have resolved to expose in a declaration their sacred and inalienable rights, in order that all citizens being always able to compare the Acts of the Government, with the ends of every social Institution, may never suffer themselves to be oppressed and degraded by Tyranny; and that the people may always have before their eyes the basis of their liberty and happiness; the magistrates, the rule of their conduct and duty; and legislators, the object of their mission.

They acknowledge therefore and proclaim in the presence of the Supreme Being, the following declaration of the Rights of Man and Citizens:

1. The end of Society is common happiness. Government is instituted to secure to man the enjoyment of his natural and impresceptible rights.

2. These rights are Equality, Liberty, Safety, and Property, natural and acquired.

3. All human beings are equal by nature and before the law, and have a continual and inalienable property in the Earth, and its natural productions.

4. The law is the free and solemn expression of the general will. It ought to be the same for all, whether it protects or punishes. It cannot order but what is just and useful to Society. It cannot forbid but what is hurtful.

5. Social laws, therefore, can never proscribe natural rights.

6. Thus, after a Parish, out of its Rents, has remitted to the State and County, its legal quota towards their expenses, and provided for defraying its own proper contingencies, the remainder of the Rents is the indisputable joint property of all the Men, Women, and Children having settlement in the parish, and ought to be equally divided among them.

7. All male Citizens are equally admissible to public employments. Free people know no other motives of preference in their Elections than virtue and Talents.

8. Liberty is that power which belongs to a Man of doing everything that does not hurt the right of another. Its principle is nature: Its rule justice: Its protection, the law, and its moral limits are defined by this maxim: "Do not to another what you would not wish done unto yourself."

9. The right of manifesting one's thoughts and opinions either by the press or in any other manner: the right of assembling peaceably, and the free exercise of religious worship cannot be forbidden. The necessity of announcing these rights supposes either the presence or the recent remembrance of despotism.

10. Whatever is not forbidden by the law, cannot be prevented. No one can be forced to do that which the law does not order.

11. Safety consists in the protection granted by Society to each Citizen for the preservation of his person, his rights and his property.

12. The law avenges public and individual liberty of the abuses committed against them by power.

13. No person can be accused, arrested, or confined but in cases determined by the law, and according to the form which it prescribes. Every Citizen summoned or seized by the authority of the law ought immediately to obey, he renders himself culpable by resistance.

14. Every act exercised against a Man to which the cases in the law do not apply, and in which its forms are not observed, is arbitrary and tyrannical. Respect for the laws forbid him to submit to such acts; and if attempts are made to execute them by violence he has a right to repel force by force.

15. Those who shall solicit, dispatch, sign, execute, or cause to be executed arbitrary acts are culpable and ought to be punished.

16. Every Man being supposed innocent until he has been declared guilty, if it is judged indispensable to arrest him all severity not necessary to secure his person ought to be strictly repressed by the law.

17. No one ought to be tried and punished until he has been legally summoned, and in virtue of a law published previous to the commission of the crime. A law which should punish crimes committed before it existed would be tyrannical. The retroactive effect given to a law would be a crime.

18. The law ought not to decree any punishments but such as are strictly and evidently necessary. Punishments ought to be proportioned to the crime, and useful to Society.

19. The right of property is that which belongs to every Citizen to enjoy and dispose of according to his pleasure, his property, revenues, labour, and industry. Here his property in land is excepted, which being inseparably incorporated with that of his fellow Parishioners is inalienable.

20. No kind of labour, culture, or commerce can be forbidden to the industrious citizen.

21. Every man may engage his services and his time, but he cannot sell himself; his person is not alienable property. The law does not acknowledge servitude, there can exist only an engagement of care and gratitude between the man who labours and the man who employs him.

22. No one can be deprived of the smallest portion of his property without his consent, except when the public necessity, legally ascertained, evidently require it, and on condition of a just and previous indemnification.

23. No public revenue can be established but for general ability, and to relieve the public wants. Every Citizen has a right to concur in the establishment of such revenue; to watch over the use made of it, and to call for a statement of expenditure.

24. Public aids are a sacred debt. The Society is obliged to provide for the subsistence of the unfortunate, either by procuring them work, or by securing the means of existence to those who are unable to labour.

25. Instruction is the want of all, and the Society ought to favour with all its power the progress of the public reason; and to place Instruction, within the reach of every Citizen.

26. The social guarantee consists in the actions of all to secure to each the enjoyment and preservation of his Rights. This guarantee rests on the national Sovereignty.

27. The Social Guarantee cannot exist if the limits of public functions are not clearly determined by the law, and if the responsibility of all public functionaries is not secured.

28. The Sovereignty resides in the people; it is one and indivisible, imprescriptable and inalienable.

29. No proportion of the people can exercise the power of the whole; but each section of the sovereign assembled ought to enjoy the right of expressing its will in perfect liberty. Every individual who arrogates to himself the Sovereignty, or who usurps the exercise of it, ought to be put to death by freemen.

30. A people have always the right of revising, amending, and changing their

constitution. One Generation cannot subject to its law future generations.

31. Every Citizen has an equal right of concurring in the formation of the law and in the nomination of his mandatores or agents.

32. Public Functions cannot be considered as distinctions or rewards, but as duties.

33. Crimes committed by the mandatores of the people and their agents ought never to remain unpunished. No one has a right to pretend to be more inviolable than other Citizens.

34. The right of presenting petitions to the depositories of Public Authority belongs to every individual. The exercise of this right cannot in any case be forbidden, suspended, or limited.

35. Resistance to oppression is the consequence of the other rights of man.

36. Oppression is exercised against the social body, when even one of its members is oppressed. Oppression is exercised against each member when the social body is oppressed.

37. When the Government violates the rights of the people, Insurrection becomes to the people, and to every portion of the people, the most sacred and the most indispensible of duties.

OF THE COMMONWEALTH

1. The Spensonian Commonwealth is one and indivisible.

OF THE DISTRIBUTION OF THE PEOPLE

2. The Spensonian people are distributed for the exercise of its sovereignty and for the management of its landed property into parishes.

3. It is distributed for administration and for justice into counties and parishes.

OF THE STATE OF CITIZENS

4. Every Man or Woman born, or otherwise having acquired a settlement in a parish of Spensonia and of the age of twenty-one years complete; is admitted to the exercise of the rights of a Spensonian Citizen, as far as their sex will allow.

5. Female Citizens have the same right of suffrage in their respective parishes as the Men: because they have equal property in the country, and are equally subject to the laws, and, indeed, they are in every respect, as well on their own account as on account of their children, as deeply interested in every public transaction. But in consideration of the delicacy of their

sex, they are exempted from, and are ineligible to, all public employments.

6. Every Man, Woman, and Child, whether born in wedlock or not (for nature and justice know nothing of illegitimacy), is entitled quarterly to an equal share of the rents of the parish where they have settlement. But the public aids to the State, and the County, must first be deducted, and the expenses of the parish provided for.

7. The settlement of every man whether native or foreigner is in that parish wherein he last dwelt a full year.

8. The Settlement of every Woman when married and living with her husband is in her husband's parish.

9. The settlement of every Widow or unmarried Woman, or Woman separated from her husband is in the parish wherein she last dwelt a full year.

10. The settlement of Children while living with their Father, is in his parish — while living with their Mother only, in hers: and if Orphans or deserted their settlement is in the parish where they became so.

11. No person can receive dividends, or have a vote in two Parishes at the same time.

12. A child, though born in the last hour of the quarter, and a person dying in the first hour of the quarter, shall nevertheless each of them be entitled to their quarterly dividends. Because such occasions are expensive, and the parish must lean to the generous side.

13. The exercise of the rights of a citizen with respect to voting, or public employments, is suspended by the state of accusation, and by condemnation to punishments infamous or afflictive, till recapitation; but his right to a share of the parish revenues, as a human being, can never be annulled but by death or banishment.

OF THE SOVEREIGNTY OF THE PEOPLE

14. The Sovereign people is the universality of Spensonian citizens.

15. It nominates directly its deputies.

16. It deligates to Electors, the choice of administrators, of public arbitrators, or Criminal Judges, and Judges of appeal.

17. It deliberates on the Laws.

OF THE PARISHES

18. The land with its natural appurtenances, (according to the law of nature)

is the common estate of the inhabitants, a parish is therefore a compact portion of the Country, designedly not too large that it may the more easily be managed by the inhabitants with respect to its revenues and police.

19. A parish can levy no tolls or assessments, but the rents of its territory.

20. Its police appertains to it.

21. It nominates its own officers.

22. It supports a public school.

23. Farmers and such as are able to build and repair their own houses, must have leases of twenty-one years, but no longer, that the most desirable situations may not be always engrossed in the same hands, and that Farms and other Tenements may now and then find their value in order that the Parish Revenue receive no damage, by places being let for less than they will bring.

24. For the more effectual preservation of justice in this business, all considerable Farms and Tenements, must at the Expiration Lease be let by public auction, after due Advertisement in the Public Prints.

25. Every Lease-holder must build according to the regulations laid down by the Parish for the sake of order and duration.

26. They must also leave their Buildings, Fixtures, Fences, etc., at the end of their Leases in good tenantable repair and condition, and their lands in good tilth becoming the public spirit of Spensonia.

27. No deputy Landlords are allowed. Therefore no leaseholder can parcel out his houses or lands to sub-tenants. All unfurnished lodgings or parcels of land can only be let by the parish.

28. Nevertheless an innkeeper or private person may occasionally accommodate strangers or others, with lodging in their own furnished apartments, and their cattle with pasturage, etc.

29. And a settlement may be gained by thus residing a great part, or even the whole of the year in the parish in such furnished lodgings.

30. Strangers from abroad, or Spensonians from other parishes, who may become necessitous through sickness or otherwise before they have gained a settlement, must be supported by the parish in which they then sojourn. But such poor being accounted the poor of the nation at large the parishes before they send off their quarterly poundage to the state, shall deduct therefrom the expenses they have been at in supporting such poor strangers.

31. Parishes in Towns, must always keep a sufficiency of small and

convenient apartments in good repair for the accommodation of Labourers, Journeymen Mechanics, Widows and others who desire and require but little room. These shall be let by the quarter at equitable rents.

32. Country Parishes shall have a sufficiency of cottages or small and convenient dwellings with little parcels of land adjoining for gardens, etc., to accommodate Labourers in Husbandry, Smiths, Cartwrights and other Tradesmen and people wishing to live in the Country. These to be let by the year at equitable rents.

33. If a Competition arise about one of these small Tenements in Town or Country on account of its more than common desirable situation, etc., it shall be let by auction, and a lease granted. This will prevent murmuring, and also the Tenements from being let under value to the detriment of the parish.

34. If any parish in town or country should become so full of inhabitants as to have all its small tenements occupied, and yet more should be wanted, then it shall divide the first large sort of tenement that becomes vacant by the expiration of its lease into such small tenements, that the free course of population be not impeded.

35. It shall not be deemed unconstitutional to hold more tenements or leases than one, and even in sundry parishes — because a person's health or business may require him to occupy Tenements in different situations at the same time; as, for instance, in both town and country: — or he may wish to secure the possession of some desirable tenement, that is to let before the lease of the place he holds at present expires.

36. In such cases as this where settlements in more parishes than one are acquired, such pluralist shall yet vote and receive dividends but in one parish, which parish shall be that which he makes choice of. This restriction is necessary to check the natural ambition and rapacity of the rich.

37. A lease-holder may give up his lease when he pleases to the parish, or sell it for the remainder of the term it has to run to another person.

38. The parishes shall receive rent quarterly from the state, and the county, for the ground which they may have occasion respectively to occupy by their buildings, at a fair valuation: — as State Palaces, Castles, Fortifications, Magazines, Dockyards, etc., County Halls, Hospitals, Jails, etc.

39. Every parish shall constantly have a quantity of corn laid up in store, in proportion to its population, as a reserve against famine or scarcity from bad seasons: and by selling off yearly the oldest, and replacing the quantity with new corn, have it always in the best state.

40. To prevent the parishes from imbibing hereby a spirit of speculation in corn, to the detriment of the country at large, the law will properly regulate this business.

41. The parishes shall take care, that all the hedges do consist only of standard and low spreading grafted Fruit Trees, Shrubs valued for their Fruits and Flowers, and Trees indispensably necessary for their wood, instead of Thorns, Briars, and Brambles. The Spensonians, being the Landlords, are so much interested in the welfare of the Husbandman, and so public-spirited from their childhood that they will never break his fences or trespass on his grounds, and therefore he may safely cultivate the most inviting vegetables close to the highway side. He has only cattle to guard against.

42. Hunting is forbidden, being inadmissible in a country so highly cultivated, because of the unavoidable destruction it must make. The game, therefore, is considered as going with the ground, and as the sole property of the occupier, who alone may kill all he finds on his premises.

43. All rents shall be brought to the parish counting-house by Twelve o'clock on quarter-day that the books may then be closed. On quarter-day the rents shall be paid to the Parish Officers at their Counting House.

44. During the ensuing week, the parish accounts shall be made up, and after setting aside the poundages due to the state and the county, and settling all internal parochial business, and finding how much of the rent remains to be returned to the people, the accounts shall be minutely printed, including the names of all the Men, Women, and Children, who are entitled to dividends as parishioners, distinguishing those of age to vote by an asterisk.

45. The Eighth day after quarter-day, and the two following (which are always days of festivity) the people come for their dividends, which together with copies of the parish accounts is given to the heads of families, according to the number of their respective households, and to single claimants.

OF THE NATIONAL REPRESENTATION

46. The parishes are the sole basis of the national representation.

47. There is one deputy for each parish if the number of parishes in the nation do not exceed one thousand.

48. If above one thousand, then the parishes in each county shall be classed in pairs of adjacent parishes, after first, if there be an odd parish, determining by lot which shall be it, for it will have the privilege of sending a deputy of itself, as if it were a pair.

49. If the parishes in the nation exceed two thousand, the parishes in each county are divided into classes consisting each of three adjacent parishes, after first deciding by lot as above, if there be one or two odd, which they are, and erecting it or them into a class, observing if there be two that they be adjacent. And so in like manner with any number of parishes that the national representation may never exceed one thousand.

50. The election proceeds in every parish of a class on the same day, and after casting up the votes, send a Commissioner for the general casting up, to the place pointed out by the parish.

51. The nomination is made by the absolute majority of individual suffrages.

52. If the casting up does not give an absolute majority, a second vote is proceeded to, and the votes are taken for the two Citizens who had the most voices.

53. In case of equality of voices, the eldest has the preference, either to be on the ballot or elected. In case of equality of age, lot decides.

54. Every male Citizen exercising the rights of Citizens, is eligible through the extent of the Commonwealth.

55. Each deputy belongs to the whole nation.

56. In case of non-acceptance, resignation, forfeiture, or death of a deputy, he is replaced by the parish or parishes, which nominated him.

57. A deputy who has given in his resignation cannot quit his past, but after the admission of his successor.

58. The Spensonian people assemble every year in their parishes on the first of May, for the elections.

59. They proceed whatever be the number of Citizens present, having a right to vote.

OF ELECTORAL ASSEMBLIES

60. The Citizens meet in their parishes, nominate two Electors for the County.

61. The electoral assembles proceed in their elections as the parishes.

OF THE LEGISLATIVE BODY

62. The Legislative Body is one and indivisible and permanent.

63. Its Session is for a year.

64. It meets the first of July.

65. The National Assembly cannot be constituted if it does not consist of one more than the half the deputies.

66. The Deputies cannot be examined, accused or tried at any time for the opinions they have delivered in the legislative body.

67. They may for a criminal act be seized, but a warrant of arrest, or a warrant summoning to appear, cannot be granted against them, unless authorised by the Legislative Body.

HOLDING OF THE SITTINGS OF THE LEGISLATIVE BODY

68. The Sittings of the National Assembly are public.

69. The Minutes of the Sittings are printed.

70. It cannot deliberate if it be not composed of — Members at least.

71. It cannot refuse to hear its members speak in the order which they have demanded to be heard.

72. It deliberates by a majority of the members present.

73. Fifty members have a right to require the appeal nominal.

74. It has the right of censure on the conduct of its members in its bosom.

75. The police appertains to it in the place of its sittings, and in the external circuit which it has determined.

OF THE FUNCTIONS OF THE LEGISLATIVE BODY

76. The Legislative Body, proposes laws and passes decrees.

77. Under the general name of laws are comprehended the acts of the Legislative Body concerning the legislation, civil and criminal; the general administration of the National Revenues, and the ordinary expenses of the Commonwealth; the title, the weight and impression, and the denomination of money; the declaration of war; the public instruction; the public honours to the memory of great men.

78. Under the particular name of Decrees are included the acts of the Legislative Body concerning the annual establishment of the Land and Sea Forces; the permission or the prohibition of the passage of foreign Troops, through the Spensonian Territory; the introduction of Foreign Naval Forces into the ports of the Commonwealth; the measures of general safety and tranquility; the annual and momentary distribution of public succours and works; the orders for the fabrication of money of every kind; the unforeseen and extraordinary expenses; the measures local and particular to an administration, or any kind of public works; the defence of the territory; the ratification of Treaties; the nomination and

the removal of Commanders in Chief of Armies; the prosecution of the responsibility of members of the Council, and the public functionaries; the accusation of persons charged with plots against the general safety of the Commonwealth all changed in the partial distribution of the Spensonian Territory; national recompenses.

OF THE FORMATION OF THE LAW

79. The plans of laws are preceded by reports.

80. The Discussion cannot be opened, and the law cannot be provisionally resolved upon till fifteen days after the report.

81. The plan is printed and sent to all the parishes of the Commonwealth, under this title "Law Proposed".

82. Forty days after the sending of the Law proposed, if in more than one half of the Counties, the tenth of the Parishes have not objected to it, the plan is accepted and becomes Law.

83. If there be an objection the Legislative Body convokes the parishes.

OF THE ENTITLING OF LAWS AND DECREES

84. Laws, Decrees, Judgments, and all Public Acts are entitled: "In the Name of the Spensonian People, the year of the Spensonian Commonwealth".

OF THE EXECUTIVE COUNCIL

85. There is one Executive Council composed of Twenty-four Members.

86. The Electoral Assembly of each county nominates One Candidate, if the number of Counties in the nation exceeds Twenty: Four, but if under then each County nominates Two. The Legislative Body chooses the members of the Council from the general list.

87. One half of it is renewed by each Legislature in the last month of the Session.

88. The Council is charged with the direction and superintendence of the General Administration. It cannot act but in Execution of the Laws, and Decrees of the Legislative Body.

89. It nominates not of its own body, the agents in chief of the general administration of the Commonwealth.

90. The Legislative Body determines the number and functions of these Agents.

91. These Agents do not form a Council. They are separated without any intermediate correspondence between them; they exercise no personal

authority.

92. The Council nominates not of its own body, the external agents of the Commonwealth.

93. It negotiates Treaties.

94. The members of the Council in case of malversation are accused by the Legislative Body.

95. The Council is responsible for the non-execution of laws, and decrees, and for abuses which it does not denounce.

96. It recalls and replaces the Agents in its nomination.

97. It is bound to denounce them if there be occasion before the Judicial Authorities.

OF THE CONNEXION OF THE EXECUTIVE COUNCIL WITH THE LEGISLATIVE BODY

98. The Executive Council resides near the Legislative Body. It has admittance and a separate seat in the place of sittings.

99. It is heard as often as it has an account to give.

100. The Legislative Body calls it into the place of its Sittings in whole or in part when it thinks fit.

THE ADMINISTRATIVE AND COUNTY BODIES

101. There is a central administration in each County.

102. The Officers arid Administrators are nominated by the electoral assemblies of the County.

103. The administrations are renewed one half every year.

104. The Administrators and County Officers have no character of representation; they cannot in any case modify the Acts of the Legislative Body, or suspend the execution of them.

105. The Legislative Body determines the functions of the County Officers and Administrators, the rules of their subordination, and the penalties they may incur.

106. The Sittings of Administrations are public.

107. The Electoral Assemblies assess their parishes by a pound rate, quarterly, towards defraying the public expenses of the County, as in building and repairing the County Edifices, such as Halls, Hospitals, Jails, Bridges, and in making and repairing Harbours, Roads, etc.

108. The accounts of the County are settled annually, and, being as minutely printed as to give satisfaction, are sent to the Parishes.

OF CIVIL JUSTICE

109. The code of Civil and Criminal Laws, is uniform for all the Commonwealth.

110. No infringement can be made of the right which Citizens have, to cause their differences to be pronounced upon by Arbitrators of their choice.

111. The decision of these arbitrators is final if the Citizens have not reserved the right of objecting to them.

112. There are Justices of the Peace elected by the Citizens in the parishes.

113. They conciliate and judge without expense.

114. There are public arbitrators elected by the Electoral Assemblies.

115. Their number and their circuits are fixed by the Legislative Body.

116. They take cognizance of disputes which have not been finally determined by the private arbitrations of the Justices of the Peace.

117. They deliberate in public, they give their opinions aloud; they pronounce in the last resort on verbal defences or simple memorials without Procedures, and without expense; they assign the reasons of their decision.

118. The Justices of the Peace and the public arbitrators are elected every year.

OF CRIMINAL JUSTICE

119. In Criminal cases no Citizen can be tried but by an examination received by a Jury, or decreed by the Legislative Body, the accused have counsel chosen by themselves or nominated officially; the process is public; the fact and the intention are declared by a Jury of Judgement; the punishment is applied by a Criminal Tribunal.

120. Criminal Judges are elected every year by the Electoral Assemblies.

OF THE TRIBUNAL OF APPEAL

121. There is one Tribunal of Appeal for all the Commonwealth.

122. This Tribunal does not take cognisance of the merits of the case: it pronounces on the violation of forms and an express contravention of the Law.

123. The members of the Tribunal are nominated every year by the Electoral Assembly.

OF THE NATIONAL TREASURY

124. The National Treasury is the central point of the receipts and expenses of the Commonwealth.

125. It is supplied by an assessment raised quarterly of — in the pound, on the rents of the parishes by the Legislative Body.

126. This assessment being sufficient for all national purposes, and being sent up by the parishes every quarter without expenses, renders revenues, laws and officers unnecessary.

127. The affairs of the Treasury are administered by accountable agents, nominated by the Executive Council.

128. These agents are superintended by Commissioners nominated by the Legislative Body, not of its own members, and responsible for abuses which they do not denounce.

OF ACCOUNTABILITY

129. The accounts of the agents of the national treasure, and of the administrators of the public money are given in annually to responsible Commissioners nominated by the Executive Council.

130. These verifications are superintended by Commissioners in the nomination of the Legislative Body, not of its own members, and responsible for errors, and abuses which they do not denounce; the Legislative Body passes the accounts.

131. The National Accounts are printed yearly sufficiently minute to give satisfaction, and sent to the parishes.

OF THE FORCES OF THE COMMONWEALTH

132. The General Forces of the Commonwealth are composed of the whole people.

133. The Commonwealth maintains in its pay, even in times of peace, an armed force by sea and land.

134. All the Spensonians are soldiers; they are all exercised in the use of Arms.

135. There is no Generalissimo.

136. Difference of ranks, their distinctive marks, and subordination subsist only with relation to service, and during its continuance.

137. The public force employed for maintaining order and peace in the interior, does not act but on the requisition in writing of the Constituted Authorities.

138. The public force employed against enemies from without acts under the order of the Executive Council.

139. No armed bodies can deliberate.

OF THE REVISION OF THE CONSTITUTION

140. If in one more than half of the Counties, the tenth of the parishes of each regularly assembled demand the revision of the constitutional act or the change of some of its articles, the legislative body is bound to convoke all the parishes of the Commonwealth, to know if there be ground for a revision of the Constitution.

141. The assembly of revision is formed by two members from each County.

142. The assembly of revision exercises no function of legislation or of Government; it confines itself to the revision of the Constitutional Laws.

143. All the authorities continue the exercise of their functions, till the change proposed in the assembly of revision, shall have been accepted by the people, and till the new Authorities shall have been put in motion.

144. The assembly of revision addresses immediately to the parishes, the plan of reform which it has agreed upon. It is dissolved as soon as its plan has been addressed.

OF THE CORRESPONDENCE OF THE SPENSONIAN COMMONWEALTH, WITH OTHER NATIONS

145. The Spensonian people is the friend and natural ally of every free people.

146. It does not interfere in the Government of other Nations. It does not suffer other nations to interfere in its own.

147. It gives an asylum to Foreigners banished from their Country for the cause of liberty; it refuses it to Tyrants.

148. It does not make peace with an enemy that occupies its territory.

OF THE GUARANTEE OF RIGHTS

149. The Constitution guarantees to all the Spensonians, Equality, Liberty, Safety, Property, parochial and private, the free exercise of worship, a common instruction, public succours; the indefinite liberty of the Press, the right of petition, the right of meeting in popular Societies, the

enjoyment of all the Rights of Man.

150. The Spensonian Commonwealth honours Loyalty, courage, filial piety, misfortune. It puts the deposit of its Constitution under the guard of all virtues.

151. The declaration of rights, and the Constitutional Act are engraven on tables in the bosom of the Legislative Body and in the public places.

OF COLONISATION

152. Spensonia disclaims all financial benefits from foreign Provinces, Dominions, or Colonies.

153. Yet because the unparalleled encouragement to marriage, and of the influx of Foreigners, must inevitably so increase the number of inhabitants under this Constitution, that Colonies enjoying the same blessings must be established as inviting offings for the redundance of population on the Mother Country to flow to.

154. All the Colonies (therefore) that now belong to Spensonia, or shall be hereafter established by her, are declared independent states, as soon as they adopt and put in practice similar Constitutions. They shall then be considered as in the most intimate state of alliance, and entitled to all the protection the Mother Country can afford.

155. To promote cleanliness and refresh the spirit of men and labouring animals, the weeks in Spensonia are but five days each; every fifth day being a day or Sabbath of Rest. Thus will the fourth day of the week be always a market day and a pay day for labourers.

EPILOGUE

What pity Friends that we should be,
So much deprived of Liberty!
Indictments one upon another
Continually do us bother.
How carefully we're forced to seek
For words before we dare to speak!
But let what will upon me come,
I scorn to close my work quite dumb.
And though my book's in queer lingo,
I will it send to St. Domingo:
To the Republic of the Incas,
For an example how to frame Laws.
For who can tell but the Millennium
May take its rise from my poor Cranium?
And who knows but it God may please

It should come by the West Indies?
No harm I mean by this reflection;
And thus I end my application.

14
Poems and Songs

•

Thomas Spence

THE RIGHTS OF MAN FOR ME[1]
Tune – Maid of the Mill.

I

There are many fine schemes contrived by the Great,
To deceive Silly Souls d'ye see?
And render them passive for pure Conscience Sake,
And mould them to fell Tyranny.
Yet for all their fine Arts with their Priests in their Aid
Their threats and their deep Policy,
I'll laugh them to Scorn while loudly I sing,
The Rights of the Man Boys for me.

II

This World for the poor they say never was made,
Their portion in the Heavens be,
And more, that they envy them their happy Lot,
So certain's their Felicity.
But thank them for nought if the Heavens they could let,
Few Joys there the Poor would e're see,
For Rents they must toil and for Taxes to boot,
The Rights of Man then for me.

---

1 The composer of the above song, was the first, as far as he knows made use of the phrase "RIGHTS OF MAN", which was on the following remarkable occasion. A man who had been a farmer, and also a miner, and who had been ill-used by his landlords, dug a cave for himself by the seaside, at Marsden Rocks, between Shields and Sunderland about the year 1788, and the singularity of such a habitation, exciting the curiosity of many to pay him a visit, our author was one of that number. Exalting in the idea of a human being, who had bravely emancipated himself from the iron fangs of aristocracy, to live free from impost, he wrote extempore with chaulk above the fire place of this free man, the following lines:

'Ye landlords vile, whose man's peace mar,
Come levy rents here if you can;
Your stewards and lawyers I defy,
And live with all the RIGHTS OF MAN.'

III

Then cheer up all you who have long been oppress'd
Aspire unto sweet Liberty;
No Fetters were form'd for a Nation to bind
Who have the brave Wish to be free.
To Reason attend and blush at your Chains,
And throw off all vile Slavery,
And let each Man sing till loud Echoes ring,
The Rights of Man Boys for me.

IV

As for me though in Prison I oft have been cast
Because I would dare to be free,
And though in black Newgate[2] I did pen this Song
My Theme I've not alter'd you see.
In jail or abroad whatever betide
My Struggles for Freedom shall be
Whatever Fate bring I will think, speak and sing,
The Rights of Man Boys for me.

2 This song was written by Spence when a Prisoner in Newgate, under a Charge of High Treason in the Year 1794.

ALTERATION

No longer lost in shades of night,
Where late in chains we lay!
The sun arises, and his light
Dispels our gloom away.
No longer blind, and prone to lye
In slavery profound;
But for redress aloud we cry!
And tyrants hear the sound.
The pomp of courts no more engage;
The magic spell is broke;
We hail the bright reforming age!
And cast away the yoke.
Our substance and our blood no more
So tamely shall we yield;
Nor quit like slaves our native shore
To deck the monster's field.
The rotten lumber of the land,
The courtly-pension'd train;
Shall hear their sentence and disband,
As we our rights regain.
The mitred villain as he rolls
In luxury and lust,
He blinds and robs the silly souls
Committed to his trust.
Amus'd no more with empty lies,
Of bliss we never knew;
The traitors lose the stale disguise,
And closely we pursue.

SPENCE AND THE BARBER
Tune – Tally heigh ho, the Grinder.

A Barber to Spence said one Day,
The times they are still getting worse,
Nor can I perceive any way,
How we're to get rid of this curse;
In politics I took delight,
But now I'm quite in desperation,
My hopes they all sunk in night,
I care not what comes of the nation.
    Tally heigh ho ye know,
    Tally heigh the barber,
    Tally heigh ho ye know,
    The times they are getting still getting harder.

My family and I are near starv'd,
No cloaths can we get to our back,
The tax gatherers come every day,
And rents they are quite on the rack;
Great hopes of amendment I had,
But now I am all in despair,
Enough 'tis to drive a man mad,
To think how we all saddled are.
    Tally heigh ho, &c.

Chear up man said Spence, never fear,
You soon will have my constitution,
And then you will end all your care,
So happy is the fruition.
The barber then flew in a rage,
And cry'd this he should never see,
We live in too wicked an age,
To suffer such justice to be.
    Tally heigh ho ye know, &c.

Said Spence, if a few hearty men,
Said come let us have Spence's system,
What would your behaviour be then,
Would you hinder or would you assist'm?
Said Strap them I could not oppose,
My interest would not allow me,
I never can count those my foes,
Who wish with such bliss to endow me.
    Tally heigh ho ye know, &c.

Your int'rest you know now said Spence,
Is the interest of nine tenths the nation,
Then pray now if you've common sense,
Shew no more of your desperation;
The time you may shortly expect,
When men of prime courage you'll see,
Occasion then do not neglect,
When fortune will set you all free.
Tally heigh ho ye know, &c.

When all feel alike in a cause,
Small trouble's requir'd in teaching,
A song that attracts their applause,
Is better than speeches or preaching;
Let's hear then no more of despair,
But sing your dear rights to each other,
'Till all think alike every where,
Even from one Land's end to the other.
Tally heigh ho ye know, &c.

A WARNING, TO USURPERS AND OPPRESSORS, Alias — GIANTS AND MEN OF RENOWN

Ye Children of men I pray you attend,
Hear what I've to say, a willing ear lend;
I'll show the dire vengeance which on you awaits
In following the sins which a Just God most hates.
Sing Fa-la ye men of renown.

The cruelty and violence is seizing the ground,
The cause chiefly was of the old world being drown'd;
The Brutish usurpers then swelling with pride,
Thought it high renown o'er their fellows to ride.

These warriors, these giants, these heroes of old,
Corrupted the manners of all we are told;
Now violence and robbery only have charm,
All honour's confined to the curs'd trade of arms.

Now war being the fashion and Plunder the trade,
The world is as wicked as it can be made;
All now were ambitious of being mighty men,
At Butchering their fellows — oh! what a world then!

These monsters although great risk in each other's eyes,
God blush'd for, and did the proud reptiles despise;
Heart sick of their Baseness, these men of renown,
He likes rats and vermine did all of them drown.

No part in this violence and plunder had Noah,
For he was a Just man[3] the text tells us so;
Nor lost by it, No – see his vast recompense,
The whole world he had for his inheritance.
Then here if you please, is a man of renown.

A warning then take now my dear fellow men,
Don't tempt the Almighty with such deeds again;
The field getting trade abolish it quite,
Dividing your rents and then all will be right.
Nor e're strive more to be men of renown.

---

3 Noah was a Preacher of Righteousness. Was it the visionary, existing spiritual sort that our Holy Men delude us with? No – it was Substantial practical Righteousness, such as Lawyers call JUSTICE. It is this and only this sort of Righteousness that is pleasing to God, and can save a world.

AN ADDRESS TO POSTERITY, WARNING THEM AGAINST THE LANDLORD JUDAS

Ye Children unborn, hear what I've got to say,
I'll tell you some strange things have pass'd in our Day;
'Twixt Democrats, and Aristocrats,[4] there was such a Pother
The World seem'd too little to hold both together!
Singing Tol de rol &c.

Full many fell Battles were fought by these Clans,
And Vict'ry the Demos gain'd by Strength of Hands,
But Judas, the Bag-bearer, playing his old Trick,
For Fields, sold Democracy, all to Old Nick!
Singing &c.

When Run-a-way Loyalists left all their Lands,
French Judases, eagerly join'd Hearts and Hands;
Democracy meanly to Traitors then yields;
All falls before Judas in Prospect of Fields.
Singing &c.

One Poor Man in England as loud as he could,
Warn'd all against Judases, saying they would,
Destroy all our Freedom, if they had the lands;
Proposing to take them into our own Hands.
Singing &c.

But alackaday! this poor Man was not heard,
But shut up[5] and from ev'ry Comfort debarr'd;
Whilst all the good Democrats, wink't at the Matter;
Philosopher-like, he liv'd on Bread and Water.
Singing &c.

Advice then my Children, I'd have you to take,
Upset all these Judases, for your own Sake;
No Freedom with Landlords, enjoy e'er you can,
For Land, I say Land, is the whole Rights of Man.
Singing &c.

4 For the Sake of Smoothness sing Demos and Aristos.

5 Imprisoned.

Little Turnstile, Holborn, London.
The site of Spence's Hive of Liberty bookshop, which he opened in 1793, now a restaurant. Photograph by Remy Bertrand, July 2014.

15
Poems and Song
•
Keith Armstrong

Taken from his play 'Pigs' Meat: Visions of Utopia', written for Bruvvers Theatre Company in 1997 and performed in St Ann's Church, Byker, Newcastle upon Tyne.

'JACK THE BLASTER'

In the summer of 1782 an old man, eighty years of age, and his wife, made one of the caves at Marsden Rocks near South Shields their place of residence. The man known as 'Jack the Blaster' had been a miner at Allenheads, but, having removed to Shields to save the expenses of housekeeping, the old couple decided to live in this cave, which they furnished. The romance and novelty drew a number of visitors to the cave. The couple provided refreshments, and even ladies and gentlemen drove to the place and partook of their cheer. One of the visitors was Spence. He describes how he went to see the old miner who had been ill treated by his landlord. Spence, 'exulting in the idea of a human being who had emancipated himself from the iron fangs of aristocracy,' wrote in chalk above the fireplace:

> 'Ye landlords vile who man's peace mar
> Come levy rents here if you can
> Your stewards and lawyers I defy
> And live with all the Rights of Man.'
> (Thomas Spence)

I've dug this cave to be free,
To let my heart leap by the sea,
It's all for the cause of liberty,
A sanctuary for me.

The landlords are off our backs,
The bosses and the hacks,
Free from tyrants and their quacks,
I'm off the beaten tracks.

I'm Jack the Blaster,
My own master,
I'm a miner and shafter,

An Allenheads grafter.
Jack the Blaster,
Drowning in laughter,
Master crafter,
Peasant and poet.

THE HIVE OF LIBERTY

(AFTER THE NAME OF THOMAS SPENCE'S BOOKSHOP AT 8 LITTLE TURNSTILE, HOLBORN)

I am a small and humble man,
my body frail and broken.
I strive to do the best I can.
I spend my life on tokens.

I traipse through Holborn all alone,
hawking crazy notions.
I am the lonely people's friend.
I live on schemes and potions.

For, in my heart and in my mind,
ideas swarm right through me.
Yes, in this Hive of Liberty,
my words just flow like wine,
my words just flow like wine.

I am a teeming worker bee.
My dignity is working.
My restless thoughts swell like the sea.
My fantasies I'm stoking.

There is a rebel inside me,
a sting about to strike.
I hawk my works around the street.
I put the world to rights.

For, in my heart and in my mind,
ideas swarm right through me.
Yes, in this Hive of Liberty,
my words just flow like wine,
my words just flow like wine.

PIGS' MEAT

"Learning will be cast into the mire and trodden down under the hoofs of a swinish multitude." (from Edmund Burke's *Reflections on the Revolution in France*)

We are the swinish multitude,
Who feed off the Loose Meat,
Our brains are bacon,
Our balls pork chops,
We honk instead of speak.

We're pigs' meat,
Pigs' meat,
We wallow in our muck.
Our snouts deep in the stinking trough,
We don't give a toss.
Pigs' meat,
Pigs' meat,
We riot in the street.
Pigs' meat,
Pigs' meat,
We piss on the elite.

We are the swinish multitude,
With sties that blind our eyes.
No sense of direction,
Just one big erection,
We bonk instead of think.

We're pigs' meat,
Pigs' meat,
We wallow in our muck.
Our snouts deep in the stinking trough,
We don't give a toss.
Pigs' meat,
Pigs' meat,
We riot in the street.
Pigs' meat,
Pigs' meat,
We piss on the Elite.

We are the swinish multitude,
Incapable of speeches,
We drink royal blood,
We eat the rich,
We fart in Halls of Art.

We're pigs' meat,
Pigs' meat,
We wallow in our muck.
Our snots deep in the stinking trough,
We don't give a toss.
Pigs' meat,
Pigs' meat,
We riot in the street.
Pigs' meat,
Pigs' meat,
We piss on the Elite.

FOLK SONG FOR THOMAS SPENCE

Down by the old Quayside,
I heard a young man cry,
Among the nets and ships he made his way.
As the keelboats buzzed along,
He sang a seagull's song;
He cried out for the Rights of you and me.
Oh lads, that man was Thomas Spence,
He gave up all his life
Just to be free.
Up and down the cobbled Side,
Struggling on through the Broad Chare,
He shouted out his wares
For you and me.
Oh Lads, you should have seen him gan,
He was a man the likes you rarely see.
With a pamphlet in his hand,
And a poem at his command,
He haunts the Quayside still,
And his words sing.
His folks they both were Scots,
Sold socks and fishing nets,
Through the Fog on the Tyne they plied their trade.
In this theatre of life,
The crying and the strife,
They tried to be decent and be strong.
Oh Lads, that man was Thomas Spence,
He gave up all his life
Just to be free
Up and down the cobbled Side,
Struggling on through the Broad Chare,

He shouted out his wares
For you and me.
Oh Lads, you should have seen him gan,
He was a man the likes you rarely see.
With a pamphlet in his hand,
And a poem at his command,
He haunts the Quayside still,
And his words sing.

Appendices

Appendix 1

The Rights of Infants; or, the Imprescriptable RIGHT of MOTHERS to such share of the Elements as is sufficient to enable them to suckle and bring up their Young

1797

by Thomas Spence

APPENDIX

A CONTRAST Between PAINE's AGRARIAN JUSTICE, and SPENCE's END OF OPPRESSION,
Both being built on the same indisputable Principle, viz. That the Land is the common Property of Mankind.

Under the system of Agrarian Justice,	*Under the system of* the End of Oppression,
The people will, as it were, sell their birth-right for a mess of porridge, by accepting of a paltry consideration in lieu of their rights.	The people will receive, without deduction, the whole produce of their common inheritance.
Under the first, The people will become supine and careless in respect of public affairs, knowing the utmost they can receive of the public money.	*Under the second,* The people will be vigilant and watchful over the public expenditure, knowing that the more there is saved their dividends will be the larger.
Under the first, The people will be more like pensioned emigrants and French priests than interested natives.	*Under the second,* The people will be all intent upon the improvement of their respective parishes, for the sake of the increased shares of the revenues, which on that account they will receive.

Under the first,	*Under the second,*
The people cannot derive right of suffrage in national affairs, from their compromisory stipends.	Universal suffrage will be inseparably attached to the people both in parochial and national affairs, because the revenues, both parochial and national, will be derived immediately from their common property.
Under the first, The government may be either absolute monarchy, aristocracy, democracy, or mixed.	*Under the second,* The government must of necessity be democratic.
Under the first, All the complexities of the present public establishments, which support such hosts of placemen, will not only still continue, but also the evils of them will be greatly enhanced by the very system of Agrarian Justice.	*Under the second,* There can be but two descriptions of public officers, parochial and national, and those but few in number, and on moderate salaries.
Under the first, There will exist two spirits, incompatible in a free state, the insolent and overbearing spirit of aristocracy, and the sneaking unmanly spirit of conscious dependence.	*Under the second,* There will exist only the robust spirit of independence, mellowed and tempered by the presence and checks of equally independent fellow-citizens.
Under the first, The destructive profligacy of the great, and the wretched degeneracy of the poor, will still continue, and will increase, to the pitiable unhappiness of both parties.	*Under the second,* All the virtues being the natural offspring of a general and happy mediocrity, will at once step forth into use, and progressively increase their blessed influence among men.

Under the first,	*Under the second,*
Taxes, both directly and indirectly, will not only be demanded, but will be increased to the utmost the people can possibly bear, let trade and seasons be ever so prosperous.	There can be no taxes, nor expenses of collecting them, because the government would be supported by a poundage from the rents which each parish would send quarterly to the national treasury, free of all expense; thus leaving the price of all commodities unencumbered with any addition but the price of labour.
Under the first, The poor would still continue, through despair, unambitious to arise out of their hopeless state of abject wretchedness and vulgarity.	*Under the second,* The lowest and most profligate having such frequent opportunities, by the aid of their quarterly dividends, of starting into industrious and decent modes of life, could not always resist the influence of the general virtue every where displayed, without some time or other following the example.
Under the first, Children will still be considered as grievous burdens in poor families.	*Under the second,* As both young and old share equally alike of the parish revenues, children and aged relations living in a family will, especially in rich parishes, where dividends are large, through high rents or the productions of mines &c., be accounted as blessings.
Under the first, If the aristocratic assistance afforded by charity-schools, in the education of poor children, be withdrawn, the labouring classes must inevitably degenerate into barbarous ignorance.	*Under the second,* If the people are not generally learned it must be their own fault, as their inexhaustible means of comfortable subsistence must furnish also the means of education.

Under the first,
The poor must still look up for aristocratic benefactions of rotten potatoes and spoiled rice, and other substitutes for bread in the times of scarcity, to preserve their wretched existence.

Under the second,
What with the annihilation of taxes and the dividends of the parochial rents, together with the honest guardianship of their popular government, we may reasonably suppose that the people will rarely be driven to the dire necessity of using a substitute for bread.

Under the first,
After admitting that the earth belongs to the people, the people must nevertheless compromise the matter with their conquerors and oppressors, and still suffer them to remain as a distinct and separate body among them, in full possession of their country.

Under the second,
After insisting that the land is public property, the people's oppressors must either submit to become undistinguishable in the general mass of citizens or fly the country.

Under the first,
If foreign and domestic trade increase, the productions of the land with increase in price, of which the landed interest will reap the advantage, by raising the rents in due proportion until the whole benefit thereof centers in them.

Under the second,
If foreign and domestic trade increase, the price of commodities will in proportion also increase, and rents of course will rise, but this increase will revert back to the body of the people, by increasing their quarterly dividends.

Under the first,
All the aristocratic monopolies in trade, in privileges, and government, will continue.

Under the second,
There can be no monopolies; but a fair, salutary, and democratic competition will pervade every thing.

Under the first,
A timid and acquiescing spirit must be promoted among the people as now, lest they should discover the dissimilarity between their natural rights and enjoyments.

Under the second,
The justness and consistency of affairs will invite, nay, challenge, the most rigorous and logical enquiries, and will draw forth, uncramped, the utmost powers of the mind.

Under the first,
Domestic trade will be far from its natural height, because multitudes of the people will be poor and beggarly, and unable to purchase numberless articles of use and luxury that their wants and inclinations would prompt them to wish for.

Under the second,
Domestic trade would be at an amazing pitch, because there would be no poor; none but would be well clothed, lodged, and fed: and the whole mass of rents, except a trifle to the government, being circulated at home, in every parish, every quarter, would cause such universal propensity as would enable every body to purchase not only the necessities of life, but many elegancies and luxuries.

Under the first,
The fund proposed by Paine will require a great number of placemen of various descriptions to manage it, and who being chosen, as they must be, by the ministry and their friends, will very much increase the already enormous influence of governments.

Under the second,
The government can have very little influence by places, because the parish officers will be chosen by the parishioners; and all the complex machinery of financiering and stock-jobbing; all the privileged trading companies and corporate towns, which are the nests of influence and corruption, would be abolished.

Under the first,
The rich would abolish all hospitals, charitable funds, and parochial provision for the poor, telling them, that they now have all that their great advocate, Paine, demands, as their rights, and what he exultingly deems as amply sufficient to ameliorate their condition, and render them happy, by which the latter of our reformation will be worse than the beginning.

Under the second,
The quarterly dividends, together with the abolishment of all taxes, would destroy the necessity of public charities; but if any should be thought necessary, whether to promote learning, or for any other purpose, the parochial and national funds would be found at all times more than sufficient.

Appendix 2

Spence's Tokens

'PIGS MEAT PUBLISHED BY T • SPENCE LONDON' A boar treading upon the emblems of royalty, parliament, and the church.

'ROUSE BRITANNIA' Britannia confounded, and the Cap of Liberty falling to the ground.

'TREE OF LIBERTY' Four men dancing around a liberty pole, the head of Prime Minister William Pitt upon the pole.

'HALF PENNY' A guillotine set up outside a town-house.

'ADVOCATES FOR THE RIGHTS OF MAN' Thos. Spence, Sir Thos. More, Thos Paine. 1795.

'PIGS MEAT PUBLISHED BY T. SPENCE LONDON' A boar treading upon a coronet, crozier and staff.

'A SNAIL MAY PUT HIS HORNS OUT'
A snail, tree, and bridge over a river.

A stag under a tree.

'THE END OF OPPRESSION'
Two men exulting over a bonfire of title deeds, etc.

'BEFORE THE REVOLUTION'
A skeleton of a man in chains, gnawing on a bare bone.

'EVEN FELLOWS'
The heads of the Devil and Pitt.

'ODD FELLOWS: A MILLION HOGG, A GUINEA PIG. 1795'
The heads of an ass and George III.

'T SPENCE. 7 MONTHS IMPRISONED FOR HIGH TREASON' 1794.

'AFTER THE REVOLUTION'
Three men dancing and a fourth feasting below a tree.

'JOHN THELWALL'

'LIBERTAS 1796'
A Cap of Liberty on a pole, radiated.

'MAN OVER MAN HE MADE NOT LORD'
Two half-naked figures.

'PIGS MEAT PUBLISHED BY T. SPENCE LONDON' A boar treading upon a coronet, crozier and staff.

'IF THE LAW REQUIRES IT WE WILL WALK THUS'
A man walking on all fours.

'END OF PIT'
A man hanging, torture implements lying on the ground, house with banner in the distance.

'RT. HE. C. J. FOX'

'LET TYRANTS TREMBLE AT THE CROW OF LIBERTY'
A lion trembling at the crowing of a cock.

'COALY X TYNE'
A man in a Tyne keel.

'AM I NOT THINE ASS'
Bull turned jack-ass. A bull having an asses head, bearing a king.

'A TRUE HEARTED SAILOR'
A sailor holding out a bowl.

'REMEMBER ME WHEN THIS YOU SEE'
An anchor, two hearts, and a crown.

'MY FREEDOM I AMONG SLAVES ENJOY'
A cat.

'MUCH GRATITUDE BRINGS SERVITUDE'
A dog.

'BRITISH LIBERTY DISPLAYED'
A press-gang dragging away a pressed man.

'A FREE BORN ENGLISHMAN'
A man shackled, his hands tied behind his back, his mouth padlocked.

'A BLUE COAT BOY'
A figure.

'A BRIDEWELL BOY'
A figure with a stick in his hand.

'LITTLE TURNSTILE HALFPENNY, 1796'
Two boys on a turnstile.

'THE GALLANT GARB OF SCOTLAND'
A highlander.

'LD GEO GORDON DIED IN NEWGATE NOV 1 1793'
Lord George Gordon in broad-brimmed hat.

'WE WERE BORN FREE AND WILL NEVER DIE SLAVES'
A caduceus with a crown at one end and a Cap of Liberty at the other.

'MUM 1796'
A padlock.

'T SPENCE BOOKSELLER, DEALER IN PRINTS & COINS, No. 8 LITTLE TURNSTILE, HOLBORN, LONDON'

The Thomas Spence Trust

The Thomas Spence Trust was founded by a group of Tyneside activists intent on celebrating and promoting the life and work of Thomas Spence.

The Trust organised a mini festival to celebrate Spence in 2000 when it published a booklet on his life and work, together with related events, with financial aid from Awards for All.

The Trust successfully campaigned for a plaque on the Quayside in Newcastle upon Tyne, where Spence was born. The plaque was unveiled on Monday June 21st 2010, Spence's 260th birthday, with a number of talks, displays and events coinciding with it.

Further information from:

Dr Keith Armstrong,
The Thomas Spence Trust,
93 Woodburn Square,
Whitley Lodge,
Whitley Bay,
Tyne & Wear NE26 3JD
England

Index

A New Grammar, *see* Fisher, Ann
A Supplement to the History of Robinson Crusoe, *see* Spence, Thomas
Abercrombie, David, 105
  Forgotten Phoneticians, 105
Age of Reason, *see* Paine, Thomas
Agrarian Justice, *see* Paine, Thomas
An Advice to Patriots, 39
Annual Register, 111
agrarian reform, 17
Alexander, Jeffrey, 110
All Saints Church, Newcastle, 107
Alston, R. C., 100
American Colonies, 29
American Revolution, 17, 107
Anti-Malthusians, 66-7
Anti-Poor Law Movement, 73
Archon, Lord, 47
Ashref, Mary, 82, 86, 87

Babeuf, 67
Baxter, John, 61, 62
Beal, Joan, 123
Beer, Max, 86, 118
Bewick, Thomas, 43, 45, 51, 91, 106, 111
  fight with Spence, 43-4
  Memoirs, 43
The Bible, 33, 84, 95, 98, 99, 120-1
Blackett, Sir Walter Calverly, 35, 37, 39, 43, 44, 51, 112
Blake, William, 80-1
Bolingbroke, viscount, 51
Bolshevism, 75
Bone, John, 62
Bonnett, Alastair, 112
Botany Bay, 54
Bow Street Runners, 55
Boym, Svetlana, 75
Brick Lane, 22
British Convention, 60
British Library, 100
British Naval Mutiny of 1797, 17
Burgh, James, 29
Burke, Edmund, 4, 54, 58, 84, 113-14, 117
  Reflections on the Revolution in France, 54, 117

Ḉa Ira, 121
Calhoun, Craig, 79, 80, 122
  The Question of Class Struggle, 79
Calvinism, 15
Calypso, ou les Babillards, *see* Rutledge, Jean-Jacques
Carlile, Richard, 13, 15, 20, 21
Catholicism, 65
Cato Street Conspiracy, 28
Cawdrey, Robert, 94
  A Table Alphabeticall, 94
The Chains of Slavery, *see* Marat, Jean Paul
Charles I, 38, 42
Chartism, 13, 14, 15, 21, 22, 23-4, 25, 28, 73, 85
Chartist Land Plan, 23, 24
Chase, Malcolm, 84, 85, 112, 120
  The People's Farm, 85
children's rights, 4-5, 17
Christianity, 33, 65, 84, 99, 120
class consciousness, 76, 79
Clerkenwell prison, 55
Cobbett, William, 6, 17, 18, 23, 24, 73, 76, 77, 78, 83, 101
  Rural Rides, 77
  A Grammar of the English Language, 101
  Political Register, 77, 101
Cole, G. D. H., 87-8
Colley, Linda, 78
Combination Acts, 21
Common Sense, *see* Paine, Thomas
The Commonwealth of Oceana, *see* Harrington, James
communal rights of ownership, 16
The Communist Manifesto, 86
Condorcet, 67
The Contest, *see* Murray, Rev. James
Cook and Debrett, booksellers, 100
Cooper, Thomas, 34
Cordeliers Club, 52

Davenport. Allen, 22, 73
Defoe, Daniel
  Robinson Crusoe, 29
Delaval, Sir Francis, 36, 37, 39, 51
Delaval, John Hussey, 36
Delaval, Thomas, 37
Deptford, 13
Derry, John, 77
Dickinson, H. T., 83, 89, 103, 111
  Political Works, ed., 89
Dictionary of National Biography, 103
Dictionary of the English Language, *see* Johnson, Samuel
Dry Club, 41
Duck, Stephen, 62
Duke of Portland, ix
Duke of Richmond, 53-4
Dyck, Ian, 78

Eaton, Daniel Isaac, 57, 59, 60, 61
  Politics for the People, 57, 60
Edinburgh, 60

Edinburgh Select Society, 41
Education Reform Act, 1988, 103
Elizabeth I, 65
The End of Oppression, *see* Spence, Thomas
Engels, Frederick, 13, 14, 86
    The Communist Manifesto, 86
English Jacobins, 117
English Land Restoration Society, 22
English Poor Law, 65-6
English radical tradition, 1, 6, 14, 20, 75, 79, 123
The Enlightenment, 15
Epstein, James, 59
Evans, Thomas, 124

fascism, 78
Fisher, Ann, 100
    A New Grammar, 100
Forgotten Phoneticians, see Abercrombie, David
Franklin, Benjamin, 107
The Freemen's Magazine, see Murray, Rev. James
French Revolution, 15, 16, 17, 54, 67, 121
Friends of the Liberty of the Press, 17, 55, 62

Gallop, G. I., 112
Garden of Eden, 16
Garden City movement, 22
Gardner-Medwin, David, 1
Genesis, 15, 30, 100
George II, 122
George III, 36, 57, 95
George, Henry, 22
German Democratic Republic, 86, 87
Gerrald, Joseph, 60
The Giant-Killer; or Anti-Landlord, *see* Spence, Thomas
Godwin, William, 29, 56, 59
Golden Age, 83
Glassites, *see* Sandemanians
Glynn, Serjeant John, 39
Goodrich, Amanda, 116
government spies, 124
Gracchus, Tiberius Sempronius, 28
Gray, Alexander, 87
    The Socialist Tradition, 87
Gray, Gilbert, 91
Grenville, George, 36
Grieve, George, 39
Gulliver's Travels, *see* Swift, Jonathan

Habermas, Jürgen, 124
Hall, Charles, 32
Hardy, Thomas, 53, 54, 59, 60, 61
Harney, George Julian, 13, 14, 21, 22
Harrington, James, 4, 19, 29, 35, 44-52
    Aphorisms Political, 50
    The Commonwealth of Oceana, 29, 44-52, 56
    The Prerogative of Popular Government, 50
Harrington, John, 54
Harringtonian republicanism, 28
Hatton Gardens, 55
Hetherington, Henry, 13
    Poor Man's Guardian, 13, 77
Hexham, ix
Hill, Christopher, 83-4
Hobbes, 33
Hobsbawm, Eric, 76
Hone, William, 3
Horne Tooke, John, 61, 62
Howard, Ebenezer, 22
Hume, David, 51
Hyndman, H. M., 22, 85, 86, 89

The Important Trial of Thomas Spence, *see* Spence, Thomas
Independent Labour Party, 22, 80
industrial revolution, 65, 76
International Phonetic Alphabet, 108

Jack the Blaster, 3
John Horne Tooke Stripped Naked and Dissected, and his Political Anatomy Exposed, 62
Johnson, Richard, 78
Johnson, Samuel, 91, 92, 93, 95, 106
    Dictionary of the English Language, 91, 101
Johnston, Kenneth, 112
Jones, Ernest, 76
Joyce, Patrick, 79-80
    Visions of the People, 79-80

Karr, David, 59
Knox, Thomas, 88, 112

Labour Leader, 22
Lambeth Loyal Association, 4, 110-11
Lee, Richard 'Citizen', 62
Leviticus, 95, 99, 120
Lilliputian Magazine, *see* Newbury, John
Lloyd, William F., 67
Locke, John, 16, 30, 32, 33, 41, 55, 56
London
    British Convention, 60
    Little Turnstile, Holborn, 55, 111, 170
    Oxford Street, 18
    Parliament Street, 18
    radical sub-culture, 3, 53
    radical politics, 22
    Spence and Paine, 27
    Spencean graffiti, 6
    Spence's arrival, 17
    St. George's Field, 62
    St. George's Field Massacre, 1768, 36

taverns, 113
London Corresponding Society, 14, 17, 53-63
London Democratic Association, 13, 22
London Evening Post, 38
London Reforming Society, 62
Longfield, Mountifort, 67
Luddite movement, 79
Luttrell, Harry Lawes, 36

Malthus, Thomas, 2, 21, 66, 67, 82
Essay on Population, 21, 66
Maoism, 75
Marat, Jean Paul, 15, 40
The Chains of Slavery, 41
Margarot, Maurice, 54, 60
Marsden Rocks, 3
La Marseillaise, 121
Martin, John, 61
Marx, Karl, 13, 14, 22, 75, 76, 79, 81, 86
The Communist Manifesto, 86
The German Ideology, 22, 81
Theories of Surplus Value, 81
Marxism, 27, 75, 79, 87
McCalman, Iain, 112, 123
The Meridian Sun of Liberty, 33-4
Methodism, 27
Middlesex, 36-7, 39
Mill, John Stuart, 21, 66, 76-7, 79
Milton, 55
Moises, Rev, H., 107
Moral and Political Magazine, 58
Moravians, 29
More, Hannah, 108, 109
More, Thomas, 29
Morning Chronicle, 61
Moses, 15
Moyle, Walter, 48
Essay Upon the Constitution of the Roman Government, 48
Muggletonians, 80
Murray, Rev. James, 37, 39, 43, 44, 51
The Contest, 37-8, 39, 51
The Freemen's Magazine, 37-8, 39, 41, 43, 51

National Front, 78
Natural Fund, 68
The Needful Attempt, to Make Language and Divinity Plain and Easie, 99
Neesom, Charles Hodgson, 22
Newbury, John, 97
Lilliputian Magazine, 97
Newcastle freemen, 38-9, 41, 46
Newcastle Literary and Philosophical Society, 1-2, 7, 35, 41-4, 45, 50, 51, 52, 104, 118
Newcastle upon Tyne, 2, 3, 7, 17, 35, 36, 37, 43, 50, 51, 88, 97, 100, 107, 108, 113
freemen, 36-7, 50
Quayside, Spence's birthplace, 2, 88
statue of Earl Grey, 14
Spence's first lecture, 1775, 28
Newcastle Weekly Chronicle, 14, 43
Nodder, Frederick Polydore, 4, 111
Norman Yoke, 83, 114
The North Briton, 36
Northern Star, 13, 22, 25
Nothumbria, 38

O'Brien, Bronterre, 23, 24
O'Connor, Feargus, 23, 24, 73
Obama, Barack, 27
Ogilvie, William, 29, 34
Owen, Robert, 19, 21, 23, 29
Owenites, 73

Paine, Thomas, 3, 14-15, 17, 18-19, 20, 27, 29, 31, 32, 33, 53, 55, 62, 68, 69, 116-17
Age of Reason, 28
Agrarian Justice, 15, 18-19, 21, 28, 31, 32, 67, 68
Common Sense, 28
The Rights of Man, 3, 14, 20, 27, 28, 31, 33, 53, 55, 96, 116
trial for seditious libel, 14
Paineites, 34
Parliament, 36-7, 39, 60, 101
Parssinen, T. M., 84
Peace of Paris, 36
Phipps, Constantine John, 36, 39, 51
Pigott, Charles, 117
Pigs' Meat, see Spence, Thomas
Pitt, William, 2, 60
Place, Francis, 2, 4, 21, 59-60, 100, 112
Autobiography, 59
Political Register, see Cobbett, William
Politics for the People, see Eaton, Daniel Isaac,
Poor Man's Guardian, see Hetherington, Henry
Pope, Alexander, 56, 57
Porter, Thomas, 5, 113
'Spence's Plan', 5
Porteus, Beilby, Bishop of London, 109-10
Preston, Thomas, 73
private property, 15, 16, 29, 31, 32, 69, 86-7
Property in land Everyone's Right, see Spence, Thomas
Protestant Reformation, 65
Pufendorf, Samuel, 30, 33, 56
Whole Duty of Man, 30

Quakers, 27

Radical meetings, 124
Ramsay, Allan, 41
Recantation of the End of Oppression, see Spence, Thomas

Read, Samuel, 67
The Real Reading-Made-Easy, see Spence, Thomas
Reeves, John, 54, 55, 56, 59, 60, 61
Reflections on the Revolution in France, see Burke, Edmund
Renaissance, 28
The Repository of Common Sense and Innocent Amusements, see Spence, Thomas
The Restorer of Society to its Natural State, see Spence, Thomas
Ricardians, 73
Ricardo, David, 66
Richter, John, 61
Ridley, Matthew, 35, 37, 39
The Rights of Infants, see Spence, Thomas
'The Rights of Man', *see* Spence, Thomas
The Rights of Man, see Paine, Thomas,
Robespierre, 67
Robinson Crusoe, see Defoe, Daniel
Roman Republic, 28
Rota Club, 45
Rudkin, Olive D., 103
Rural Rides, see Cobbett, William
Rutledge, Jean-Jacques, 52
    Calypso, ou les Babillards, 52

Sadler, Michael, 67
Saint, Thomas, 96
St. George's Fields, 62
    Massacre, 1768, 36
Sedition Meetings Act, 2
Sandemanians, 27, 84, 121
sans-culotte library, 110
Scrivener, Michael, 113, 114
Scrope, Poulett, 67
Seaton Delaval Hall, 36, 37
Second Report of the Committee of Secrecy, 58
Shakers, 29
Sheridan, Thomas, 92, 101, 102, 104
    Complete Dictionary of the English Language, 102
    Dissertations on the Causes of the Difficulties Which Occur in Learning the English Tongue, 92
    General Dictionary of the English Language, 104
Sherwin, William, 20
Shields, 3
Shrewsbury prison, 111, 118
Skedd, S. J., 108
Smith, Adam, 31, 66
Smith, Olivia, 101
social contract, 16
socialism, 75, 78, 85, 112
Society for Constitutional Information, 60-1
Society for Promoting Christian Knowledge, 99
Society for Protecting Liberty and Property against Republicans and Levellers, 54-5
Speenhamland system, 65-6
Spence, Thomas,
    A Supplement to the History of Robinson Crusoe, 30, 96, 98, 99, 104
    animal kingdom, 84-5
    on aristocracy, 69
    Blue Plaque, 88
    bookselling, 18, 27, 54, 61, 62, 111, 113
    critique of Paine, 17-19
    Crusonea, 108
    Spence's debating society, 45
    The End of Oppression, 14, 17, 62, 81
    family, 2
    fight with Thomas Bewick, 43-4
    first lecture, 1775, 28
    funeral, 1, 18
    gaoled, 3, 17-18, 56, 61, 82, 111
    The Giant-Killer; or Anti-Landlord, 5, 101
    graffiti, 2, 6, 113
    The Grand Repository of the English Language, 89, 92, 93, 94, 95, 96, 99, 100, 101, 107, 108, 114
    children's education, 95-6
    gradualism, 69
    The Important Trial of Thomas Spence, 104
    Jubilee, 30, 56, 63, 99, 120
    national fund, 18-19
    New Alphabet, 107
    the people's farm, 13, 21
    phonetic system/spelling reforms, 89-102, 103-8
    The Pronouncing and Foreigners' Bible, 100
    on property in land, 15-16, 27-34
    Pigs' Meat, 3-4, 29, 50, 55, 56, 57, 60, 61, 62, 84, 98, 113, 114, 116, 117, 121
    political songs, 109-25
    Property in land Everyone's Right, 1, 35, 42-3, 45, 50, 53, 81
    The Real Reading-Made-Easy, 98
    Recantation of the End of Oppression, 17, 18
    The Repository of Common Sense and Innocent Amusements, 98
    The Restorer of Society to its Natural State, 17, 29, 90, 111, 125
    right to subsistence, 65, 67, 68-73
    The Rights of Infants, 4, 17, 28, 31, 32, 67, 68, 73
    'The Rights of Man', 1, 5, 14, 27, 52, 56, 117, 118
    school room, Broadgarth, 43, 100, 104
    on use of force, 17
Spence's coins, 2, 17, 113
Spence's Plan, 2, 4, 6, 17-18, 21, 28, 53, 81, 82, 83, 84, 85, 118

Spenceanism, 19, 21, 22, 23, 30-1, 63, 82, 118
Spencean Philanthropists, 2, 6, 17, 22, 82
Spenser, Edmund, 57,
    The Faerie Queen, 57
Stafford, William, 86
    The Historical Basis of Socialism, 86
Stanhope, Lord, 56, 61
Statute of Artificers, 65
Street, John, 122
Sunday School movement, 98
Sunderland, 3
Swift, Jonathan, 56, 57
    Gulliver's Travels, 29
'swinish multitude', 4, 58, 84, 113-14, 117

tax reform, 20, 21, 23, 69
Thelwall, John, 59, 61, 62
Thompson, E. P., 76, 78, 80, 87, 112, 117, 124
    The Making of the English Working Class, 81
    Witness Against the Beast, 80-1
Thomson, Robert, 57, 58, 59, 60
    A Tribute to Liberty, 57
The Times, 13
Tilly, William, 113
Toland, John, 51
Town Moor Affair, 36, 39, 41, 50

United Englishmen, 63, 111
universal suffrage, 21, 53
USSR, 86
Utopia, Thomas More, 29, 32, 56

Vegetarian Society, 22
Venice, Republic of, 47
Volgin, V. P., 86
Volney, 4
Voltaire, 4

Waddington, Samuel, 73
Walker, John, 102, 107
    Critical Pronouncing Dictionary and Expositor of the English Language, 102, 104, 107
Wallace, Alfred Russel, 27
Wallace, Robert, 29
Webster, Noah, 107, 108
Welford, Richard, 107
White Ridley, Sir Matthew, 35-6, 39
Wilkes, John, 36-7, 38, 39, 41, 51
women's rights, 4, 17, 69
Wood, Marcus, 113, 122
Woodward, Richard, 65, 67
    An Argument in Support of the Right of the Poor in the Kingdom of Ireland, to a National Provision, 65

Also from
BREVIARY STUFF PUBLICATIONS

Ralph Anstis, Warren James and the Dean Forest Riots, *The Disturbances of 1831*
£14.00 • 242pp *paperback* • 191x235mm • ISBN 978-0-9564827-7-8

John E. Archer, 'By a Flash and a Scare', *Arson, Animal Maiming, and Poaching in East Anglia 1815-1870*
£12.00 • 206pp *paperback* • 191x235mm • ISBN 978-0-9564827-1-6

Victor Bailey, Charles Booth's Policemen, *Crime, Police and Community in Jack-the-Ripper's London*
£17.00 • 162pp *paperback* • *2 colour and 8 b/w images* • 140x216mm • ISBN 978-0-9564827-6-1

Victor Bailey, Order and Disorder in Modern Britain, *Essays on Riot, Crime, Policing and Punishment*
£15.00 • 214pp *paperback* • *5 b/w images* • 191x235mm • ISBN 978-0-9570005-5-1

John Belchem, 'Orator' Hunt, *Henry Hunt and English Working Class Radicalism*
£14.00 • 248pp *paperback* • 191x235mm • ISBN 978-0-9564827-8-5

Bob Bushaway, By Rite, *Custom, Ceremony and Community in England 1700-1880*
£14.00 • 206pp *paperback* • 191x235mm • ISBN 978-0-9564827-6-1

Malcolm Chase, The People's Farm, *English Radical Agrarianism 1775-1840*
£12.00 • 212pp *paperback* • 152x229mm • ISBN 978-0-9564827-5-4

Malcolm Chase, Early Trade Unionism, *Fraternity, Skill and the Politics of Labour*
£14.00 • 248pp *paperback* • 191x235mm • ISBN 978-0-9570005-2-0

Nigel Costley, West Country Rebels
£20.00 • 220pp *full colour illustrated paperback* • 216x216mm • ISBN 978-0-9570005-4-4

Catherine Howe, Halifax 1842, *A Year of Crisis*
£14.50 • 202pp *paperback* • 156x234mm • ISBN 978-0-9570005-8-2

Barry Reay, The Last Rising of the Agricultural Labourers, *Rural Life and Protest in Nineteenth-Century England*
£12.00 • 192pp *paperback* • 191x235mm • ISBN 978-0-9564827-2-3

Buchanan Sharp, In Contempt of All Authority, *Rural Artisans and Riot in the West of England, 1586-1660*
£12.00 • 204pp *paperback* • 191x235mm • ISBN 978-0-9564827-0-9

Dorothy Thompson, The Chartists, *Popular Politics in the Industrial Revolution*
£16.00 • 280pp *paperback* • 191x235mm • ISBN 978-0-9570005-3-7

E. P. Thompson, Whigs and Hunters, *The Origin of the Black Act*
£16.00 • 278pp *paperback* • 156x234mm • ISBN 978-0-9570005-2-0

David Walsh, Making Angels in Marble, *The Conservatives, the Early Industrial Working Class and Attempts at Political Incorporation*
£15.00 • 268pp *paperback* • 191x235mm • ISBN 978-0-9570005-0-6

Roger Wells, Insurrection, *The British Experience 1795-1803*
£17.50 • 372pp *paperback* • 191x235mm • ISBN 978-0-9564827-3-0

Roger Wells, Wretched Faces, *Famine in Wartime England 1793-1801*
£18.00 • 412pp *paperback* • 191x235mm • ISBN 978-0-9564827-4-7

Lightning Source UK Ltd.
Milton Keynes UK
UKOW02f2024180914

238852UK00002B/11/P

9 780957 000599